The Life of
Brother André
The Miracle Worker of St. Joseph

C. Bernard Ruffin

Our Sunday Visitor Publishing Division
Our Sunday Visitor, Inc.
Huntington, Indiana 46750

Acknowledgments

In the composition of this book I wish to acknowledge the kind
assistance of the family of St. Joseph's Oratory, who, on my two
visits there, welcomed me into their midst and unstintingly
provided me with their time and assistance, making available to
me all the primary sources for the life of Brother André
that were available to them. In particular, I wish to thank
Father Marcel Lalonde, Father Roland Gauthier, Father Bernard
Lafrenière, Father Henri-Paul Bergeron, Brother Laurent Boucher
and Brother Robert Montcalm. I wish also to thank my friend,
Gordon Eugene Bennett, who compiled my index.

INTERNATIONAL STANDARD BOOK NUMBER: 0-87973-492-2
LIBRARY OF CONGRESS CATALOG CARD NUMBER: 88-61112

PRINTED IN THE UNITED STATES OF AMERICA

Cover design by Rebecca J. O'Brien

492

*This book, with love and gratitude,
is dedicated to my aunt
LOUISE JONES HUBBARD, Ph.D.
retired professor of Romance Languages
who translated nearly all the French works
used in my research*

Contents

1. The Miracle Man — 1
2. The Misfit — 12
3. The Doorkeeper — 24
4. The Oil and the Medal — 40
5. A Chapel on the Hillside — 48
6. An Expanding Ministry — 65
7. The Healer — 80
8. A Humble, Pious & Jolly Man — 121
9. A Miracle a Day — 152
10. The Traveler — 162
11. St. Joseph Finds a Roof — 175
12. My Work is Done — 190
13. Blessed Brother André — 199

Chapter Notes — 209

Index — 216

Chapter One

The Miracle Man

It was in August, 1960 when, as a boy of twelve, I first beheld the Oratory of Saint Joseph in Montreal. With my parents and aunt, I was on a bus tour of Quebec and Montreal. A visit to the Oratory was not a part of our itinerary, but the bus stopped at "the finest wax museum in North America," and there the tour guide encouraged us to admire the magnificent Oratory across the street. I carried with me back to Washington, D.C. the memory of that immense white church crowned with its stupendous bronze dome, accessed by an outdoor stairway which pious souls ascended on their knees, breathing a prayer on each step. During the course of that trip we visited the Church of Ste.-Anne-de-Beaupré, and there I was struck by the multitudinous crutches, canes, and braces displayed in one of the chapels there, attesting to miraculous cures. Some years afterward I was told that the Oratory of St. Joseph had a similar collection of discarded orthopaedic devices and that this sanctuary was even more renowned for miracles than the Church of Ste. Anne. Apart from this information, however, St. Joseph's Oratory remained fixed in my memory simply as a big white-domed church in Montreal whither the devout came to worship, mounting flights of stairs on their knees.

More than a quarter century after my visit, after my publish-

1

ers asked me to write a book about Brother André, I stood once more before St. Joseph's great basilica. Until I was asked to write about him, I had never heard of Blessed Brother André Bessette, the founder of the shrine, and never associated the miracles reported there with the ministry of any particular individual. In 1986 and 1987 I had the privilege to stay at the rectory of the Congregation of Holy Cross, the same house in which Brother André lived the last two decades of his life. There the members of the community did everything possible to assist me in my research, even taking me on a thirty-mile drive to see the rural site of Brother André's birth, the building where he was baptized, the house where he lived as a child, and the approximate spot where his father was killed.

Who was this Blessed Brother André? Let us go back in time to the early 1930s, when he is perhaps the most well-known man in Canada. In this time, the section of Montreal called Côtes-des-Neiges is not nearly so urban as it became a few decades later. The Oratory, which means "place of prayer," lies on the slope of Mount Royal, the towering peak that dominates the city of Montreal. The steep outdoor stairway leads, to a large sanctuary known as the Crypt Church. Behind and above it rise the walls of a still-incomplete upper church which, one day, will be the "Basilica." As the visitor turns off Queen Mary Road and walks up St. Joseph's Boulevard, the lane that leads up the steep hill to the church, he can see, to the right of the crypt, the modest four-story rectory, the home of the religious community that serves the Oratory. To the rear and up the hill, and not so obvious from the street, is the tiny "primitive chapel" that originally comprised the Oratory. To the right of the rectory, and more evident, is a simple, one-story frame building which serves as the site of the gift shop, as well as the office of Brother André.

Brother André's office is entered through a waiting room. Here, as in the office of a physician, the sick, without appointments, wait to see "the miracle man" on a first-come-first-served basis. Brother André's hours are usually from about nine until twelve noon, and from three until five in the afternoon. Long before Brother André is scheduled to arrive, the waiting room is packed with people, and, if it is summer, the crowd overflows into a line outside. In the waiting room, the visitor sees people of all ages in all states and stages of illness and disability. In one corner of the room we see a mother with her young child whose limbs are grotesquely animated with an incessant convulsive twitching. Across the room is a man whose eyes are covered with white scars. To the right is another man whose legs are encased in braces, who eases himself into his chair with the aid of crutches. To the left is a woman in a wheelchair. Beside her, gaunt and haggard, is a man who looks like a skeleton in a suit. Next to him is another visitor from whom everyone tries to avert their eyes so as not to be nauseated by the huge, oozing sore on his head.

Just before nine o'clock a very tall, impressive-looking man in a black suit posts himself at the door that leads to Brother André's office. Those visitors who come frequently to see Brother André recognize the tall man as Azarias Claude, a Montreal businessman who for several years has volunteered his time to serve as Brother André's receptionist. At nine, Brother André himself appears, walking through the waiting room. "The Miracle Man" is an unassuming little figure, dressed in the black robe, worn by nearly all Canadian Catholic clergy, known as a *soutane*. The Brother's frame, shrunken to a height of less than five feet, is contorted with age. He walks slowly, yet with a firm and steady step, his shoulders back and his abdomen thrust out. A reverential hush falls over the crowd in the waiting room as he moves silently into his office. Almost immediately, Monsieur Claude calls for Brother André's first visitor of the day.

The pilgrim enters a ten-by-eighteen-foot, wood-paneled room where the old gentleman stands behind a counter upon which he leans with both elbows. A reporter recently has noted the worn soutane and the bright, bird-like eyes peering from a sere and leathery face crisscrossed by "ten thousand lines." Another interviewer has described the Brother as "a little man as dry as a vine shoot," noting the "luminous and limpid" eyes surrounded by the network of wrinkles.

"Comment ça va?" mumbles the old man in a thin, feeble, quavering voice. This is, of course, French for "How are you?" For Americans, Brother André, like most French-Canadians, can switch into a passable English.

"Well, I was in an accident," the visitor says, "and I hurt my shoulder." He is obviously still in pain.

"Have you seen a doctor?" The old man's voice is so weak that the visitor has to ask Brother André to repeat his question. He seems irritated at having to repeat himself, but does so.

"Yes, I've seen a doctor, but I've gotten no relief."

"Get some oil consecrated to St. Joseph and get a medal of St. Joseph and rub your shoulder with the oil and with the medal. Make a novena to St. Joseph. Pray to him a lot. Pray to the Good God."

For several seconds there is silence, then the little man, who seems to be in a kind of reverie, mumbles, "Is there anything else?" Before the pilgrim has time to reply, Brother André rings a little bell on his desk, signaling the end of the sixty-second interview.

Such was a typical visit to Brother André. "The Miracle Man's" healing ministry centered around the curious practice of rubbing the sick or injured with oil that had been placed in a lamp burning before an image of St. Joseph and begging the intercession of the foster father of Jesus. Should any happy results ensue, Brother André refused to take credit. "It was St. Joseph and not I who cured you," he insisted to those who returned to thank him for restoring their health.

It is widely claimed that not a day went by without a miraculous cure. Joseph Pichette, a well-to-do merchant who was one of Brother André's closest friends declared after André's death that in the thirty years he knew the celebrated working-brother, he himself had personally witnessed nearly one thousand healings.

Sometimes startling cures occurred before the astonished eyes of the crowds on Mount Royal, as on an August day in 1918 when the holy man left his office at noon and passed an American waiting his turn, lying totally paralyzed, strapped to a stretcher. Brother André took one look at the invalid and said quite casually to the man's companions, "Untie him," and climbed the steep, winding stairs of the Rectory, apparently oblivious to the explosive cries of "Miracle! Miracle!" from the thronging crowds as the paralytic, now untied, rose and walked.[1]

Around 1929 a man from Garson, Ontario by the name of Desjardins was in an accident which left him paralyzed from the waist down. His doctors told him that he would never walk again. In fact, it took Desjardins thirteen months of therapy to regain enough function just to sit up in a wheelchair. In 1931 Desjardins decided to visit Brother André. So depleted were his finances that he had to beg money from his friends, to whom he vowed, "I'll not return to Ontario unless I am cured!"

When Desjardins arrived at the Oratory, he learned, to his dismay, that Brother André was ill and receiving no visitors. It was, in fact, a month before the old man was able to see the sick again, but Desjardins waited. When at last his opportunity came to meet Brother André, Desjardins was alarmed.

"You come to me so that I can heal you," said the Brother curtly. "But I am not a doctor."

"But the doctors can no longer do anything for me."

"Yes, but you no longer have legs. They are entirely dried up. One cannot make what is dead walk."

"I'll not leave without being cured!" insisted the paraplegic.

This was the sort of response which normally drew an angry rebuke from Brother André, but this time he spoke gently. "Well, if you have faith, in the name of St. Joseph, get up and walk."

Desjardins rose and stood. His legs supported him. With tremendous effort, he took one step, then two, then managed to traverse the length of the office. Exhausted, he collapsed into his wheelchair, drenched with perspiration. Lending him a handkerchief, Brother André exhorted him, "You're a good boy! Now get up again." This time Desjardins was able to walk with less effort. "Go now, pray to St. Joseph, and come back," charged the Brother.

There was "indescribable astonishment and enthusiasm" on the part of the hundreds of people waiting in line that day when they saw the man, who had entered the office in a wheelchair moments before, leave walking unassisted. Not believing their eyes, a group of Protestants from the United States crowded about him. "How did it happen?" one of them asked him. "What did he do to you? Up to now, we didn't believe in miracles."

All Desjardins could tell them was, "He told me, 'Get up and walk,' and I got up and walked."[2]

Ludger Boisvert was in his early forties in 1916 when he developed bladder problems that grew increasingly severe over the next two years. In 1918 when he was hospitalized for tests at Montreal's Hotel-Dieu, urologists found two ulcers in the bladder, one of which was obstructing the flow of urine. Although Boisvert, when he told his story nearly thirty years later, did not mention the word "cancer," he recounted that his doctors had told him that without surgery, he would quickly die. With surgery, he had the cheery prospect of living a year or two as an invalid. "In that case," he said, "I prefer to die." He left the hospital with his doctors predicting his death within three weeks. When Boisvert came to Mount Royal, Brother André told him to get a medal of St. Joseph and some oil consecrated to him and to rub. Not satisfied with André's three-second advice, Boisvert went back to the end of the line in the waiting room. It was wartime and there were only twenty people, and so Boisvert was able to see Brother André again that day. But when the sick man reappeared, Brother André was gruff. "Get out! Go!" he ordered. When Boisvert appeared a third time, the holy man seemed angry and rude. "Do I have to send for the police?" he demanded. Boisvert promised to go out, but only to re-enter the line and to "keep coming back until you listen to me!" This time Brother André softened and said, smiling, "You've got a hard head! Sit on the bench outside my office and wait till I tell you to come in. When I'm ready to see you, I'll tell you."

And so the sick man sat all afternoon until the last visitor had gone, at which point Brother André came out, took Boisvert by the shoulders and escorted him into the office. When Boisvert told him the details of his illness, Brother André said, "Bah! You're afraid of dying?"

"I'm not afraid of dying, but if I can still be useful to my family, I'd like to live. If not, I prefer to die as soon as possible. I've been suffering for a long time."

"I'm going to ask the community to make a novena to St. Joseph," said André, "Pray with us."

Ludger Boisvert, father of eleven children, was healed and survived at least another twenty-seven years.[3]

"I never brought a sick person to Brother André who did not come back satisfied," Joseph Pichette declared in the 1940s.

"Some were cured. Others died a short time afterward, but Brother André comforted them."[4]

Even those who were not cured were relieved in mind and spirit. For instance, a deaf woman came one day to see the good Brother.

"Do you have a good husband, Madame?" asked André.

Reading his lips, the deaf woman replied, "Oh, very good."

"Do you have children?"

"Wonderful children."

"Do you have money?"

"Certainly, Brother. Providence lets us lack for nothing."

"Then, Ma'am," replied Brother André, "you've got to have something to bear for the love of the Good God."

The woman — who remained deaf — later recounted, "If anyone else had said all that to me, I would have been outraged."[5]

Another time Brother André went to the Hospital of the Sacred Heart to see a young man named Desjardins, apparently no relation to the cured paraplegic. "What's the matter with you?" asked the Brother. When the man replied, "Consumption," Brother André told him bluntly, "You're going to die tomorrow. The Good God wants you with Him."

The tubercular told André that he had a wife and young children, but André told him not to worry about them, that St. Joseph would look after them. "Your death will be sweet and calm," he assured him. Desjardins, who had been in a state of despair, died the next day, happy and in peace.[6]

At times Brother André told his visitors, especially if they were strong Christians: "It is better to suffer" or "God will have all eternity to console you" or "We must be strong in trials, we must endure everything for the love of God who suffered so much for us." Frequently he said that it is especially fitting for priests and other religious to suffer, in union with the Passion of Christ.

Brother André's day was not over with the conclusion of his office hours at the Oratory. "My life is not yet earned," he would say. "I have not earned my living yet." Almost every evening, except for Fridays, Brother André visited hospitals, nursing homes, and private residences in and around Montreal to call on the sick and troubled. Each evening the superior of his community gave him a list of people to visit. In the beginning of his ministry, Brother André used a horse and buggy, public transportation, or even went on foot, but after the second decade of the century he relied on lay volunteers to drive him. Usually he dined at the home of his companion for the evening before making his calls. On those visits many wonderful events have been reported.

For example, one day André was en route to visit a patient on his list when, looking out the car window, he saw a man hobbling along the street on crutches. Bidding his driver stop, he leaned out the window to ask the cripple what was the matter with him. When the man explained that he was the victim of an accident, Brother André ordered him to "Walk! Let go of your crutches and walk!"

"I can't."

"I said, let go of your crutches and walk!"

The injured man let his crutches clatter to the street and he was able to walk without them. "I know you are not the Good God," cried the man, transported with amazement and joy, "but you must be someone great!"

"Thank St. Joseph, not me," replied André, drily. "Come to the Oratory tomorrow and bring your crutches."[7]

When Brother André visited the sick at home or hospital, he sometimes performed the rubbing himself, but on men only. He never rubbed women. Even with men he touched only what he called the "seemly" parts, and then only over the clothing and in the presence of at least one witness. Despite his advanced age and a heart condition which caused his chest to hurt and his lips to turn blue with the effort, the old man massaged for up to a half hour, with startling vigor and strength.

Sometimes Brother André told the sick to discontinue their medical treatment or forego an operation. Whenever he did, his judgment was said to be infallible. Whenever Brother André said a patient did not need an operation, the sick person unfailingly recovered without surgical intervention. There was an instance when Brother André called on a man of twenty-eight who was hospitalized after an accident. His leg had become gangrenous and amputation was scheduled for the next morning. Pulling up his pajama trousers to show the swollen, discolored limb, he explained to the Brother that amputation was the only way of saving his life.

"You want to have your leg cut off?" growled André. "Bah! It's not necessary. Pay your hospital bill tomorrow. Take these medals of St. Joseph and the oil. St. Joseph is going to heal you!" Much to the rage and consternation of the surgeons, who promised the patient that he would be dead in five weeks, the injured man signed himself out of the hospital. Within five weeks he was not only alive but completely healed.[8]

Between nine and ten Brother André returned to the rectory, where he lived with approximately ten priests and ten other brothers. Before retiring, he took his companion to the Crypt Church or to the little chapel for an hour of prayer. Despite the fact that he was seldom in bed before eleven, Brother André was always up by five, when he cleaned his room and then went to the little chapel to pray for two hours. When asked, "Don't you ever get tired? Don't you rest during the day?" Brother André typically responded, "Yes, I am tired. Sometimes I see and speak to a thousand people in turn all day. That makes me very tired. But lie down and rest? There is too much work. I have no time."[9]

Brother André did not always find his work pleasurable. Of his conversations with pilgrims, he was known to remark to intimates, "Never anything joyous, never anything amusing." In extreme old age, Brother was rather crotchety and many visitors complained that he seemed downright ill-tempered at times. André confided, "If people realized how it is not pleasant for me to remain for long hours, hearing their complaints, they would be shorter in their questions." Many pilgrims were frankly obnoxious. Some came only out of curiosity and others chattered non-stop. When people became abusive or refused to leave unless they were cured, Brother André was liable to have harsh words. To such persons he frequently said, "It is not I who cure. It is God and St. Joseph." To those, who, like the stupid woman who said she had a right to demand a healing from God because she attended Mass every day, insisted that the Lord was obligated to cure them, André typically snorted, "The Good God owes you nothing!"

Many people — hundreds, even thousands — returned to thank Brother André. Again, his response was always self-effacing. "How wonderful the Good God is! How good St. Joseph is! God is everything, I am nothing, and it is because the Good God wills it that I can do it."

Frequently people left donations. All contributions were strictly voluntary and never solicited. Whenever anyone asked, "What do I owe you?" the good Brother promptly affirmed, "You owe me nothing."[10] Brother André immediately transfered any money placed in his hands to a black velvet bag which he kept with him, to be presented at the end of the day to his superior. He never even counted the money.

Physical sickness was not the only target of Brother André's ministry. More numerous perhaps than those who professed a release from physical disabilities were those who were led from indifference or unbelief to a faith in Jesus as their Lord and Savior. The good Brother considered his mission to save men's souls even more important than his calling to heal their bodies. "Some may think this is a pleasure [to minister to the sick], but it is not. I visit the sick because I can perhaps help some people whom I would not be able to reach otherwise."[11] Brother André's ministry of healing, then, he saw, not only as an end in itself but as a means of leading people to God through devotion to St. Joseph. If Brother André was questioned about his mission, invariably he insisted that his life-work consisted of instilling in humanity a love of St. Joseph. After Brother André's death, a colleague wrote of him: "Brother André spoke of St. Joseph with such fervor that he aroused in his listeners the same devotion," insisting that he "contributed immensely to giving full rise to devotion to St. Joseph in our province, in Canada, in the United States, and even in Europe."[12]

Brother André, though intelligent, quick of wit, and nimble of mind, never had the opportunity to have an education. He read slowly and painfully and could write nothing except his name. He knew the Bible, which he was always quoting and urging others to read,[13] and three other books: "The Imitation of Christ"; a collection of prayers by St. Gertrude of Helfta; and a devotional work by Sister Marie-Marthé Chambon. These works he virtually memorized.

Having begun life in abject poverty, Brother André had great sympathy for the poor and oppressed. St. Joseph, the carpenter of Nazareth, he saw as the patron of the workingman. Brother

André felt more comfortable in the presence of the poor than of the rich. Wealth and rank left him unimpressed. For instance, one day the chaplain of His Royal Highness, King George V was introduced to him. Unmoved by the personal greetings of the king, Brother André greeted the eminent churchman with curt brevity and after a few seconds moved on to the next person who claimed his attention.

The story of Blessed Brother André Bessette is the story of a man who began life amidst poverty and deprivation, who entered religious life in his mid-twenties after living the life of an itinerant laborer — almost a hobo — from his early teens. He was a man whose collected written works number exactly three dictated letters, a man who never read a newspaper or magazine and was so indifferent to world affairs that in the 1930s he told a reporter that he had not heard of Roosevelt, Mussolini or Hitler.[14] Nonetheless, Brother André inspired a widespread prayer movement, directed the development and construction of one of the largest houses of worship on earth, and offered to heaven prayers that resulted in the healing of thousands of bodies, minds and souls.

Blessed André of Montreal is surely one of the twentieth century's most fascinating characters, yet in many ways there is little to say about him. Up to the age of about fifty, his life is bare of almost any interesting external events, and since he said little of his intellectual and spiritual development and wrote nothing, that aspect of his life remains veiled to the world. In contrast with many reputed "healers" of the late twentieth century, Brother André was not a "personality." This was surely because there was, in a real sense, very little of self in the humble Brother of Holy Cross, who spent so much of his life in the service of his Good God and his fellow human beings that he had no time left for himself. He was truly "a man for others" in whom personality, as it is normally understood, was crucified along with self-will in his Lord Christ.

Chapter Two

The Misfit

Brother André was a man of few words, but his friends and associates felt that he was especially spare of comment about his childhood. When questioned about the beginning of his life, the Good Brother was apt to smile sweetly and remain silent. Were Brother André the only source of information about his early life, we would know next to nothing. But thanks to statements made by his nieces and nephews and by former associates, as well as information from church and land records, researchers have been able to piece together a picture — albeit sketchy — of Brother André's background and childhood.

André was a "religious name." In the nineteenth and early twentieth century, members of many religious orders were often required to accept a new name as a token of their severance of ties with "the world," as a sign that they were a "new creation." The man known to the world for sixty-six years as "Brother André" began life as Alfred Bessette in a one-room cabin about a mile north of the village of St.-Gregoire d'Iberville, thirty miles southeast of Montreal, on August 9, 1845. The cabin is gone today, but the site of Brother André's birth was, when visited in August, 1986, in a virtually unspoiled condition of delightful rusticity, amid field and meadow and forest. In 1845 it was mostly forest, with very little cleared land. The cabin stood at a crossroads. One road led east to Ste.-

Marie and west to Richelieu, both a few miles away, and, branching off from it, another road led south to St.-Gregoire, and, beyond that, to Farnham. From their cabin, twenty feet by seventeen, the Bessettes could look south and see, rising from a forested plain, a hill shaped like a loaf of bread, known in those days as Mount Johnson. Nearby, across the road, stood the cabin and smithy of Alfred's paternal uncle, Eusèbe Bessette.

Little Alfred, whom tradition describes as so small and weak an infant that the midwife baptized him on the spot, was taken the day after his birth to St.-Gregoire, where the Sacrament was formally administered by the local priest (who served three rural parishes) in an all-purpose stone building that served as the community's church and town hall.

The Bessettes, like all their neighbors, were of pure French extraction. Although he learned not a word of English until he went to work in the United States as a teenager, Alfred was born a subject of Great Britain's twenty-six-year-old Queen Victoria in the colony of Lower Canada in "British America." What is now the Province of Quebec was settled by the French in the early 1600s, but was acquired by the British through the Treaty of Paris of 1763, which ended the Seven Years War. By the mid-nineteenth century, Britain's North American holdings, which were peopled by only about a million souls, were divided into the colonies of Upper Canada (which included what is now Ontario) and Lower Canada.

Alfred's father was Isaac Bessette. Although he and his celebrated son probably knew little and cared less about their "roots," church records prove their descent from a man named Jean Bessette or Bessède, a French soldier from Aquitaine known as "The Wrecker," who came to Canada in 1665 with the Carignan Regiment for a three-year tour of duty and decided to stay when his term of enlistment ended. "The Wrecker" married one Anne Seigneur and received a grant of land in an area called Chambly. Most of his descendants — sturdy, long-lived folks — were farmers, like Isaac's parents. Joseph Bessette, Alfred's grandfather, died in his seventies in 1851, and his wife, born Angelique Georges, lived until 1885 when she must have been at least 100 years old.[1] In September, 1831, in his home town of St.-Mathias, Isaac Bessette, twenty-four years old, married Clothilde, the seventeen-year-old daughter of Claude Foisy and his wife, the former Ursule Barsalou. The Foisys traced their roots back to one Martin Foisy, who came from Champagne in 1663.

At the time of Alfred's birth, Isaac Bessette owned a long, narrow strip of land behind his cabin, one mile long but only three *feet* wide. It was largely infertile and he scraped out a living as a carpenter. Nearly everything that could be done with wood, he did. He cut it, he hauled it, he fashioned it into furniture, barrels, and wagon wheels, and he did repairs. The few statements about his personality that his children cared to make in later years give one the impression that he was quiet and undemonstrative. He doubtless spent all his waking hours working and was forced to leave to his wife nearly all the responsibility for rearing and nurturing his numerous children. About the only thing that Brother André ever said about his father was that he worked at the same trade as St. Joseph.

The Good Brother, on the other hand, did occasionally speak of his mother and how much he loved her. Once he remarked: "My mother, knowing that I was very frail, seemed to have more love and care for me than for the others. She kissed me more often than was my turn, and frequently gave me little delicacies in secret. In the evening, when we recited family prayers, I was next to her, and followed the prayers on her Rosary. In those days I never saw my mother when she was not smiling — and what a lovely smile!"[2]

The hardworking Isaac and his fragile wife had twelve children. The eldest, Clothilde, born in 1833, died as a baby. The first child to live was Léocadie, born in 1835. She was followed by four boys: Isaïe, Napoleon, Joseph, and Claude. Then came Marie Rosalie, Alfred, Alphonsine, Josephine, Virginie (who died in infancy), and finally Elise, who died at four. Neighbors recalled the Bessettes as very poor, but hardworking — just as most of the people around them — and especially pious. Madame Bessette came from a particularly devout family. Two of her distant cousins, Marie-Rose Durocher and Marguerite d'Youville, have been beatified! Brother André recalled that his mother taught him to pray by teaching him to invoke the names of Jesus, Mary and Joseph, and it was to her that he attributed his lifelong devotion to Mary and Joseph.

In 1849, when Alfred was four, the family moved nine miles south to the larger community of Farnham, which had been settled at the time of the American Revolution by loyalists to the British crown. By the mid-nineteenth century, its long-standing population of English, Scots and Irish was being augmented by an influx of French Canadians. Isaac Bessette's brothers Basile, Benoni, and Xavier were already living in Farnham when he brought his family there and settled into a house on Queen's Road beside the Yamaska River.

Six years later, on February 20, 1855, an event occurred that remained forever etched in Brother André's memory. Alfred was nine years old that snowy morning when Isaac and his oldest son, eighteen-year-old Isaïe, went to cut wood on a plot of land about a mile from their home. Later that day neighbors carried Isaac's crushed and bleeding body into the cabin. A felled tree, in falling had become entangled in the branches of another, toppled the wrong way and, in Brother André's words some fourscore years later, "crushed my poor father to instantaneous death." Poor Isaïe, struck with "profound horror," was unable to speak for days. Clothilde seemed as if she were "frozen," the happy smile forever vanished from her face.[3] Evidently she was already suffering from "consumption," or tuberculosis, and Léocadie said that "the shock of that accident" was the direct cause of her mother's eventual death. Brother André said that after the accident, his mother seemed slowly to pine away.

Dire times descended upon the Bessette family, deprived of its breadwinner and headed by a mother too ill to work. The older boys went to live as hired help on nearby farms. Léocadie and Marie remained with their mother and younger siblings, probably doing domestic work in neighboring households. Clothilde hoped that little Alfred, her youngest boy, who seemed so frail and delicate, could learn a trade and thus avoid heavy manual labor. To do this, however, he would have to become an apprentice and for this a fee was required. Clothilde had no money and so, at the age of eleven, Alfred, while living at home, began to work as a day laborer on neighboring farms.

An education was not possible for most boys of that time and place. An educational system in Lower Canada was non-existent. When Great Britain acquired Quebec in 1763 the French school system was dismantled in an attempt by Parliament to anglicize the natives. A few Protestant schools were set up, with instruction in English, but these were shunned by the populace, and by the time Brother André came along, there was no public school system at all. If parents had money (although the Bessettes did not), they could send their children to private schools in the cities of Montreal or Quebec. Otherwise, there were only a few private schools here and there, most run by religious orders. Curiously, most of these schools were for girls, as reading and writing in nineteenth-century Quebec was considered "women's work." Boys were sent to work in the fields, while girls had the leisure to go to school for a few years to learn how to read, write and figure. Indicative of this custom is the fact that while Isaac Bessette could not even sign his name, Clothilde could write hers. Because of the lack of free public education, Alfred, like most of his family, did not go to school.

More trouble befell the Bessette family in 1855. Fifteen-year-old Joseph was living with a family who cruelly abused the frail lad. One day Clothilde received the news that Joseph had disappeared. Much later it was learned that he had walked to the Richelieu River and stowed away on a boat headed for America by way of Lake Champlain. A cook discovered the tiny, fragile boy, and, having heard his story, cared for him until the boat docked at Plattsburgh, New York. Then, filling his handkerchief with food, the cook directed him to a man who found him work in the iron mines. It was many years, however, before any of Joseph's brothers or sisters saw him again. As long as Clothilde lived, Joseph remained a "missing child." In November, 1857, although she was only forty-three, she felt that her appointed time on earth was drawing to its close and sent for her remaining boys, and, as all the children gathered around her bedside, she bade them: "Believe in God. Never abandon your faith. Never fail to go to Mass on Sundays."[5] On November 20, she died. "How good she was!" mused Brother André in later years. "I have rarely prayed *for* my mother, but I have often prayed *to* her."[6]

And so the Bessette family was further broken up. Isaïe, Léon, Claude and Marie went their separate ways. Léocadie kept the three youngest girls, and Alfred was taken in by Clothilde's sister, Rosalie Nadeau, who, with her husband

Timothée and their children, lived in the neighboring town of St.-Césaire. The Nadeaux, who owned a store, were able to send twelve-year-old Alfred to school for the first and only time in his life, a favor that he would never forget. He proved a good student, but shortly after he made his First Communion in June, 1858, Alfred was apprenticed to a shoemaker and his days of schooling forever came to an end. In later years gossip circulated that Timothée Nadeau was cruel to the boy, but Brother André, while conceding that his uncle was "hard" and "demanding," always professed a great love and respect for him.[7]

The life of a shoemaker did not suit young Alfred. "Working at shoemaking, almost on all fours, striking the hammer all day, is not good for the digestion,"[8] Brother André later remarked, referring to the stomach problems that frequently plagued him all his life. Next, Alfred tried his hand working as a tinsmith for a man named Garceau, and then worked for a while as a baker's assistant. By this time Timothée Nadeau had decided to go to California to look for gold and Alfred was on his own. He wandered to Farnham, where he found work as a blacksmith, then to Ste.-Brigide, where he hauled wood, and to Ste.-Angele, where he did construction. Then he returned to St.-Césaire, where, a farmer named Louis Ouimet took him in as a hand.

Although Alfred Bessette spent his early years as a wandering laborer — almost a hobo — nobody who met the scrawny little youth ever doubted the excellence of his character. "He was so sweet the whole world loved him," his elder sister Léocadie recalled.[9] His younger sister Alphonsine later recounted, "Alfred was a good boy and an excellent young man. He was very pious. He took communion often. He spent all Sunday in church."[10] Indeed, it was Alfred's piety that struck all who knew him.

"He was pious, that young man!" remembered an employer. "Nobody could be any more pious!"[11] Another employer recalled, "He never went out. He was always praying. But he was very kind."[12] Alfred sang hymns while he worked and used every spare moment to pray. He seemed to be in church the moment the door was open. For a while he roomed with a boy by the name of Pierre Demers. Pierre liked to go play cards at night and repeatedly urged Alfred to come along. "Sorry, that doesn't interest me," Alfred insisted. When Pierre came back late at night, invariably he found Alfred praying.

One night Alfred consented to go with friends, and returned to his room at a late hour, despite the fact that his mother, when alive, had counseled her boys against keeping late hours. As he was going home, he later told a friend; "Near a ditch I saw something like a human form. I believed it to be an apparition of my mother, and I took it as a warning not to return home so late any more. After that I was always in by nine."[13] Another time Alfred was cajoled into accepting an invitation to go to a party. He arrived early, but instead of going into the house, he began to walk around in the fields. Stopping by a stream, he heard a noise which he could not explain, coming from he knew not whence. Concluding that it must be his mother trying to contact him from the other world, Alfred asked, "Mama, is that you? If you don't want me to go, let me hear that noise again." He heard it again and, refusing to go to the party, he went back to his room to pray.[14]

The boys with whom Alfred worked noted that at the table he always refused dessert and made it a point to walk barefoot in the snow, even though he owned a pair of shoes. While he was living with the Nadeaux, Aunt Rosalie was horrified to find the boy wearing, under his shirt, a belt studded with tacks.[15] One day a roommate, seeing Alfred undressed, cried, "Dammit, what are you doing with that?" referring to a chain link that was cutting into the flesh about his waist and making him bleed.[16] These eccentricities were mortifications, whereby, like many religious people of the day, Alfred hoped to subdue the flesh and quicken his mind and soul to the things of heaven. In later years, Léocadie insisted that Alfred's self-imposed dietary restrictions had ruined his digestion forever. Alfred, was never interested in girls, and no one who ever knew him ever had the slightest doubt of his lifelong virginity. He played apostle to the boys, telling them Bible stories and trying to win them to faith-filled and godly living. "Pray to St. Joseph! He will not fail to obtain all your requests!" he urged them. Many of the other boys laughed at him, calling Alfred "The Fool."[17]

It was with priests and religious that Alfred loved to consort. He became a close friend of Father Sylvestre, and spent many hours with him in the parsonage, asking him such questions as, "What prayers are most pleasing to God?" (To which Sylvestre answered: the Our Father and the Hail Mary.) Father Sylvestre even took Alfred with him on trips to neighboring towns. Around this time Alfred confided to Léocadie that for as long as he could remember, he had wanted to become a religious.[18] But with no education he could not even consider the priesthood, and his ascetical practices had played such havoc with his digestion that he feared his uncertain health would make him unacceptable even as a working brother.

In 1863 a catastrophic civil war was raging in the southern United States, with the result that the industries that provided shoes, firearms, cloth for uniforms and other material used in the war effort were booming in the North. On the other hand, there was a depression in Canada and many of Alfred's relatives and friends were pouring across the border in search of work. One of his father's brothers, Clovis, had been living in Manchester, New Hampshire for some time and by now Alfred and his siblings had learned that brother Joseph was working in the mines near Plattsburgh, New York. By the end of the Civil War, most of Alfred's brothers and sisters had moved to New England. Alfred himself, boarding the train at Iberville, journeyed to Nashua, New Hampshire, to work in a factory there for a while, before joining his brothers Napoleon and Claude and his sisters Marie and Josephine in Connecticut, to work with them in the cotton mills of Moosup and Putnam. Work was from six in the morning till six in the evening, with an hour for lunch. Two or three times a week two hours of overtime was required. In later years Brother André said nothing about his work in the States, but most of the factories of the period were infernally hot, dirty, dangerous and unsanitary. Reformers of the day called such sweatshops "the graveyards of the poor." One of the deadly hazards of the cotton mills where Alfred toiled, was the dust, which, inhaled over a period of years, often led to tuberculosis and other lethal or debilitating respiratory problems. Wisely, Alfred would work in the mills for only a few months at a time, then quit to take a job as a farm laborer, where, although the pay was less, the conditions were more healthful. Then, physically restored, he would return to the mills for another stint of several months. Although he continued to lead a sober and austere life, spending the little free time he had in church or in prayer, Alfred seems to have made many friends in America.

In 1867, two years after the end of the Civil War, young Bessette, now twenty-two, returned to Canada. His brother Claude later said that he did so because his health would not permit him to continue in the mills. Many of the Canadians who had gone south during the war returned to Canada during this period, and Claude was one of them. This was the year when the British North American Act created the Dominion of Canada. Canada, with four provinces (New Brunswick, Nova Scotia, Ontario and Quebec) was granted autonomy in domestic affairs (although Parliament would continue until 1931 to supervise foreign policy). Many Canadians felt that the independence of their fatherland would lead to more jobs, and so they returned. In later years, about all that Brother André had to say about his sojourn in the States was that it prepared him for his future ministry because he was forced to learn to speak English.

Alfred now went to work in the town of Sutton, Quebec, near the Vermont border, where Claude and his wife had preceded him and Léocadie was also residing. Her husband, Joseph Lefebvre, was the brother of Claude's wife. Only eight miles away at Richford, Vermont, Isaïe, the eldest brother, had settled with his family. Alfred took a job as a yardman and gardener for the parish priest, Edward Springer. After Father Springer was transferred, his successor decided that he did not want a handyman, and so the little hobo was back on the road, finding work as a stableboy and farmhand for the same Louis Ouimet of St.-Césaire who had employed him several years earlier.

Between the ages of thirteen and twenty-five Alfred Bessette lived in at least nine different towns in two countries and tried his hand at ten different trades (at least). What was the problem? Surely, a large part of the reason for his continual changes of employment and residence was the fact that Alfred was an unskilled laborer and much of the employment that he was able to obtain was seasonal. In this respect he was no different from many men and women of his time and place. Alfred's brothers were similarly peripatetic before they settled down in the States and married. Joseph, in fact, seems to have wandered over half the continental United States. With Alfred, this situation was compounded by the fact that he was dissatisfied with the life of an itinerant laborer. It is true that his physique did not look particularly suited for sustained heavy labor. He never stood more than 5'3" and weighed, at most, 110, and was given to headaches and indigestion. Many men, however, nurtured in the harsh environment which characterized the life of the poor in those days grew up with stunted bodies and ailments resulting from malnutrition and overwork, but did not (and could not) allow such physical limitations to stop them from engaging in a round of toil that would exhaust the most carefully trained and nourished athlete of the present day. Despite his feeble appearance, people who knew André testified that the little fellow, even well into middle age, was "strong as an ox."[19] What is important in Alfred's case is that he longed to devote his life entirely to God and never gave his heart entirely to his secular work. He discovered that he was happiest in the presence of those who had made religion their career, and while he was in worship and prayer.

Alfred was called a "fool" by some of his companions, and many moderns might be tempted to write him off as a "loner," a "neurotic," or a "misfit," a young man who, after the death of his parents, seemingly drew into a shell and a dream world of his own creation. Before we dismiss the young Bessette as a madman, a dreamer, or a candidate for a mental hospital, we need to pause and consider the words of Sacred Scripture: "The foolishness of God is wiser than men" (1 Cor. 1:25) and "God chose what is foolish in the world to shame the wise" (1 Cor. 1:27). Often the response to God's call in a man's life appears foolish in the sight of the world. A young man who is not interested in girls, in going to parties, or in making lots of money and who spends every spare minute in prayer is often considered "foolish" by his contemporaries. Yet Alfred Bessette was a fool *only* if we presuppose that there is *not* a spiritual world invisible and imperceptible to most, which was real and tangible to him. Alfred believed himself to be not so much "turned off" to the reality of the world around him as "turned on" to the reality of a world beyond this world, a world far more real to him perhaps than the one of his physical senses.

Jesus, St. Joseph and St. Mary were as real to the young Bessette as the men for whom he labored, and heaven was as real to him as the shops and factories in which he toiled. Clearly, if there is no God, if there is no heaven, if Jesus, Mary and Joseph are only heaps of dust mouldered away in long forgotten graves, Alfred Bessette was mad. Then, too, there are people who, disenchanted by the frustrations of daily life, invent a fantasy world of make-believe in which they choose to take refuge from the unpleasant vicissitudes of daily existence. There are also persons whose brains are poisoned with drugs or damaged by disease who see things that have no basis in reality and hear things that exist only in their disordered minds. Alfred Bessette's character never at any time, then, or when he was Brother André, had anything in common with that of a man with a mental disorder. Unlike the typical pathological dreamer, Alfred, though timid, reserved and nervous, was never self-centered. All the men with whom, or for whom, he worked insisted that he was always kind and concerned with others. He was the young man who was "so sweet the whole world loved him," the boy whose "heart was literally filled with [a] love that left no place for self-love."[20] Alfred Bessette, to use the words of Henry David Thoreau, heard the beat of a different drummer. He had a set of priorities that were not the same as those of most other people.

In 1870 Bessette's life took an important turn. His employer, Louis Ouimet, recalled:

> After work I would send him to the barn to care for the horses. He did not come back. 'What is he doing?' Every evening it was like that. One evening I decided to go to see. He had placed a cross in the back of the barn. He was on his knees, praying. That happened many times. When I realized he was like that, I spoke of it to Messire Provençal, who told me, 'Bring him to me.'[21]

André Provençal, a native of Quebec, was fifty-three years old. The balding priest with the owl-like visage had been pastor in St.-Césaire since 1850 and served there until his death in 1889. A dynamic, hard-working man concerned with the spiritual well-being of his flock, Provençal was concerned with their material needs as well. One was the need for education. With his own hands, he built a school for girls at St.-Césaire and later concerned himself about creating one for boys. In 1869 he obtained the services of six members of the Congregation of Holy Cross, which since 1847 had operated a school in St.-Laurent, near Montreal, to organize a boys' school at St.-Césaire. This was the man who wanted to see Louis Ouimet's pious farmhand, telling him, "I'll know where to put him."

When Father Provençal met Alfred Bessette, the first thing the pastor noted about the young man was the iron chain fastened to his waist, which showed through his clothing. "You have no right to wear that!" he told Alfred, warning him against unsupervised mortifications. During their conversation, Bessette explained that he had always wanted to be a religious. "I want to enter Religion to serve the Good God and sanctify myself. I want to be able to pray more easily. It is only among the priests at church and at devotions that I feel happy."[22]

Provençal met with Bessette many times. Alfred had just about given up on the possibility of a religious vocation when Provençal persuaded him that he could be accepted by the Congregation of Holy Cross as a working brother. Alfred Bessette jumped at the opportunity and made preparations to travel to Montreal to enter the novitiate. In November, Provençal wrote to the superior of the College of St.-Laurent, who had charge of the novices, declaring, "I'm sending you a saint."[23]

Chapter Three

The Doorkeeper

The Congregation of Holy Cross derives its name, not directly from the instrument of torture upon which the Savior died, but from the town of Sainte-Croix in France, near Le Mans, where the Order was organized eight years before the birth of Alfred Bessette. This Order, the official name of which is *Congregatio a Sancta Cruce* (abbreviated CSC), was formed by Basile Moreau (1799-1873), a French priest who created a merger of two congregations. The Congregation of the Brothers of St. Joseph had been established to provide primary education for children in rural French villages, and the Auxiliary Priests of Le Mans had as their purpose to provide assistance to diocesan clergy through preaching and holding retreats. Father Moreau united the two orders, each of which kept its own government and administration, but submitted to a single constitution and General Council in which members of both societies were represented. Father Moreau intended the two groups, in conjunction with an order of sisters that he founded, to function as a family.

The priests of Holy Cross were known, in Brother André's day, as Salvatorists. Their habit consisted of the black soutane, over which they wore a small black cape modeled after that worn by the pope. They wore a clerical collar and on a cord around the neck, a pectoral cross. The brothers, known originally as Josephites (not to be confused with another Order, founded in 1866 to minister to persons of color) wore the collar and the soutane but no cape. They girded their waist with a double cord and round their neck, on a black cord, instead of a cross they wore a medal of St. Joseph, which they kept tucked unobtrusively into their soutane.

The brothers were never known as "monks." In the nineteenth century there were two types of brothers, very different from each other. The teaching brothers, highly educated men, ran the schools, and the coadjutor or "working" brothers, who were drawn, usually, from among the less academically endowed, did menial tasks. Most of the schools run by the CSC were self-supporting and relied on the working brothers to keep the grounds, maintain a farm to support both students and staff, and care for the buildings. The coadjutor brothers were trained in a separate novitiate, in which a great deal of their preparation consisted of memorization, since many of them were unlettered.

The CSC had been in Canada since 1847 when Archbishop Ignace Bourget (1799-1885) of Montreal had persuaded Father Moreau to send some of his community across the sea to assist him in his attempt to build an educational system in his archdiocese. Bourget had difficulty at first, because his request was for only teaching brothers. Moreau, in keeping with his concept of his Order as a family with priests, brothers and sisters functioning as a unit, wrote back, "If ever you want brothers, you have to accept the priests and the sisters as well " Bourget gave in and eight brothers, four sisters and two priests arrived from France. The parish at St.-Laurent, outside Montreal, donated land on which the Order could set up a school. By 1870 the CSC ran three institutions in Canada, a high school at St.-Laurent, the primary school in St.-Césaire and another grammar school, only recently opened, in the little village of Côte-des-Neiges, between St.-Laurent and Montreal. This last was called the College of Our Lady of the Sacred Heart (College de Notre-Dame du Sacre-Coeur).

Bessette entered the CSC as a postulant, or candidate for admission, on November 22, 1870. A month later he was admitted to the novitiate, in which the candidate begins a period of probation which leads, if successfully completed, to the taking of final vows. On December 27, twenty-five-year-old Alfred Bessette and twenty-year-old Joseph Buchand were received into the novitiate at the chapel at the College Notre-Dame. The two candidates slowly approached Father Jules Gastineau, the master of novices, each holding an unlighted candle and chanting, in unison, Psalm 121, which begins:

> I will lift up mine eyes unto the hills:
> from whence cometh my help.

After dedicating the young men to St. Joseph, Father Gastineau took and blessed the candles, returning them lighted as a symbol of the good works and "perpetual praises" expected of them. Following his sermon, Gastineau sang Mass. After the singing of the hymn called the *Veni Creator,* in which the Holy Spirit is invoked, Gastineau proceeded to question the postulants individually, asking, "My son, what do you want?"

"Reverend Father," said Bessette and Buchand, in turn, "I ask you for the habit of this holy society and the grace to be tested by the training of the novitiate."

Blessing the collar, which for clergy of all denominations symbolizes the "yoke of Christ" by which religious are bound to their Lord as slaves, Gastineau repeated: "The only Son of God took for us the form of a slave. Let us put on the Lord Jesus Christ." Next, the soutane was blessed and given to the young men as a symbol of purity and humility.[1]

Until the 1940s, coadjutor brothers of the Congregation were given religious names. Although priests of the Order were allowed to retain both their baptismal and family names, never again, except for strictly legal purposes, were brothers called by their original names. Joseph Buchand became Brother Henri. Then Alfred was told: "Your name in the world was Alfred Bessette. Henceforth you will have the name Brother André." It is not clear whether Alfred himself chose the name or whether it was chosen for him, but certainly it was given in honor of Father André Provençal. The novices now chanted verse fourteen of Psalm 132: "This is my rest forever. Here I will dwell, for I have desired it." The Congregation of Holy Cross proved not to be Brother Henri's rest forever, for he left before taking final vows. Although he desperately wanted to become a permanent part of the community, Brother André, as we shall shortly see, very nearly lost the opportunity to make his final vows.

Brother André the novice was required to arise at 4:30 each morning and pray to his Guardian Angel who had awakened him from sleep, calling upon the angel to enlighten, protect, direct, and govern him. He had then to invoke Jesus, Mary and Joseph. As he put on his soutane, he was to think about putting on everlasting life. Then he was required to recite by heart Psalm 63, which begins: "O God, thou art my God. Early will I seek thee. My soul thirsteth for thee, my flesh longeth for thee in a dry and thirsty land where no water is, to see thy power and thy glory, so as I have seen thee in thy sanctuary. . . ." Leaving his cell at last, Brother André was to pray, "O Good Jesus, do not allow me ever to separate myself from Thee." He then joined the community for Matins, the service of morning prayer, and after that he participated in or "assisted at" the Mass.

There was a great emphasis on devotion to St. Joseph. First of all, the Order was consecrated to him. Secondly, the very month that Brother André was received into the novitiate, Pope Pius IX proclaimed St. Joseph the Patron of the Universal Church. St. Joseph was also the Protector of Canada. Brother André had always identified with St. Joseph. St. Joseph had to leave his native land, just as Brother André did. Like André, St. Joseph was humble, silent and poor. Moreover, St. Joseph was a carpenter, just like André's father. For all these reasons, Brother André always had a strong love for the saint as a powerful and benevolent friend who lived with God.

In July, 1871 several other novices joined the community and the novitiate for the coadjutor brothers was transferred to the College at St.-Laurent. Brother André, however, remained at Notre-Dame, where he was given janitorial duties. Nobody knows why André did not accompany the other novices, but it is believed that the reason was that the novice-master had made up his mind that Brother André was not suited to remain with the community. This was not because of his illiteracy. The novitiate for the working brothers was geared for the unlettered, and Brother André was very quick in memorizing the

Psalms and other portions of Scripture that were required of him. In fact, he memorized all four Gospels and much of the New Testament. The problem lay in his health. The young man was subject to episodes of extreme stomach pain (attributed by the doctors to very slow digestion), pains severe enough to confine him to bed for days at a time. The community expected its coadjutor brothers to be capable of heavy manual labor and this seemed beyond the physical capabilities of Brother André, despite his diligence and piety.

In that same summer of 1871 there occurred a serious outbreak of smallpox. Although a vaccine had been developed for this highly infectious disease in the 1790s by Edward Jenner in England, health authorities throughout the civilized world were extremely slow in inaugurating programs for mass immunization, and deadly outbreaks still occurred, even in North America. A number of students and staff at St.-Laurent developed symptoms of the disease, four seriously enough to be hospitalized. Of these, two died, a novice and a teaching brother from New Brunswick. Brother André was transferred temporarily to St.-Laurent to help as a nurse in the crowded infirmary. There he suggested that members of the community who were still on their feet carry a statue of St. Joseph in procession around the infected school, invoking the saint's protection. Appealing to a saint for assistance in time of trouble by means of a procession had long been popular among the pious. Only the year before Brother André's arrival, on the occasion of another epidemic a procession had been organized at St.-Laurent. After the procession in the summer of 1871, no new cases of smallpox occurred and, within two days, everyone had recovered. No one at the time attributed the cessation of the pestilence to the piety of the little novice who suggested the procession. At the time the feeling in the community was that the two men who died in the hospital had offered up their lives for the health and safety of their fellows.

On January 8, 1872, a year after Brother André's admission to the novitiate, the Provincial Council of the Congregation, which had jurisdiction over all three communities in Canada, made a decision. Presided over by the Superior Provincial, Father Joseph Rézé, it ruled, "Brother André is not admitted to temporary religious professions because his state of health would hardly seem to warrant hope for admission to perpetual vocation."[2] Needless to say, Brother André was devastated. He begged his superiors to be allowed to stay just a little longer. He found an ally in Father Pierre Guy, who had just replaced Father Gastineau as novice-master. Guy told Father Camille Lefebvre, the new Provincial Superior, "If this young man becomes unable to work, he will at least know how to pray."[3] When Archbishop Bourget paid a visit to the college early in 1872, Brother André asked to speak to the prelate. Falling on his knees and placing his hands on the archbishop's lap, André told him of his desire to remain in the community. Bourget was sympathetic and assured him, "The community will keep you."[4] In August, the Provincial Council, with Father Lefebvre as chairman, met again, and this time decided to allow Brother André to take his vows. The minutes of the meeting read: "All members of the Council are present. The chairman proposes that Brother André be allowed to take his vows. All members of the Council are agreed to approve Brother André's admission to the religious profession, whilst remarking that though his health is rather weak, the Brother nevertheless remains quite capable of rendering fine services to the Congregation in view of his zeal and piety."[5] And so, on August 22, Brother André made his temporary vows:

> I, Brother André, named Alfred Bessette in the world, all unworthy that I am, supported nevertheless by the desire to serve the adorable Trinity, make for one year to God Almighty the vows of poverty, chastity, and obedience, according to the meaning of the rules and constitution of this congregation, in the presence of Our Lord Jesus Christ, the Blessed Virgin Mary, conceived without sin, her praiseworthy husband St. Joseph, and all the heavenly court, promising to accept whatever tasks it pleases my superiors to assign me.[6]

A year later, on August 27, 1873, the Council voted unanimously to permit Brother André to take his final vows. Final approval had to be obtained from the General Council in France, and this took several months. At last, on February, 2, 1874, Brother André, now twenty-eight, made his final vows.

Since André was deemed unsuited for manual labor on the farm that adjoined the College, he had been assigned in December, 1871 the "obedience" of Doorkeeper, or Porter, and the profession of his final vows confirmed him in this position indefinitely. His superiors felt that his quick mind and cheerful disposition made him an ideal choice to serve as the community's liaison with the public. In later years, Brother André, who loved puns, used to joke about the fact that his superiors were first bent on sending him away and then made him doorkeeper. He said, "My superiors showed me the door and I stayed there."[7] He was also given to remarking, "I was at the door forty years without going out."[8]

Notre-Dame College was located in what was then the little village of Côte-des-Neiges, or Snow Hill, which was named for a club which owned the Bellevue Inn, the rundown establishment which the CSC had purchased and converted into a school. Côte-des-Neiges, located at the foot of Mount Royal, was very much in the country, and the community had deliberately chosen a rural site for the school so that the students would be spared the temptations of the city. The Congregation had transformed the ballroom on the second floor into a chapel. A refectory, or dining room, was built on the first floor. The rest of the building was used for classrooms. The term "college" in the nineteenth century simply meant a private school and the two dozen boys who were enrolled in the early 1870s were between eight and twelve years old. So Notre-Dame College in Côte-des-Neiges was an elementary school, set up, in the words of a brochure printed by the community, for "families desirous of raising their little ones in the country under the wing of religion." Here nothing would be spared "for the development and moral faculties of these young people."[9]

The operation ran on a "shoestring." The staff, which included priests, teaching brothers, working brothers, as well as the handful of nuns who lived in the vegetable cellar and did the laundry and cooking, subsisted on bread and potatoes and shared everything in common, even overcoats and umbrellas. The College rapidly gained a favorable reputation, however, so that after little more than a decade of operation, the Bellevue Inn was razed and the school was moved into a large Victorian Gothic building that was erected. By 1895 the student body had expanded from two dozen boys to more than 300, about half of whom lived on campus, supervised by a staff of about thirty religious.

The CSC Constitution set forth a detailed job description for the Doorkeeper, or Brother Porter, as he was usually called. "Worthy of confidence, with a modest and natural exterior, active and intelligent," he was to be "polite and honest, accustomed to receiving everyone respectfully, knowing how to make a refusal accepted and not sending anyone away unhappy." He was not to speak "except when fitting and then to the proper authority." The Doorkeeper was to live in a "lodge" near the door, where, somewhat segregated from the rest of the community, he would eat, pray and do his spiritual exercises.[10]

Brother André seemed happy in this confining job, not only because he was free forever from a life of wandering, but more because he now had a chance to grow closer to God, shut off from the vanities of the world. He had come to the Congregation of Holy Cross, in pursuit, not of comfort or worldly pleasure, but of God. Father Henri-Paul Bergeron, who knew Brother André in his latter years, wrote that André was from the start "convinced that his vocation was such an inestimable grace that it could not be requited even by the most complete sacrifice of self."[11]

The only letters preserved from the "pen" of Brother André date from his early years at the College. Actually, never having learned to write, he had dictated his messages. The first he wrote to his Aunt Rosalie and Uncle Timothée, in St.-Césaire. On August 13, 1874, a few months after making his final vows, Brother André declared:

Dear Aunt and Uncle,

It has been a long time since you've heard from me. But I am happy in the state of life I have chosen, without, from all that, forgetting my benefactors. I trust you did not expect me to come and visit you during the vacation season, because, as I had mentioned to you, I can no longer go out on visits. Actually, I did not go out very much except downtown a few times on errands. Incidentally, I did pay a quick visit to Louis while running an errand some time ago.

31

I intend to abide by my promise because the happiness I have found in the Lord's house is so great in view of the fact that additional favors are granted me, thus making it that much easier for me to renounce all worldly satisfactions.

How I wish I had more time to spare to pray to God for more graces of all kinds, and to thank Him and serve His interests.

If you do come here to see me, I'll be the one who will be answering your summons at the door, and, needless to say, we'll chat at length together.

Your loving nephew,
Brother André, C.S.C.

A few months later, on January 22, 1875, Brother André wrote again to the Nadeaux:

Forgive me for my delay in replying to your kind letter of the 12th instant, I was waiting for just an opportunity that afforded me today, namely, the feast of your glorious patron St. Timothy. Since it is customary in families to present a bouquet to the head of the household on the feast of his patron saint, I could think of no more precious and scented bouquet to be offered to you than my remembrance of your countless benefactions on my behalf. What lovelier bouquet could I send you than the memory of all the worries and cares to which you consented for my welfare. As you can see, this bouquet is enhanced with the crown of the two religious vocations that have blossomed among the youngsters you have raised [apparently one of the Nadeaux children had become a nun]. In fact, a religious vocation is an outstanding grace, regardless of the unworthiness of him to whom it is given . . . What greater happiness can there be than that of sharing in the religious life apparently so sacrificial but in reality replete with consolations.

Your nephew never failing to pray for you,
Brother André, C.S.C.[12]

From these letters to the Nadeaux we learn that Brother

André maintained contact with his aunt and uncle, that he had apparently been to see them in the past, that he was too busy to do so for the foreseeable future and that his aunt and uncle evidently came to visit him. It is also clear that Brother André was extremely happy in his religious vocation.

How often Brother André was allowed to take vacations in the early years is not clear. It is apparent that he visited his sister Léocadie and her family in Sutton, Quebec in 1878. A year after his visit he dictated to his "beloved sister":

> I'll bet you feel somewhat offended that I've put off for quite a while my reply to your kind letter of Jan. 5 last. But please rest assured that my delay was due neither to indifference nor neglect; my numerous occupations have actually prevented me from attending to my personal mail.
>
> I was delighted to hear that all of you are enjoying good health. I hope and pray that God in His divine goodness will continue to render you ever happier, because I consider good health a source of happiness . . . I am quite well and looking forward to visiting you during the holidays.
>
> You request me to pray for you and your little ones. Needless to say, it always remains such a pleasure for me to pray for my family that I could hardly forget to do so. However, I shall pray more zealously and more fervently still during the lovely month of March, which will open shortly. This particular month is dedicated to good St. Joseph. In return, I'm sure, you will support me with your fervent prayers because I feel that parents' prayers for their children are most powerful on the Sacred Heart of Jesus.
>
> Goodbye. Best wishes to the entire family and a great big hug for the youngsters whom I am most anxious to see again.
>
> Devotedly yours,
> Brother André, C.S.C.[13]

At this point in his life, Brother André seems to have been happy and healthy, if very busy. What is interesting in this third letter is the fact that he refers to Léocadie as a "parent," confirming statements made in later years by his nieces that his relationship to his eldest sister was almost that of a son to a mother.

Content though he was, Brother André's life as Doorkeeper was backbreaking with work and austere with mortifications. The stark white walls of his lodge were adorned only by a crucifix and a print of St. Joseph. Brother André's "bed" was a mere bench, with rough leather upholstery, only sixteen inches wide! He had a bowl, a pitcher, and a wardrobe, as well as a chamber pot.

Brother André's duties were many and tedious. He had just enough knowledge of letters to keep an alphabetical list of everyone in residence at the College and to see that the boys signed in and signed out. When a visitor came to the door, André had to announce the name, "in a loud and intelligible voice, not forgetting the honorific title if it is a person of importance." Until an intercom was installed in 1890, whenever a caller came to the door, he had to go through the building in search of the person requested. He had to see that visitors did not stray into the parts of the building that were off-limits to the public, nor tarry beyond the hours of visitation. If a present was left at the door for any pupil, Brother André had to mark the gift with the student's identification number and place the gift in the steward's office or in the linen room. Whenever a member of the community returned from a trip, it was Brother André's duty to admit him and prepare something for him to eat.

Brother André also served as the community barber, shaving the priests and brothers and cutting their hair and that of the children in the only style allowed by the Congregation — one achieved by placing a bowl over the head and snipping off the locks that projected beneath it. Brother André's responsibilities did not end there, for he served as a general handyman for the community, braiding the cords of the religious, maintaining the wine cellar, sweeping the rooms, washing the windows and cleaning the outhouses. Utilizing his boyhood training, he served as the community shoemaker. He also worked as gardener.[14] Sometimes, at two or three in the morning, if he was not scrubbing floors, he was hauling rocks from the garden in two wheelbarrows. "I used two wheelbarrows to save time," he remarked later. I would push one a hundred yards and walk back to get the other, resting myself and reciting my Rosary. Several times while I was working, the cock's crowing reminded me that it was time to ring the awakening bell."[15]

The sisters complained that they did not have time to wash the boys' clothing, so to Brother André was delegated the task of taking the soiled linen of each of the boys to his respective home for his mother to launder. Every Wednesday he hitched a horse to a buggy and drove all over Montreal, leaving dirty clothing and picking up clean at dozens of homes. In addition, Brother André served as postman to the community, taking outgoing mail to the post office and returning with the day's letters and packages to distribute to students and staff.[16]

Brother André served also as a community watchman, looking out for fires and burglars. Once, at three in the morning, he had to rouse the brother who kept the stable to tell him that the horses were out and roaming in the garden.

His least favorite task was that of undertaker. Whenever a priest or brother died, it was Brother André who washed and dressed the body and prepared it for burial. Sometimes he was called upon to perform the same service for poor people in the village, or even in Montreal, who could not afford a professional undertaker. Nights after he laid out the bodies of the dead, Brother André had difficulty sleeping and heard frightening noises in his room.

When Brother André finally allowed himself a few winks on his narrow board-bed, it was with the knowledge that he had to rouse himself before the other members of the community. Each morning at five he rang the bell that signaled the beginning of the day, then knocked on the door of each of the religious, with the greeting *"Benedicamus Dominio"* (Let us bless the Lord), which was to elicit the response *"Deo gratias"* (Thanks be to God). After all the priests and brothers were awake, it was time for André to rouse all the pupils.

During the 1880s the superior of the College was Father Augustin Louage. This hot-tempered Frenchman also served as Provincial (supervising all three communities in Quebec) and as bursar (or treasurer) of the College Notre-Dame. He was remembered as an evil-natured martinet with "a very violent disposition towards everybody."[17] Very often Brother André was the victim of his tyrannical caprice. For instance, one day Louage sent the doorkeeper to the post office, assigning Brother Osée Coderr the task of watching the door until his return. For some reason, Brother Osée left the door momentarily, and it so happened that in his absence there was a knock on the door, and there was no one in earshot except Father Louage. When Brother André returned Louage exploded with wrath, demanding to know where he had been. André reminded the superior, "You sent me to the post office." Nevertheless, Louage snapped, "Is that so? I am the Provincial, the Superior, the Bursar, and now I must be doorkeeper as well! Kiss the ground, Brother André!" Without a single word of protest, Brother André kissed the ground.

Another time one of the pupils gave Brother André a piece of candy. At this time in his life, Brother André's normal sustenance consisted of one crust of bread a day dunked in milk. During Lent he dunked the bread in water. Not to hurt the boy's feelings, Brother André ate the candy — just as Father Louage walked by. The superior turned on André and accused him of "having a weakness for sweets," reprimanding him for gluttony. "I won't do it anymore!" Brother André promised.

On yet another occasion, a pupil complained to Father Louage that Brother André had spanked him. The superior summoned the doorkeeper, and without giving him a chance to explain himself, right in front of the boy and his father, he scolded André severely and ordered him to kiss the floor.[18]

"I never refused to do what was asked of me," Brother André later said of this time in his life. "I always answered, 'Yes,' and I finished at night what I couldn't do in the day."[19] No one ever heard a complaint cross the lips of Brother André. No matter what was asked of him, no matter how unreasonable his superior, André was always cheerful and even-tempered, even self-effacing, declaring of himself, "A good-for-nothing is good for everything."[20]

Despite his eighteen-hour work days and his ascetical diet, Brother André's health seems to have been reasonably good in his thirties and forties. He would often say later that the key to a long and healthy life was to "eat as little as possible and work as much as possible." When he was forty-three, however,

Brother André collapsed with pneumonia, spitting up blood. A doctor ordered two months of complete rest. Moments after the doctor left Father Louage entered the sickroom. "Would it bother you if I died quietly here at the house, or while washing windows?" André asked. Louage said nothing. Thereupon André said, "If it doesn't make any difference to you, it doesn't make any difference to me." So, without any protest by the superior, he disregarded the orders of the doctor and went to work again. When the physician returned a few days later he was horrified to find his patient not only out of bed but washing windows. Warned that he was endangering his life, André laughed and said, "If I die, the community will be well rid of me!"[21] Brother André suffered no lasting effects from this episode, and despite his frail appearance and "capricious stomach," many of his confreres were of the opinion that he was "strong as an ox."[22] Not only did he consider incessant work, an austere diet and little rest ingredients for a long and healthy life, he resorted to such other eccentricities of ascetical hygiene as taking baths in the snow in the midst of winter![23]

As the years relentlessly succeeded one another and Brother André grew from a young to a middle-aged man, he gained the love and respect of his community, of the students and of the parents for his quiet piety, his good cheer and his helpfulness. When not interacting with others, Brother André seemed constantly in prayer. Even while he worked, he prayed or sang hymns. Scrubbing floors in the wee hours of the morning, he nonetheless found time to repair to the chapel for an hour of prayer before he retired. If they happened to be about in the depths of the night, sometimes his confreres found him asleep on his knees in the chapel. But no matter how little sleep he allowed himself, Brother André was never remiss in providing the community its morning reveille.

Brother André was popular with the students and formed many lasting friendships with them. A number of parents from New England sent their sons to Notre-Dame for their primary education. Several of these boys eventually became priests in the States. Years later, when Brother André traveled in America, these former students acted as host to him in their parishes. One student, Maurice Duplessis, pursued a different career, one in politics, and Brother André lived to see him elected Prime Minister of the Province of Quebec. The boys loved the little Brother because he was kind and friendly, and took time to listen to their problems, their hopes, and their dreams. He taught them little prayers and talked to them of "The Good God" and about St. Joseph and the need for frequent Communion. "For us, Brother André was perfection," a former student wrote later. "We respected him, we greeted him, and he always had a beautiful smile."[24] Sometimes his pious platitudes annoyed some of the tougher boys. For example, the man, who, when asked in later years whether the Brother had "a pious word" for him from time to time while he was at Notre-Dame, replied: "Oh, almost too many! I had enough to last me for the rest of my life!"[25] Some expressions he taught his young friends were: "The wounds of Jesus are a book from which you can get more knowledge than from the wisest men,"[26] and "The suffering Jesus is the door to union with the Trinity."[27] He taught them devotion to the Holy Spirit saying, "What the Holy Spirit did for the Apostles, He will do for you."[28] Of course, he taught them to love St. Joseph and to imitate him as closely as possible, praying these words: "O Good St. Joseph, grant me what you yourself would ask if you were in my place on earth. O Good St. Joseph . . . be my help and listen to my prayer."[29] Most moving were Brother André's remarks on heaven. "When he described heaven," a former pupil recounted, "he seemed to see it, so brightly did his countenance beam with joy."[30]

Brother André was, moreover, beloved by visitors to the College. Some of the fathers were wont to stop in at the doorkeeper's lodge and pass the time of day, smoking their stinking cigarettes and cigars without a protest from their austere friend who always had a kind word and a funny story. (If anyone had the insensitivity to tell him an off-color joke, André said nothing, but glared so coldly that the teller never repeated the mistake.) Whenever he visited private homes to deliver laundry or on some other errand, Andre distinguished himself for his kindness and willingness to listen to the recitation of troubles. Tramps used to come to the door of the College for handouts and it was Brother André, as doorkeeper, who spoke with them. Doubtless remembering his years as a wandering laborer, he invariably went to the kitchen to fetch a bowl of soup or a few slices of bread and stood, talking to the tramp with the same respect he accorded to doctors, lawyers, clergy and other "persons of importance."

In later years, the rumor spread that Brother André had been the community doormat. Gossip had it that during the tenure of Father Louage and even later, Brother André was called the "beaten dog," or scapegoat. The men who lived at Notre-Dame at the time denied that André had ever been abused or mistreated. In the early years, the entire community had to work extremely hard and all priests and brothers had multiple responsibilities. By the time Brother André was in his forties, he was known as the "lightning rod" of the community, not so much because he tended to draw the superior's wrath (which apparently was blasted with equal force and frequency upon everyone in his path), but because his holiness and devotion, in particular, his long and fervent prayers, kept the community from harm. Even so, as Brother André approached his fifth decade, he was known only to his confreres, to the pupils and their parents and to the members of his biological family as one of many holy religious who were dedicating their lives to educate the youth of Canada. He was celebrated for his piety, his humility, his diligence, and his humor, but there were other religious — especially among the working brothers — who had a similar reputation for sanctity. It was only with time, after his hair had turned silver and furrows had come to mark his craggy brow that it became apparent to others that Brother André had a special mission.

Chapter Four

The Oil and the Medal

T he Brothers of Holy Cross, who were deeply devoted to St. Joseph, had brought with them from France the folk custom of anointing the sick with oil that had burned before the image of St. Joseph and rubbing them with a medal of the saint. The use of oil to anoint the sick is authorized in the New Testament by St. James, who wrote: "Is there any among you sick? Let him call for the elders of the church, and let them pray over him, anointing him with oil in the name of the Lord, and the prayer of faith will save the sick man, and the Lord will raise him up; and if he has committed sins, he will be forgiven" (James 5:14-15). The use of the medal is reminiscent of remedies mentioned in Scripture such as the waters of the River Jordan in which the prophet Elisha bade Naaman, the Syrian leper, bathe for healing (2 Kings 5:1-14) and the paste of mud and spittle with which the Lord anointed the eyes of a blind man (John 9:1-7).

From the beginning of his vocation, Brother André seems to have been particularly fond of using this remedy to combat sickness. Whenever he himself was ill he asked a confrere to anoint him with "St. Joseph's oil," and rub him vigorously with a medal wrapped in cloth. As time went on, he came to recommend this procedure to any of the students who complained of sickness. If he was cutting a boy's hair, for example, and the boy complained of a toothache, Brother André touched the boy's face with a medal. If he found one of the pupils in the infirmary with a stomach ache, he applied the oil and rubbed him. He did the same with his confreres and it was not too many years after he came to Notre-Dame that his companions realized that the ministrations of their unassuming little doorkeeper often had dramatic results.

The first clear documentation of Brother André's reputation as a healer dates from June, 1878, when one of his confreres, Brother Aldéric Manceau, wrote an article for *The Annals of the Saint Joseph Association,* a type of newsletter circulated among the various CSC communities. Brother Aldéric, a native of France, then fifty-one, was a teaching brother who was serving as bursar at Notre-Dame. Aldéric wished to glorify St. Joseph by recounting "some of the numerous favors he accorded us here with that liberality which extends everywhere to those who invoke him with confidence and love." The first instance Brother Aldéric recounted concerned his own recovery from illness.

On February 5, 1877, Brother Aldéric cut his right leg to the bone on a piece of iron. He neglected the injury, with the result that after a week, the limb was swollen with an infection that resisted all the remedies proposed by his doctor. By the end of March, the leg was in such a state that Aldéric was being warned about the possibility of amputation. At this point

> No longer having any confidence in [his medical treatments] I turned to the friend of the unfortunate, Saint Joseph . . . I did not want to end the month consecrated to our holy protector without asking him for my complete cure. I promised him that if he deigned to hear my prayer I would work with new ardor to propagate his cult . . . On March 31 . . . I asked little Brother André to get me a little oil from St. Joseph's lamp, that oil that he had told marvels of. Good Brother André did not think that he was authorized to grant me the object of my request, and to get it I had to have recourse to Brother Ladislas . . . , the sacristan of Notre-Dame. In the evening I poured some drops of my precious flask on the wound in my leg, praying to St. Joseph to heal me and

promising him, if my prayer was heard, to partake of
Communion the next day in Thanksgiving. When I woke
up I did not feel any pain in the leg, and, after two days
without uncovering the wound, when I took off the bandages, I saw a dry crust on the scarred wound. Each of my
visitors can state from observation that I am radically
cured. Glory, love, and gratitude to Saint Joseph! From
then on I have taken up my usual work.[1]

Brother Aldéric related other instances of cures affected
through St. Joseph's oil. One of his confreres, Brother Alexander, had been a victim of the smallpox epidemic of 1871. A
pustule had formed on his leg which never healed and after
several years his entire limb was "swollen, black, and livid —
terrible-looking." The afflicted man found it painful even to
stand, and he, like Brother Aldéric, was threatened with amputation. After a novena, however, during which he "oiled his
leg with St. Joseph's oil," Brother Alexander found himself
"suddenly cured from an inveterate illness and a chronic condition."[2]
A man from the village of Côte-des-Neiges named Monsieur
Cadat had a severe eye infection that threatened to result in
blindness. Using St. Joseph's oil as an eyewash, "the second
day he was cured and resumed his job, blessing the foster father of Jesus and the holy husband of Mary."[3] Another man had
an arm almost totally immobilized by arthritis. When, at
Brother André's suggestion, he rubbed the arm with St. Joseph's oil, he obtained prompt relief.[4] A woman, apparently the
mother of one of the pupils, contracted diphtheria, a highly infectious throat disease which at the time was associated with a
30% mortality rate. She had "lost all hope" when "they" gave
her some St. Joseph's oil. "Her confidence in the holy protector of Christian families was immediately regarded. She was
cured and the deadly contagion disappeared from the house."[5]
Brother Aldéric concluded his article: "I stop. I would not fin-
ish if I tried to tell you all the marvels and graces done here by
our good and powerful St. Joseph."[6]
Several things are important about Brother Aldéric's letter.
This is the first documentation of cures wrought through the
ministration of Brother André. However, in only two of the

cures, is André mentioned as being directly involved, once in "telling of the marvels" of the oil of St. Joseph, and again, in urging an arthritic man to rub his arm with the oil. The use of St. Joseph's oil as a remedy for sickness did not originate with Brother André, but the doorkeeper, out of his powerful devotion to the saint, enthusiastically recommended the practice. The dramatic results were attributed both by him and by his confreres to the mercy of St. Joseph, and to that alone. Throughout his life Brother André would insist that he had no special gift save for a mighty confidence in St. Joseph.

As time went on, however, Brother André came increasingly to be identified with the cures that were taking place in Côte-des-Neiges. Another early miracle was reported in 1884. Brother André was scrubbing the floors when one of his confreres told him of a woman who had come to see him. Without even looking up, much less going to see the woman, who was a total stranger, Brother André mumbled, "Let her walk." When the woman received this curt message, she was instantly cured of the condition that had necessitated the use of crutches. This lady, who was said to have been wealthy and prominent told her friends about this marvel wrought by the little doorkeeper of Notre-Dame.

When questioned in the last year of his life about the first cures wrought by St. Joseph at Notre-Dame, Brother André mentioned the case of a Monsieur St.-Laurent, "who lived at Pointe-Saint-Charles." André recalled: "His wife was very sick. We made a novena together in honor of St. Joseph. One evening, M. St.-Laurent was surprised to find his dear wife at the offices, on Visitation Street, of her doctor. He was surprised because up to that time she was incapable of leaving the house. 'How did you come to be here?' he asked her. 'I came,' she said to the doctor, 'to announce my cure, due to the intercession of St. Joseph.' And she went home, perfectly normal.'"[7]

Azarias Claude had a fuller, but slightly different version of what must surely be the same case. In 1942 he recounted what Brother André had told him twenty years before concerning an incident that had transpired four decades previously. According to Claude, the man, whose name he did not remember, had two sons at the College. When he visited them each week, he met Brother André at the door. André, troubled because the man seemed invariably irritable, stopped him one day and asked him how he was.

"All right," mumbled the disgruntled man.

"How's everything at home?"

"What's that to you?" he snarled.

Brother André pressed him further, saying that it was apparent that something was wrong, since he always seemed upset. The man broke down and told him, "I have enough problems to be in a bad mood!" explaining that his wife was a chronic invalid who required a nurse to take care of her and whose astronomical medical bills were jeopardizing his ability to pay for his boys' schooling. He started to walk away towards his carriage, but André followed him, with the assurance: "At this very hour, things are better with you at home. Tell me about it the next time you come to see your boys. Goodbye."

In Claude's version, the man reached his home two or three hours later, after attending to some business. At the very moment when Brother André had assured him that things were better at home, his wife had asked her nurse, "Bring me a chair. I would like to sit in my room." When the nurse objected, "You can't get up!" the sick woman insisted that she felt better. When the nurse placed a chair on a balcony overlooking the street, the invalid, bedfast for months, took a seat there to await her husband.

As the husband approached his house in his buggy he wondered who the woman was sitting on the balcony, never once dreaming that it could be his wife. When he drew closer, he realized that it was indeed his wife and that she had been healed, just as Brother André had predicted.[8]

In the same 1936 interview in which he gave his version of the healing of the sick wife, Brother André recounted the cure, around 1880, of a ten-year-old boy whose family name was Clément. According to André, this child suffered from "an incurable fever in his legs" (un fièvre incurable aux jambes). "The doctor despaired of his case," André recalled. "Our sick boy made a novena to St. Joseph . . . who obtained his cure before he finished his prayers . . . He lost his crutches when he returned to class and they were never again found. But their owner was not upset at all, because he saw that his cure was complete and permanent."[9]

A case better documented in that it was described in writing immediately after it occurred by the man it concerned, was recounted in a CSC newsletter in 1890. Brother Ovide Ianneville, then thirty-two years old, had been at one time the community tailor, but had been forced to relinquish that "obedience" because of his failing eyesight and make his contribution by sweeping the floors. The specific ailment that afflicted Brother Ovide was not named, but it was characterized by the formation of white spots on the cornea and a chronic inflammation of the entire eye. Despite the ministrations of two general practitioners and an ophthalmologist, Brother Ovide became almost totally blind and was forced to give up even his janitorial duties. His eyes hurt so fiercely that it was impossible for him to sleep or rest. Then, on the morning of August 15, 1890, while praying "to calm his pain," he "followed the advice the brothers were giving him," namely, "Put on your eyes some of the olive oil from the lamp that burns in front of St. Joseph and promise that great saint something in gratitude." Confidently, Brother Ovide put the oil in his eyes during a novena and promised that, if cured, he would receive Communion and tell all his friends and companions about "the power and favors" of St. Joseph. He was completely cured and recounted his story in fulfillment of the promise he made to the saint.[10] It should be noted that no specific mention was made of Brother André, only "the brothers," an indication that the use of the oil was not merely an idiosyncrasy of the doorkeeper, but a devotional practice embraced by most of the community.

Yet, as we have seen, because Brother André was the most enthusiastic promoter of the practice, it was he who was identified with the cures that were occurring in the 1880s with increasing frequency. Parents of the pupils came to him seeking relief, and soon, total strangers were knocking on the door of the school to see the "healer." Brother André, embarrassed and bewildered at the attention directed to him, was adamant that all credit for any unusual favor go to God and St. Joseph. "Don't thank me. It is St. Joseph you must thank. Go and say a prayer to him,"[11] he urged those who thanked him for healing them. Of his rubbings he insisted, "The medal is only metal. The oil is just olive oil. But it makes [people] think more about

St. Joseph and so strengthens their faith."[12] He complained: "How stupid people are to think that Brother André makes miracles. The Good God makes the miracles, St. Joseph obtains them, and I am only the wire which transmits their blessings."[13] The more his fame grew, the more humble and self-effacing Brother André seemed to become. "It is with the smallest brushes," he said of himself, "that the Artist paints the most exquisitely beautiful pictures."[14]

The people of Quebec tended in those days to great piety and were receptive to the ministry of Brother André and the devotion to St. Joseph that he taught. St. Joseph, the Protector of Canada, was the object of intense popular devotion even before Brother André came on the scene and many miracles were attributed to the intervention of the saint that in no way involved the little doorkeeper at Côte-des-Neiges (at least as far as was apparent). For instance, in April, 1896, a community near Montreal was menaced by floodwaters. The parish priest took a one-inch statuette of St. Joseph and flung it off a bridge into the boiling waters, shouting, "Save yourself and save us!" It is not recorded whether the figurine was recovered, but the waters subsided immediately.[15] Nor was Brother André the only religious of his time and country to whom miraculous cures were attributed. The Franciscan Father Frédéric Jansoone of Ghyvelde (1838-1916), who became an admirer of Brother André, was reputed to have manifested miraculous powers of healing. The Rev. Albert Hughes, a pastor at the High Park Baptist Church of Toronto in the early years of the twentieth century was another contemporary to whom favors of healing were attributed. Colonel George Ham, an early biographer of Brother André, preserved a comment about the ministry of Pastor Hughes: "I have seen miracles performed before my very eyes within the last seven days. I have seen lame men get up and walk. I have beheld men whose eyes have been blind for years see wonderful things, and I have heard the dumb speak."[16]

Not unique among his contemporaries in his reputation as a healer, nor the originator of the practice of rubbing the sick with St. Joseph's oil, Brother André was remarkable in the intensity of his faith in God and devotion to St. Joseph. If he had any special mission, he said, it was to teach devotion to the saint. The dramatically proliferating favors, the miracles (which soon came, in fact, to surpass in number and magnitude of those attributed to any other person and place in Canada) were, he said, a sign of St. Joseph's response to a people's prayers. Brother André's mission was to exhort the faithful to go to St. Joseph: *Ite ad Joseph.* The favors that brought swelling crowds to seek him occurred, he said, because St. Joseph was using him in the same way an electrical generator makes use of a wire.

By the 1890s Brother André was more than merely one of several devout men whose prayers were alleged to effect miracles. It was increasingly clear that he was set apart for a unique mission, the mission of making known the power of St. Joseph through the favors the saint deigned to work through him.

As his fame increased, problems of various kinds thrust themselves in the path of the little doorkeeper of Côte-des-Neiges. But in the early days, the most pressing problem and concern was the increasing stream of visitors who beat a path to the College of Notre-Dame to seek the prayers of Brother André.

Chapter Five

A Chapel on the Hillside

In the early 1890s, visitors to Brother André at the College numbered only three or four a day, and this posed no problem. As the numbers grew, the question arose as to how and where Brother André should meet with the sick so as to disrupt his duties and the life of the school as little as possible. Most of the religious were highly supportive of Brother André's work, sharing his devotion to St. Joseph and his belief that Canada's patron was making his presence felt through cures wrought through the application of holy oils and holy medals. Brother André now had a firm supporter in Father Louis Geoffrion, who had succeeded Augustin Louage as Director of the College and Superior of Religious in 1888. Geoffrion, a spare, balding man with a clean-shaven upper lip and white chin whiskers in the Amish style was about eight years older than Brother André, and, if possible, even more austere and ascetical. He spent long hours in prayer, mended his own clothing, took no vacations, ate little and suffered from constant digestive problems. "You want to live to be old? Eat less!" was a favorite counsel.[1] (He lived to be nearly 100.)

But there were dissenting voices. One of the most strenuous was that of a teaching brother named Henri Dureau, the acerbic, chain-smoking counselor of the College, whose duty it was to supervise the discipline of the boys. He was concerned that sick people — many of them total strangers — were finding their way into the building when Brother André's myriad duties took him away from his lodge, and that they were wandering through the halls in search of the "miracle man." Concerned that a constant stream of unauthorized, unsupervised visitors made it difficult for students to study without distraction, Brother Henri complained to Father Geoffrion. The superior supported Brother André, but asked him to confine his visits with the sick to an empty storeroom near the lodge. Anyone could walk into the building, however, and if Brother André was not in immediate evidence, there was nothing to stop visitors from roaming around the building in search of him. Even when callers were escorted to the storeroom, the visits still proved disruptive to the academic activities of the school.

Even more vociferous opposition came from Dr. Joseph Albini Charette, the school physician. A large, impressive, dignified man, Charette was a devout Roman Catholic and a dedicated civic worker. Although described as a sensitive, good-hearted gentleman, he was disturbed by the large number of sick persons, many of whom were suffering from tuberculosis and other contagious diseases, who were allowed free access to a school for children. "This is not a hospital," Charette complained to Geoffrion. "Keep the sick people away." Pious Christian though he was, Charette looked askance at Brother André's practice of anointing the sick with St. Joseph's oil. Speaking as a scientist, he objected, "This is no way to heal people!" and began to accuse Brother André of being a "quack doctor." One incident particularly enraged Charette.

There was a boy in the infirmary with a raging fever. The physician had ordered complete bed rest. Brother André went to see the child, applied the medal and oil, and told him, "You're not sick," and sent him out to play. When Dr. Charette found the boy outside, he was wild with rage, even though, upon examining the child, he found that his fever had vanished and he was perfectly well. Perhaps the boy's illness was not as serious as he first feared, but he, Dr. Charette, and not Brother André, was the school physician, and the doorkeeper, who had no degree in medicine or in anything else for that matter, had no right to butt in, recklessly endangering the lives of his patients with his whimsical medical judgments and his crude folk remedies.

So, at some point in the late 1890s someone complained to the new archbishop of Montreal, Monsignor Paul Bruchési (1885-1939), who summoned Father Geoffrion. Bruchési, a large majestic man of impressive intellect who gazed at the world through a lorgnette (eyeglasses mounted on a long handle) made Geoffrion aware of the concern about the risks involved in receiving diseased persons in a school for young children. "Tell me," asked the archbishop, "if Brother André were asked not to receive the sick at the school, would he obey?" Geoffrion insisted that he had no question at all but that André would "obey immediately."

This was all Bruchési wished to know. He was apparently more concerned about the possibility that one of his religious was becoming the subject of a cult than he was about questions of public health. The assurance that Brother André was totally submissive to his superiors prompted the archbishop to paraphrase the words of Rabbi Gamaliel about the first Christians: "Let him continue. If his work is human, it will collapse of itself. If it is of God, it will last."[2]

It was agreed, however, that it was best for Brother André to meet the sick across the street from the College in a large, ornate ginderbread-gabled, late-Victorian trolley shelter. Thus, for several years, Brother André's office was a public streetcar station. Interestingly enough, no one complained at this time, not the trolley company, nor the town fathers, nor the Board of Health, nor the commuters, who grew accustomed to waiting for their streetcar in a shelter jammed with sick people ministered to by a little man who rubbed them with religious medals and holy oil.

Soon, however, a definitive solution was at hand to the problem of where Brother André was to carry on his ministry, as a tract of land had just been acquired by the College, across the street, just behind the streetcar stop, on the western slope of Mount Royal. This heavily wooded slope had for years belonged to a kindly old Scotsman by the name of Alexander Gunn, who allowed the boys, when properly supervised, to play on the property. In the mid-90s, however, Gunn sold out to a man named Michael Guerin, who despised the school and its pupils, and turned his vicious dogs on boys, and even religious, who dared trespass. Father Geoffrion was quite alarmed when he learned in 1896 that Guerin wanted to sell the land and refused even to consider an offer from the CSC. Côte-des-Neiges, now that the streetcar line had been extended from Montreal, was undergoing rapid suburbanization, and Geoffrion was apprehensive about the use to which the land might be put once it was sold and developed. Concerned that his pupils thrive in an environment in which they would be shielded from the vanities of the world, his ascetical soul was aghast at the thought that the land might be sold to developers who might build a bar, or gambling hall, or, worse, an amusement park.

Father Geoffrion was convinced that St. Joseph would obtain the land for his community. So was Brother André. When Brother Aldéric (whose infected leg had been healed years earlier) told Brother André that whenever he left the statue of St. Joseph in his room facing away from the mountain, he would return to find the image pointed towards Mount Royal, the doorkeeper calmly observed, "That's because St. Joseph wants to be honored there."[3]

One day Father Geoffrion and Brother Aldéric decided to brave Guerin's dogs and walk up the hillside to bury a medal of St. Joseph in the hollow of a large pine. The two men besought the saint to remove the obstacles to the purchase of the land. Their orisons were not in vain, for within days Guerin changed his mind and sold the land to the Provincial Council of the CSC. The religious, jubilant, named the tract St. Joseph's Park. At the time, plans called for converting the lower part of the slope into a garden for the school and community but leaving the upper slope untouched as a place of sylvan recreation for students and faculty.

As soon as the land was acquired, the priests and brothers of the College went up to clear the land set aside for the garden, constructing a path up the steep slope, a little driveway they named St. Joseph's Boulevard. The next year a small wooden pavilion, or belvedere, was constructed on the hill to serve as a picnic area for the boys and a place of meditation for the religious. A year after that a little stage for school pageants was erected.

It was about 1900 when Brother André asked permission of

Father Benjamin Lecavalier (who had succeeded Father Geoffrion as superior in 1898) to build a shrine to St. Joseph on the mountain. This would be, André explained, a capital way of getting the growing numbers of sick out of the streetcar shelter. He proposed to use the five-cent fees he received for cutting hair (which were routinely turned over to the treasurer of the community) as a means of raising the funds to construct a small chapel. Lecavalier was at first cool to the proposal, but Brother André began to drop medals of St. Joseph all over the mountain, telling everyone he encountered, "St. Joseph wants me to promise to build him a chapel here." About a year after he first made his suggestion, Brother André found himself sick in the infirmary with Father Lecavalier as his fellow patient. During the time he had the superior as his captive audience, André was able to convince Lecavalier to authorize the construction of a chapel on the hill. The doorkeeper was authorized to set aside his haircut fees to finance the project. During the next few years, Brother André augmented this meager source of income by placing a statue of St. Joseph on the mountain with a bowl beneath it for donations. These modest contributions, as well as donations of cash and kind from interested laypersons, were all permitted by André's superior to finance the chapel on the hill.

By 1904 Brother André had $200 and the father of one of the pupils, who ran a lumber yard, had pledged to supply all the wood needed for the shrine. Now the exact site had to be designated. André rejected Lecavalier's choice of a site, insisting that he had "seen" the chapel in another spot. Lecavalier allowed the doorkeeper to put his chapel where he wanted it.

Before the chapel could be constructed, a large plateau, or level area, had to be built up where there was only a narrow jutting promontory, or cliff, surrounded by deep ravines. Brother André had to hire workmen to do this considerable project of landscaping. The Brother hired the workmen himself on Monday and paid them Saturday afternoon. After a short time his savings had been exhausted and he had to pray for further donations to pay the workmen each week. It so happened that at the beginning of each week, André had no idea where he was going to obtain the money to pay his men on Saturday, but he was always confident that St. Joseph would come through for him on time. Invariably, by Saturday afternoon, he had the cash in hand. After he paid the laborers, the foreman would ask Brother André, "Shall we come back to work on Monday?" When the Brother replied, "I don't know. I haven't got any more money," the foreman always said, "Bah! We'll come back. Next Saturday, if you have the money, you'll pay us. If you haven't, we can wait."[4] They never had to wait.

The chapel itself was constructed by Brother Abundius Piché, the community carpenter. In his mid-forties, Abundius was a thin little man whom some described as looking like a bearded version of Brother André. He, too, had a reputation for great saintliness. It took Brother Abundius seven or eight days to construct a little wooden shed measuring sixteen feet by twelve. The modest interior decorations, along with a large statue of St. Joseph painted blue and white, were donated by a local sculptor named Dufresne. The chapel was opened in October, 1904, with a solemn High Mass and a procession by the religious and students of the College. It was announced then that the chapel, known as The Oratory (or place of prayer) would henceforth be "a place of pilgrimage for the favors obtained from heaven by the intercession of St. Joseph."[5]

Actually, the need for a shrine to St. Joseph had been recognized fifty years before by Archbishop Bourget, who had declared: "St. Joseph must have a church which will . . . supply the service of all the others and in which he may receive every day the public honors due to his eminent virtues . . . [to serve as] a place of pilgrimage whither the faithful will come to visit him."[6] The tiny chapel was situated on the edge of the bluff built up on the mountainside by Brother André's workmen. It had room only for an altar made of pine by Brother Abundius and ten chairs. For this reason, the back of the chapel (facing the mountain) was comprised of big double doors which opened outward so that a larger congregation, seated on backless benches, could follow the service. The chapel had no windows and was illuminated through a skylight. Since it was unheated, no services could be held in winter. Nonetheless, Brother André saw that a light burned day and night before the statue of St. Joseph, and he himself climbed the mountain, in all kinds of weather, nearly every day, to pray before it during the winter of 1904-1905.

In the spring of 1905 an anonymous benefactor donated a set of wall reliefs comprising a way of the Cross, and on June 1 of that year, an Ascension Day Mass was offered there. Later that summer the very first pilgrimage was directed to St. Joseph's Oratory, from a parish in the town of St.-Laurent. It was not until the following May that the existence of the Oratory caught the attention of the press, when an article in *La Presse* of Montreal appeared, declaring:

> A most impressive religious ceremony took place . . . yesterday morning at Côte-des-Neiges. It was . . . the day of the annual pilgrimage to the chapel of St. Joseph of Notre-Dame-des-Neiges, a pilgrimage that has been taking place for several years. [Actually this was only the second year]. The chapel is . . . situated on the side of the mountain, facing the college of the Holy Cross Fathers . . . The temperature was superb and the congregation numerous and reverent. The divine service was celebrated in the open air under the great blue sky. The spectacle was most edifying and left an indelible impression on the spirit of the faithful . . . Despite the late hour, many persons approached the Holy Table to receive Communion.[7]

That same year (1906) Father Lecavalier was succeeded as superior by Father Georges Dion, a short man of middle years known for his dignified and icy reserve. He was at least once characterized as "not a man but an icicle."[8] He was also described as "a man of great prudence" who felt it necessary to restrain the enthusiasm of some of André's lay friends so that the doorkeeper and his Oratory could enjoy the good graces of Archbishop Bruchési. One of Dion's first acts as superior was to remove the collection of crutches, canes, and braces that had been left in the chapel by persons professing cures. "We don't want to be accused of superstitution," he explained.[9] Eventually Brother André persuaded the new superior to allow the display of these ex-votive offerings.

Brother Henri had been somewhat mollified now that Brother André was ministering to the sick across the street and not in the school, but Dr. Charette was still hostile to "the Oily Brother" with his "Religion of Massage." Along with certain others, he complained to the Montreal Board of Health. A physician was dispatched to make inquiry and determine if Brother André was doing anything illegal. The doctor from the Board of Health asked Brother André if it was true that he ministered to the sick. André admitted that he did. How did he minister to them? The Good Brother gave the doctor a medal of St. Joseph and a bottle of the oil, saying: "This is what I give. You can use it. It could be useful to you." Taken aback by the Brother's disarming ingenuousness, the physician, whose name has not been recorded, remarked: "If it is like that, you needn't worry, at least for what concerns City Hall. I don't see anything wrong in what you give."[10]

Brother André was deeply hurt by Charette's hostility and the criticisms of others who accused him of being a "fakehealer," a "charlatan," and a "mountebank." To a certain extent he was oblivious to criticism, believing that St. Joseph was in charge and would deal with opponents, but when his own good faith and integrity were questioned, he was deeply wounded. When he learned that a local priest had written an article ridiculing him for creating a "religion of massage," Brother André burst into tears. "I don't know what I did to them. I don't know why they give me such a hard time. Is it then such a great harm to pray to St. Joseph with the sick?"[11] While Brother André was ready to accept criticism that he was silly and ignorant, he was wounded when his mission to lead people to St. Joseph was attacked.

Events soon transpired to hurl Dr. Charette into Brother André's camp. Madame Charette was stricken with a severe nosebleed that her husband was unable to check. She insisted on seeing Brother André, but the physician refused to listen to her until he was afraid that she would bleed to death. Then he went to Brother André and explained the situation. The Charettes lived in a large house on the main street of Côte-des-Neiges, just a few blocks from the College. The doctor explained to Brother André that he had been such a bitter opponent for so long that he would feel foolish if people saw him bring the "fake healer" into his home. André told Charette, "She will not die," and walked away. When Charette returned home a few minutes later, he found that is wife's hemorrhage had ceased — at the very moment when Brother André announced that she would not die. At once the Brother gained an enthusiastic supporter in Dr. Charette, who thereafter encouraged André to accompany him in his car on visits to the sick. He even urged his patients to go to the Oratory. When Charette was killed in a 1914 automobile accident, however, people shook their heads and murmured, "He spoke too much against Brother André."[12]

Shortly after the visit of the representative from the Board of Health, Brother André pressed Father Dion for permission to further enlarge the chapel. After some deliberation, the superior authorized the Brother to spend the $300 that was on hand, not to enlarge the chapel, but to extend St. Joseph's Boulevard. When André received a gift of $500 a short time later, Father Dion granted him permission to use this to enlarge the Oratory. "What is this?" asked the superior. "Do you want to build a basilica up there?" To Dion's amazement, André nodded.[13]

Dion now had to seek the permission of Archbishop Bruchési, who insisted: "Before I can permit the erection of a public sanctuary, I must see its plan and know its approximate cost. I moreover insist that the sum necessary for the construction of this church be well guaranteed beforehand." Explaining that because of the many building projects in the archdiocese which had to be supported by the faithful, Bruchési said that he could not authorize collections for the Oratory in any of the parish churches. Money would have to be raised through the College and by the friends and supporters of Brother André. He gave permission to use raffles to raise money, however. It was agreed that the ownership of the Oratory would reside with the College, which would be responsible for the services of worship.[14]

The five hundred dollars proved inadequate to finance the enlargement of the sanctuary, but a group of Montreal businessmen came up with the money, forming a group known as "The Work of the Oratory." Father Dion cautioned that the archbishop had given only tentative approval. Bruchési would have to be approached with the specific plans. It was still uncertain whether they would meet with his approval. "Have you got a St. Joseph medal?" asked André. When Dion replied that he did not, the doorkeeper gave him one, charging him to "hold it tightly in your hand while talking to His Exellency."[15] It worked. Bruchési approved the plans and authorized the enlargement.

It was probably in this project that Brother André drew upon the help of a carpenter by the name of Calixte Richard, who came to the mountain for healing. Richard was so ill with what he insisted was a stomach tumor that he could hardly walk. Brother André announced to the carpenter that he was not sick. Richard indignantly insisted that he was, refusing André's invitation to accompany him across the street to the College for a bowl of soup. "I can't eat," he said.

"If St. Joseph healed you, would you come work on the mountain?" André asked.

"Willingly," replied the ailing carpenter.

So Richard agreed to go with André to the College kitchen to partake of some soup. André dismissed him and told him to report for work the next morning. At 6:15 a.m. the next day Richard appeared, totally cured, and began work.[16] (This incident is often associated with the 1904 construction, but Brother Abundius testified that he built the original chapel unassisted.)

A wooden canopy was constructed over the place where the faithful had previously worshipped in the open air, and, later, wooden walls sheeted in tarpaper were constructed to enclose it. In 1906 a harmonium (reed organ) was installed, and a small charcoal stove was set up in the fall of 1908 so that services could be held year round. Then electric lights were installed and the walls of the nave, which was enlarged to one hundred feet in length by forty in width, were enclosed in sheet iron, and a large bronze bell was installed.

In July, 1909 Brother André was nearly sixty-four years old. He had served as doorkeeper of the College for nearly forty years, although in the last decade the number of menial tasks assigned to him had been considerably reduced as he gave increasing time to ministering to the sick and supervising the operation of the Oratory. He was now relieved of his duties as doorkeeper and given the new "obedience" as guardian, or caretaker, of the Oratory. Now Brother André could devote all eighteen hours of his workday to his mission. He moved his few possessions to a little shed near the chapel, where, after forty years of sleeping on a narrow bench, he was given a folding bed, as well as, wonder of wonders, a telephone!

Over the next few years the chapel was slowly expanded, bit by bit, as gifts trickled in. A tower was constructed to house the bronze bell, and sanitary facilities were constructed on the mountain. Then, on Ascension Day, 1910, more than 3,000 people followed in procession a new statue of St. Joseph which had been blessed by Pope Pius X.

The year 1910 marked an "explosion of cures" that made headlines in major newspapers and gained Brother André national notoriety. On Monday, January 10, 1910, Brother André's picture appeared on the front page of the Montreal *La Patrie,* beneath the headline: "A MIRACULOUS HEALING AT ST. JOSEPH'S ORATORY." The newspaper reported, "A poor cripple walking painfully with the help of crutches, went to ask [Brother André] to give him back the use of his legs and he left nimbly without the aid of crutches or even a cane."[17] The recipient of the cure was a middle-aged, railway freight inspector, injured more than a year before when his legs were crushed by blocks of marble. (We will hear more of his case later.) On February 10, *Action Sociale,* a Quebec City paper, announced the cure of Antoinette Mercier, a teenaged girl whose eye had been blinded the year before. In May that same paper reported: "Mlle. Gagnon of Quebec, daughter of M.J.A. Gagnon, a plumber of Beauport, Quebec, was cured at the Oratory of St. Joseph in a remarkable way that astonished everyone who saw it on her prilgrimage to Côte-des-Neiges. The young girl . . . nineteen years old, was incapable of using her limbs and was unable to eat because of a stomach ailment. On her return from the Oratory, she walked without assistance and was returned to normal health."[18] That same month *La Patrie* reported the cure of ten-year-old Yvonne Guertin, who, since the age of three, could walk only with the help of crutches, her legs encased in braces. At the Oratory, she abandoned the crutches and walked without assistance.[19] *La Presse* reported on August 1, "Mrs. Brownrigg of St. Jean, Terreneuve, age twenty-five, was suddenly cured after walking with crutches since she was young. Mrs. Brownrigg suffered from [an unhealed] fracture of her left leg. She [intended to go] on pilgrimage to Ste.-Anne-de-Beaupré but desired, before her departure, to address a prayer to St. Joseph at his Oratory. As soon as she finished praying, Brother André approached her and told her to put her crutches away and remove the bandages that swathed her leg — and to walk, which she did, without difficulty. A great number of persons were witness to this miracle."[20]

By now Brother André was receiving hundreds of letters a day and Father Dion assigned Brother Marie-Auguste the task of answering the correspondence. Brother André needed still further assistance and told Dion; "I need a priest. People come and they ask blessings from an old thing like me."[21] And so, on July 16, 1910 Father Adolphe Clément was assigned to the Oratory as chaplain. A short, squat swarthy man with somewhat negroid features, Father Clément at thirty-three was suffering from an eye ailment, never even vaguely identified by historians of the shrine, which was causing progressive blindness. So sensitive were his eyes to light that the young priest was comfortable only in semi-darkness. When he reported to Brother André, Clément apologized, "They're sending you a blind man as chaplain."

"Aren't you happy to come to the Oratory?" asked André.

"Yes, but just the same, I'm a priest and I would like to say Mass . . . and recite the breviary."

"Rest," counseled the Brother. "You'll begin tomorrow morning."

Next morning Father Clément was still unable to see, but on the second day he was able to read his breviary. His eyesight improved rapidly and dramatically, but, curiously, when he consulted his eye specialist he was told: "Your eyes are the same as before. You're blind." "But I can see!" objected Father Clément, who was now able to celebrate Mass and was to enjoy such good eyesight that he did not need spectacles until he was more than fifty.[22] From the time of his cure, Father Adolphe Clément was "the right arm of Brother André."

That same year — 1910 — the first International Eucharistic Congress ever to meet in the New World assembled in Montreal. This massive influx of the faithful added to the fame of Brother André and his little Oratory, as hundreds of people attending the Congress learned of the shrine and its cures and made their way to Côte-des-Neiges to ascend Mount Royal to worship at the chapel on its heights. A visiting priest, in a letter to a local paper, declared, "The sanctuary on the mountain promises to become the Lourdes of Canada."[23] During this time Father Clément noted in his diary: "Nearly every day, in the presence of religious and many pious faithful, the sick leave their crutches or some other instrument and go down the mountain, saying they're healed. Also many conversions."[24] In just one month, Clément read ninety-four letters reporting complete or partial healings. Of these cures, the chaplain concluded that thirteen were perhaps miraculous.[25]

Problems persisted. That same year a group of physicians made a public declaration that Brother André was endangering the health of Montreal, complaining that he was practicing medicine without a license. They characterized him as an ignorant man. When Brother André learned of this he remarked: "They are right. I am ignorant. That is the reason why the Good God concerns himself with me. If there was anyone more ignorant than I, the Good God would choose him instead of me."[26]

That fall Archbishop Bruchési set up a commission to investigate Brother André and his ministry. On November 17 he put together a commission comprised of Canon J.T. Savaria, Father Joseph Lalande and Abbé Philippe Perrier, charging them with the following responsibility:

> For several years there has been a considerable movement of pilgrims to the Oratory Saint-Joseph at Notre-Dame-des-Neiges. Many people say they have obtained particular favors there. It has also been reported to us that extraordinary cures have occurred there.
>
> Since now it seems opportune to us to proceed with a serious examination of the facts, in order that we may enlighten the piety of the faithful, we charge you to make a complete inquiry into everything which goes on at the Oratory Saint-Joseph and also the extraordinary happenings which have occurred there.
>
> We give you all the power necessary to this end, especially that of interrogating under oath all persons whom you judge will be able to inform you.
>
> You will report to us on this inquiry and submit your conclusions.[27]

The commission interviewed all the religious at Notre-Dame and many laypersons. Father Dion stoutly defended Brother André, whom he characterized as "the approved instrument of St. Joseph." Dion furthermore told the commission that he often warned the faithful not to place excessive confidence in Brother André, to the detriment of St. Joseph, and declared that he had counseled André to avoid any words or actions that might lead the credulous to assume that he was personally the cause of any of the wonders that were occurring. The superior characterized Brother André as an exemplary religious: humble, innocent, artless, and without guile.[28]

The commission worked for several months. On March 11, 1911 they interviewed four persons who professed miraculous healings. Three of them had suffered from orthopaedic problems, and the fourth claimed to have been cured of a tumor and peritonitis. This cure had taken place May 6, 1910, when the sick woman's father begged Brother André's assistance. "I'm busy. Come back tomorrow," had been the Brother's somewhat brusque reply. When the father objected that his daughter was so ill that she was likely to be dead by the morrow, André's response had been, "No. Right now she has stopped suffering." On the spot, he had begun a novena with the father. The man returned home to find the daughter markedly improved. By the end of the novena the tumor had disappeared entirely and the peritonitis had disappeared.[29]

Finally, Brother André himself was called in for an interview. When asked, "Why don't you stop treating these people and leave them to God alone?" he replied, "I do what I feel I must." When questioned whether he felt that the cures were his own doing, André responded: "It is through St. Joseph. I am nothing but his little dog."[30]

On March 20, 1911 the commission submitted its report to Archbishop Paul Bruchési:

> We are happy to be able to declare to Your Grandeur that everything we have found there appears to be well done to edify the piety of the faithful and develop their confidence in the powerful protection of St. Joseph.
>
> From what we have heard of the Reverend Father Dion, provincial, as well as of the good Brother André,

they seem to us to be animated by the highest spiritual ideals.

The most extraordinary happenings which we have studied seem indeed to be the result of a supernatural intervention due to the goodness and power of St. Joseph. However, in these cases we cannot render an absolute judgment because the proofs are insufficient.

We think a permanent bureau, where theological science and medical science are concentrated — since we dare to hope that Saint Joseph will continue to manifest the marvelous examples of his bounty — would be able to reach absolutely certain conclusions.[31]

So Brother André was given a green light in his ministry to the sick. An official medical bureau to investigate the cures, such as was already in existence at Lourdes in France, never came about at the Oratory. Brother André said that the cures were just too numerous to record. For many years, however, those who professed to be recipients of divine favors were urged to submit medical affadavits about their conditions before and after their cure. Some did, but most did not.

The Oratory continued to grow structurally. In October, 1910 the foundations of the rectory were begun adjacent to the Oratory. This building would house the priests, brothers and nuns who worked at the shrine. When it was completed the College and Oratory became two separate communities. Next to the rectory a one-story frame building was constructed which served as Brother André's office, or "bureau," as well the Oratory gift shop. In 1912 the chapel was enlarged again and Brother André moved from his shed into a room above the renovated sanctuary. It was the most luxuriant home he had known in all his sixty-seven years. Accessed by means of a spiraling staircase leading from the rear of the church, it was a simple room, with walls and ceiling made of sheet iron, containing two beds, a pitcher, a basin, a chamberpot and a plain wooden cupboard for clothes and medicine. Brother André even had a stove on which he could prepare his meager meals, and the room even had electric lights, something of a luxury in those days. When the new rectory opened in 1915, Brother André was assigned a room there, but, from time to time, almost until his death, he would be given permission by his superiors to spend a night or two in the room above the little chapel, so he could counsel or pray with the sick or troubled.

It was in November, 1912 that Archbishop Bruchési came to the Oratory to bless the enlargement of the chapel. In his address he declared:

It would seem that St. Joseph wishes to be honored in a special manner in this Oratory on Mount Royal, just as Mary Immaculate wished to be honored in a special manner at Lourdes in France . . . I see here a pious movement that consoles me. This grain of mustard seed, at first so small, will soon produce a large tree . . . I foresee in the not distant future a church — a basilica — built in honor of St. Joseph on this beautiful spot on Mount Royal . . . Shall I say that miracles are wrought here? If I denied that such were the case, the ex-votive offerings in yonder pyramids would belie my words. I need make no investigation, I am convinced that extraordinary occurrences have taken place here: corporal cures, perhaps, although it is quite easy to suffer illusion in such cases; and spiritual cures still greater have been wrought. Sinners have come here, have prayed, and, after prayer, have purged out their iniquities and gone away at peace with their God! . . . Come here, then, and pray! Come here often, to implore the aid of the all-powerful and all-generous St. Joseph.[32]

The day of Bruchési's visit, Brother André was in the kitchen of the College, peeling potatoes. When told, "Brother André, fix yourself up a bit. You're to eat with the Archbishop," he shrugged his shoulders and said indifferently, "Imagine that!"[33] When they were alone, Bruchési said: "Brother André, is there anything supernatural in what you are doing? Do you believe that you've had a vision? Did St. Joseph speak to you to order you to build him a basilica on Mount Royal?" Brother André denied that his mission was the result of a vision. "There has been nothing of the kind," he insisted. "I have nothing but devotion to St. Joseph. That alone is what guides me and gives me utter confidence in the project."[34]

Archbishop Bruchési was now thoroughly convinced that Brother André's project was the will of God, and from that day on, the Oratory of Saint Joseph enjoyed the unreserved support of the archbishop, who reportedly, at least on one occasion, asked the Brother to rub him with the medal of St. Joseph. The little doorkeeper's dream of a basilica — one of a select group of large churches accorded special privileges by the Vatican — moved closer toward reality.

Chapter Six

An Expanding Ministry

At the age of nearly seventy Brother André moved into a ministry that extended beyond the College and the Oratory. So many sick persons confined to home or hospital requested the "miracle man" to come to them that Father Dion decided to authorize Brother André to go on evening visits. Each day he prepared a list of sick people who had requested a visit and directed André to see as many of them as possible. At first the Brother, who was sixty at the beginning of the automobile age and had never learned to drive, went on his calls by foot or trolley, but within a few years laymen were volunteering to drive him about in their cars. Brother André incurred criticism from some for riding in an automobile, which, before the First World War, was considered a luxury. Defending the practice, Brother André insisted that his evening excursions were not pleasure trips and declared that he would not venture even a mile from the Oratory — even on foot — except on an errand of mercy. If he walked or took a trolley, he could see at the most two or three people an evening. Driven, he could visit twice that number, and for this reason, Brother André justified the excessive speed he sometimes encouraged his drivers to attain, explaining that he wished to travel at great speeds, not for the thrill, but "to do more good." The police rapidly came to recognize him and never issued a citation to a speeder whose passenger was the little man in the worn black overcoat and "pot-pie" clerical hat who was now celebrated as "The Miracle Man of Montreal."

The roads were poor in those days, and well into the 1920s many streets, even in the city of Montreal, were unpaved. On several occasions, going at high speeds, André's volunteer chauffeurs came within a hair's breath of wrecking. On one occasion, the car in which André was riding nearly collided with a horse and wagon and, in fact, came so close that the print of the animal's nose was left on the windshield. Yet, as in this instance when the Brother, unflappable, calmly prayed his Rosary, never did a car bearing Brother André ever meet with a mishap.

By now all Brother André's immediate family were living in the States. Since 1878 Léocadie and Joseph Lefebvre had been living in West Warwick, Rhode Island, and their five children had scattered all over New England. Isaïe had remained in Richford, Vermont where he raised his family. Joseph, whose contact with the rest of the family remained slight, had moved west with his wife and several children and died in 1905 in Centerville, Minnesota. Claude, after his brief return to Canada in 1867, moved back to Connecticut, where he and his wife reared a family of nine. Both Claude and Napoleon, who had three children, lived in the town of Sterling. Marie and Josephine had also settled in Connecticut, where they married brothers by the name of Cayer, but both sisters were dead by the second decade of the century. Alphonsine, who married Néré Boulet and bore him eight children, was living as a widow near Léocadie, in Natick, Rhode Island.

Louis Cayer of New Bedford, Massachusetts, son of André's long-dead sister Marie, was amazed when his wife showed him a newspaper article about "The Miracle Man of Montreal." "Louis, that's your Uncle Fred!" she said. "Your Uncle Fred is getting famous!"[1] Even André's surviving sisters were startled by his celebrity status.

One day, around 1911, Mrs. Eugenie Miville, whose husband had been healed through the ministry of Brother André, was visiting Alphonsine Boulet, who was a close friend. Present that day at Alphonsine's home were Léocadie and Alphonsine's daughter Suzanne. Mrs. Miville was amazed that the Bessette sisters made light of their brother's reputation as a healer.

"Don't laugh," protested Mrs. Miville. "What I'm telling you is absolutely true."

Léocadie told her, "Listen, my legs hurt very much. Tell him that if he heals me, I'll believe in him." Alphonsine complained about her back and promised that if she obtained relief, she, too, would believe that Alfred made miracles.

When Mrs. Miville returned to Montreal she recounted to Brother André the conversation with his sisters. "Tell them to write me themselves," he said. Three months later a letter arrived from Rhode Island, reporting that both sisters were relieved of their afflictions.[2]

In the autumn of 1912, for the first time in many years, Brother André returned to New England, to visit his family. He stayed with Léocadie and her husband. Léocadie has been described by a granddaughter as "a very proud lady, small and delicately built like her brother, Uncle Brother André; pious, always saying the Rosary and going to Mass, always 'happy go lucky,' even tempered." She and her husband Joseph took André to see the numerous other relatives and friends who were scattered about in the area. By then the reputation of the "Miracle Man" had reached New England and the Lefebvre home was besieged with callers, as some two hundred sick persons called on Brother André each night he was there. Two of them, a Mr. Lebou and a Mrs. Paradis, both of whom had been badly crippled, reported their cures to a newspaper, and overnight, Brother André was in great demand in the northern United States.

For the rest of his life, Brother André made two trips each year to America, supposedly as vacations. He would stay a night or two with relatives, friends or priests, and then move on. He traveled all over the northeastern United States, ministering to the sick in hospitals, private homes, and in churches and parish halls. Every time he returned to Montreal he brought with him canes, crutches, corsets, braces and other devices that were discarded and given to him by the sick and the injured who professed cures.

A Council of the Oratory, under the aegis of the Congregation of Holy Cross, had been formed to administer the prayer center that was emerging on the mountain, and to plan for future growth. Brother André was a member of this board, and although he never served as chairman, the other members usually deferred to his wishes. The Council was incorporated in 1916. That same year it purchased from Notre-Dame College, for the sum of $210,000 (raised by supporters) the tract of a half-million square feet on Mount Royal, in preparation for the construction of the basilica. Two architects drew up plans for a gigantic baroque structure, projecting a cost of some three million dollars. (The basilica, even after the plans had been considerably scaled back, ultimately cost nearly four times that much to construct!)

The first step was to construct what was to be called the Crypt Church, over and behind which the basilica would rise. Thus this lower church would be a kind of basement, or crypt, to the large edifice that was to follow. The cornerstone of the Crypt, which was to have a seating capacity of 2,000, was laid by Archbishop Bruchési in April, 1916. On December 6, 1917, the Crypt Church, 200 feet long and 118 feet wide with a ceiling forty feet tall, was blessed by Bruchési and opened to the public, who crowded the nave in numbers far beyond its intended capacity.

By this time "The Great War" was ravaging Europe, and Canada, still part of the British Empire, was sending her sons to bleed and die in the trenches of Belgium and France. This was very much on the Archbishop's mind as he addressed the congregation on the day of dedication:

> In the course of the war which for three years has sown in Europe so much mourning and so much ruin, millions of men have died, entire cities have been devastated and pillaged. Blood has run in torrents. And in the horrible carnage, how many churches have fallen! . . . The cruel enemy . . . dropped on them its murderous and sacrilegious bombs . . . Women have been wounded and women have been killed. . . . Brothers, the future is dark! When the European War is over, there will be in our century — I am not the only one to fear it — [another war] that will bring us more sadness and suffering.

Bruchési thought it was significant that in an era when

churches were being blasted to pieces in Europe, in North America a house of prayer was being dedicated to St. Joseph, the protector of Canada, which, he hoped, would serve as a bastion against the forces of evil that he saw unleashed upon the twentieth-century world.[3]

That same day the congregation beheld the unveiling in the Crypt of the nine-foot statue of St. Joseph, fashioned from a single block of Carrara marble by an Italian sculptor by the name of Giacomini, who donated it as a love offering to the Oratory. There had been no little concern about its safe arrival, for fear that the Germans, who earlier that year had vowed to sink all Allied ships in range of her U-boats, would find and destroy the ship on which the statue was being conveyed. Brother André supposedly calmed the fears of the members of the Council, saying that St. Joseph would protect the statue. He and his confreres gave thanks to the saint when the two-ton statue arrived on time and intact, and was hauled up the mountain by a team of horses.[4]

In January, 1918, the original chapel, now dwarfed by the new church, was moved to a site higher up the mountain and somewhat to the rear of the Crypt. It continued to function as a church, however, and, as we have seen, although Brother André had a room in the new rectory, he occasionally used his little apartment above the chapel for intensive prayer and counseling.

By this time Brother André was seventy-two years old. Most people had never known him as anything other than old. Yet there seemed to be an ageless quality in the spritely, elfin brother with his leathered face, his curly white hair, and penetrating dark eyes. A reporter left a striking word picture of Brother André in his seventies when he described: "a man dressed in black," whose slight form was "enveloped from shoulders to feet in a somber overcoat," standing at daybreak atop the steep wooden staircase leading to the Crypt, raising his face "to the splendor of the sunrise," and slowly extending his arms towards God in a gesture of adoration."[5]

During the past several years Brother André had gained the friendship of several laymen who were to assist him in his ministry and make it possible for him to extend himself to those whom he had never been able to reach before. One of the most interesting was a prosperous landowner by the name of Joseph Malenfant (name meaning "badchild" in English).

Malenfant was living "peacefully and independently" on his farm at St.-Hubert de Temiscouta, some three hundred miles east of Montreal. At sixty, Malenfant, a widower with a grown son living away from home, was at loose ends. All his life his motto had been: "Not to help others is to be useless." Now, in retirement, he indeed felt useless. He told friends about recurring dreams: "I seem to see an old man painfully trying to build a church and I hear him calling to me for help. These dreams seem to be inspired by heaven." To remove his doubts, Malenfant resolved to go in search of the old man he had seen in his dreams. And so, to the consternation of all who knew him, in 1914, Malenfant set out for Montreal. There he learned that there was indeed an old man, a member of a religious community in the suburb of Côte-des-Neiges, who was trying to build a church he called St. Joseph's Oratory. Making his way to the Oratory, Malenfant climbed the wooden steps to the Crypt. At the top of the stairs he saw a brother — André — whom he recognized as the old man in the dreams. Brother André spoke first, telling Malenfant, "You're just the man I need."

Immediately Malenfant went to Father Dion, requesting admission to the community as a lay brother, only to be told that he was over the maximum age for admission. Malenfant decided that it was the Lord's will that he travel all over the Province of Quebec, soliciting alms for the Oratory. Going first to the town of Chicoutimi, where he asked for authorization to beg in that diocese, he was told to leave because he carried no papers showing that his mission had the approval of ecclesiastical authorities. Undaunted, the country squire decided to become a "vagabond of St. Joseph," traveling from village to village, proclaiming: "Not to help others is to be useless. It is better to obey God than man."

During the next few months, this eccentric old man on his strange mission met with ridicule and insults. Moreover, he often heard the devil whispering to him: "You're an old fool, Malenfant! You had a fine farm, an assured livelihood, and now look at yourself! You're a tramp, a beggar, a good-for-nothing! You sleep in barns, you tramp the highways!" But

Malenfant answered Satan, "Begone! Not to help others is to be useless!"

When Joseph Malenfant returned to the Oratory he gave Father Dion the sum of $1,400 which he solicited in his wanderings. Dion, whom Malenfant described as an "icicle," accepted the gift, but insisted that he stop his life of vagabondage. This Malenfant refused, and now became convinced that it was his mission to raise subscriptions for the magazine, *The Annals of St. Joseph*. This journal, published by the Oratory, had first been printed on January 1, 1912, and within a year it had 4,500 subscriptions. Malenfant believed that the time had come to "analyze" the entire nation, and so for the rest of his life, until he died in July, 1924, he lived the life of a tramp for St. Joseph, wandering all over eastern Canada during the summer, soliciting subscriptions for *The Annals*, and living at the Oratory during the winter. During the ten years he "analyzed" the countryside, he procured over 35,000 subscriptions.[6] It was through this magazine that the plans for the Oratory and news of the cures reached all of French-speaking Canada. And, when an English language edition was added, the fame of Brother André and his church spread among Roman Catholics in the United States as well.

Around this same time Brother André made the acquaintance of a dealer in furniture and livestock by the name of Azarias Claude. Claude, who was then in his late forties, was a man of impressive stature and bearing. Of great physical strength, he stood 6'6" tall and always dressed in black. His photograph shows a massive bald head and a stern imposing face dominated by a big, neatly trimmed moustache. At the time Claude met Brother André, he was but a nominal Catholic and admitted to a problem with the bottle. Sceptical when he first heard of Brother André, he decided to accompany his wife when she paid a visit to the Oratory in 1912. The visit lasted only five minutes, but Brother André told Claude to come back, reminding him, "It's not necessary to be sick to visit me." Claude later declared, "That visit changed my mind about Brother André. I wanted to return. I would have gone that very evening, or the next day, but I didn't for fear of attracting remarks about me that would hurt my self-esteem." But the memory of that conversation with Brother André "haunted"

Claude's mind until he began to lose interest in his business. Then,

> One week after the first interview with Brother André, I returned to see him. Brother André received me with kindness and invited me to go to chat with him on the mountain. There he confided in me his manner of dealing intimately with St. Joseph . . . and I got into the habit of visiting him each week.[7]

Brother André had a profound effect on Claude, who attributed his "fondness for alcoholic beverages" to the tensions of his work. He was quickly cured of his addiction and soon confessed that "the orientation of my life" was completely changed. Brother André taught him "to practice renunciation and patience," and Claude became "a devotee of St. Joseph" and a daily communicant.[8]

Claude was forty-eight when he met Brother André, and he and his wife were childless. Madame Claude's fifteen pregnancies had all ended in miscarriages or stillbirths. She was now in her sixteenth pregnancy, and naturally, she and Azarias were pessimistic about the chances of having a living baby. Brother André, however, announced that this baby would live, and the daughter, Marguerite, was still very much alive in 1987.

When Brother André first met Monsieur Claude, he noticed that one of his arms was shorter than the other. Claude explained that the arm had been crushed some fifteen years earlier by an elevator door, but that the disability, such as it was, did not bother him. Brother André then asked:

> how I would like to return home with my arm healed. I answered that God probably had more important favors to grant me. Brother André asked me, 'Do you know what you are saying?' I answered, 'Yes.' He asked me the question a second time, adding, 'Do you believe you'll remain with that attitude?' I answered, 'Yes, I think I understand.' Brother André said, 'Return home with your crippled arm, but if later you want your arm healed, don't ask me to heal you. You accept the will of God and I won't be able to do anything for you.' Anyway, right after having

spoken of my arm, Brother André noticed a lump on my neck. He asked me what that lump was. I said it was nothing important, and anyway, it could easily be removed by a surgeon. He touched the lump and told me, 'It isn't necessary to operate.' I didn't notice anything and returned home. The next day my wife casually remarked that my lump had disappeared. I hadn't noticed it. That lump never came back.[9]

Brother André's first volunteer driver was probably Dr. Charette. After the doctor died, Azarias Claude offered to drive Brother André on his evening visits, and, along with several other men, formed a sort of car pool that took the good Brother on his rounds, in and about Montreal. After his retirement from business around 1920, Claude volunteered to serve as receptionist in Brother André's office, and nearly every day for the next fifteen years, when André was in Montreal, Claude took charge of the waiting room, bringing order to the interviews and enabling Brother André to see from thirty to forty visitors an hour.

Another close lay associate of Brother André was Joseph Pichette, the successful young proprietor of a shoe store. Pichette was twenty-five in 1911 when he met the guardian of the Oratory. For several years the young man had been under the care of Dr. Georges Aubry for a disease, never specifically identified, which affected both his heart and digestive system. Dr. Aubry told Pichette's sisters that he had "a heart such as I have never myself seen even in the hospitals of Paris or anywhere else I have been." In addition, Pichette suffered from kidney and intestinal troubles, spat blood, and could not digest food.

One day one of Pichette's customers, a Mrs. Lucas, told him about Brother André. She insisted that she had been cured of an ulcerated arm after Brother André directed her to place a drop of St. Joseph's oil on the ulcer, rub it with the medal, and drink a little of the oil. Shortly after he spoke with Mrs. Lucas, Pichette met a traveling salesman by the name of Bertrand, who told him of the cure of his father through Brother André. Bertrand had before-and-after photographs of his father's arm. The elder Bertrand had been suffering from a cancer which involved the entire arm, from wrist to elbow, and the first set of photographs showed a limb obviously diseased and deformed. The second set showed what Bertrand said was the same arm after the ministrations of Brother André. It was perfectly normal. These two conversations convinced Pichette to visit Brother André.

He went to Mount Royal on a Sunday, the only day of rest that he allowed himself, despite his wretched health. André advised Pichette to obtain a St. Joseph medal and to drink a little of the oil and return to him the following week. Pichette actually went to see Brother André for more than a hundred times over a period of a year, but experienced no improvement whatsoever. Finally, in 1912, Dr. Aubry told his patient that there was nothing more he could do for him. "You'd better prepare for that great journey," he warned.

"I still have someone left to see," replied Pichette, "and I'll leave him only with improvement or in my tomb."

"Who might that be?" asked Aubry.

"Brother André."

"What are you thinking about?" demanded the doctor. "What can he do? He has no education. I've heard of him. They call him the 'Crazy Old Man.'"

"But I have confidence that he can do at least as much as you can," retorted the sick man.

"I warn you," cautioned the physician, "be very careful, because, going up to the Oratory, you could fall dead any moment."

When he next met with Brother André, Pichette told him, "If you wish, I will come here and return only when I'm cured or when I'm in my tomb. I can't live like this anymore."

"As you wish," replied Brother André. "If you want to come, you can sleep in my room in the little chapel."

Brother André had the little apartment over the chapel, which at the time of his first encounters with Pichette was his exclusive residence. From time to time, with Father Dion's permission, André invited sick men to spend the night with him in prayer. When Pichette came as the guest of the Brother, there were two other men staying in the apartment. The invalids slept on little cots, separated by a curtain from Brother André who lay pillowless on a mattresss on the floor. As Pichette recounted:

For the [first] nine days I lived at the Oratory there was no change. Brother André rubbed me with his hand two or three times a day. I believe that on the ninth day he rubbed from 11:30 to 2:30 in the morning, because I told him that it was not going any better . . . About 4:25 he was awakened by his clock. He got up and we got up. The evening before he had brought in a piece of fresh pork and some veal, with spices and seasonings, and he boiled it on the stove. He boiled some potatoes and [on leaving in the morning] told me to put them in the soup around ten o'clock or ten thirty in the morning.

At midday he came for dinner. He took a big plate, filled it with meat, potatoes, and broth, and presented it to me, and, in spite of my objections, told me to eat, saying that it would go down well. 'Since you tell me, Brother André, I am going to eat.' Moreover, he added three big pieces of bread. When we had finished eating, Brother André told me I could walk. I felt very well and the afternoon passed without pain. I said to Brother André, who asked me in the evening how everything had gone, 'All is very well.' In the evening he gave me the same food — almost half of what he had given me at noon. I went to bed about 10:30 p.m. and slept until the next morning when Brother André's alarm clock woke me. I had not slept a night through during all the time of the nine days I had spent at the Oratory.

The following day Brother André told Pichette, "Since you're well, you can go." Thereupon Pichette boarded a streetcar and went home, where he discovered that his wife had gone to visit a cousin several miles away in the suburb of St. Esprit. So Pichette got on his bicycle and pedaled to Moreau Station, two miles from the house, where, taking the bike with him, he boarded the train to St. Esprit. From the station he cycled five miles to the cousin's house, where his wife was so astonished by the improvement in his condition that she wept with joy.

Pichette recuperated at home for eight weeks and gained eighteen pounds. When he returned to the Oratory to give thanks, he met the two men who had been his roommates in Brother André's apartment. "Pichette," said one of them, "if we had met you on the street, we would never have recognized you, you look so much better!''

When Brother André conferred with Pichette, he warned him, "Doctors are so much against me, you'd better not tell your doctor." Even though Pichette did not return to Dr. Aubry, the physician learned about the cure through Madame Pichette, who was also his patient. The doctor predicted that Pichette's apparent cure would last no more than a month, but a quarter century later the merchant was still active and working. In 1942 he declared, "If I still wasn't completely cured, I was able to work without too much pain."

A few years later Monsieur Pichette again had the occasion to seek a cure through Brother André. One day at the store he noticed that his thumb bled for no apparent reason. After this went on for two weeks, he consulted one Dr. Rouleau, who diagnosed the problem as a cancer and sent him to a radiologist, Dr. Panneton. Panneton used ultra-violet rays, but Pichette's thumb grew worse. It ulcerated and became extremely painful. In this condition he went to Brother André. Even after the medal was applied, the pain remained and he found no relief. After four months of fruitless treatment, his pain was so great that he could not sleep. He was able to find a few minutes of relief through a remedy suggested by a friend — namely, the imposition upon the thumb of a cold slice of potato. Pichette reasoned that the cold numbed the pain temporarily.

"I have never been so ill," Pichette complained to Brother André, who responded, "It's at that time, sometimes, that things are about to get better." He then put a white cloth over the thumb and rubbed for five or six minutes and then said, "That will be enough." When Andre removed the cloth, Pichette's thumb looked normal, except for a black scab, of which the Brother said, "Oh, that's nothing." When he scratched the scab off with his fingernail, two or three drops of blood oozed out. Then André put the white cloth back on the thumb, rubbed again, and the pain went away, never to return. When Pichette told André of the cold potato remedy, André said, "The potatoes took away the pain, the doctors took away the dollars, and St. Joseph took away everything!"

Brother André tried to dissuade Pichette from going back to Rouleau, but this time the cured man was determined to show himself to his physician. On examining the thumb, Rouleau remarked that a single treatment should not have sufficed to heal the cancer. A few weeks later a nurse who worked for Dr. Panneton visited Pichette's shoe store and asked about the thumb. When Pichette showed it to her, she was amazed and told him, "It's impossible for a single treatment to cure it." Then Pichette told her of his cure by Brother André and St. Joseph.[10]

Madame Albertine Pichette was also the recipient of a cure through the ministrations of Brother André. Shortly after her husband's healing she fell ill with an intestinal disease which involved a progressive, inoperable obstruction and pains so constant and excruciating that for nine weeks she had found it impossible to sleep or rest. Her doctor pronounced her condition inoperable. Monsieur Pichette consulted Brother André. André did not rub women, but he began a novena. The very first night Madame Pichette fell into a restful sleep, and by the time it was concluded, she was entirely well.

Pichette, like Claude, donated his time and his automobile to assist André on his evening visits. In later years, he and his wife opened the doors of their home to Brother André on occasions when he needed a few days of rest from the pilgrims who constantly demanded his attention at the Oratory. Despite their earlier illnesses, both Pichettes were still alive in the early 1960s.

Another one of Brother André's circle of lay friends was the firefighter, Raoul Gauthier, who became Chief of the Montreal Fire Department in 1923. He was in his early thirties when he met Brother André in 1911 or 1912. An athletic non-smoker devoted to physical fitness, he has been described as a kindly, happy, modest, and self-effacing man, a loving husband and father of six. His motto was, "Keep smiling." His one obvious fault seems to have been a tendency to swear. Brother André delivered him from that, teaching him to substitute the inocuous expression, *"Cheval vert!"* (Green horse!) for his favorite oath, *"Christ de Calvaire!"* (Christ on Calvary!). Gauthier was a captain when he first met André, and it was his custom to personally visit, at home or hospital, any of his men who were sick or injured. Gauthier encouraged Brother André to ride with him on these calls as he sped through the streets of Montreal in his red car with its siren howling. Through

Gauthier, Brother André became a favorite of the firemen of Montreal, who were encouraged by their chief to volunteer their services at the Oratory by welcoming visitors and assisting the sick. Gauthier also made available to Brother André a firefighter's retreat in the countryside outside of Montreal, where the Brother could rest a day or two from his grinding labors.

Gauthier knew that Brother André made the Stations of the Cross every evening. He suggested that laypersons be allowed to join him in the prayer office. And so it was agreed that Friday evenings, instead of making sick calls, Brother André would pray the Stations of the Cross in the Crypt with any people who cared to join him. From the start he was accompanied by a good-sized congregation.[11]

Still another lay assistant was Arthur Ganz, a wealthy young insurance agent. Ganz met Brother André when, as a young man of twenty, he accompanied his priest, Father Rosaire Audel, on a visit to Brother André. Audel had some ear problem, and as Brother André rubbed his ear, Audel made such an odd expression that Ganz began to laugh. "Look here," quipped Brother André, "it costs fifty dollars to laugh!" "At that price," replied Ganz, "I'll stop laughing."

After he ministered to Father Audel, Brother André asked Monsieur Ganz if he owned a car. When Ganz replied that he had two, André asked him to take ̣im to visit the sick. Ganz agreed and drove André to see a Monsieur Nadeau, a man in his early sixties who was totally blind, unable to distinguish night from day. Two specialists at the Royal Victoria Hospital had told Nadeau that there was nothing that could be done to restore his sight. When Nadeau begged Brother André to restore his sight, he was told, "Rub yourself with a medal of St. Joseph and I will come back in a week." When Ganz brought André back, Nadeau was sitting in a chair, reading a newspaper, but complained that he could read for only short periods of time. "You have to walk before you run," remarked Brother André. Nadeau's vision improved so dramatically that when he died some years later at the age of eighty, his eyesight was so good that he did not need glasses![12]

Just as the Great War seemed near its close, North America was stricken by the furious epidemic of influenza known as the

Spanish flu, which would ultimately claim over twenty million lives throughout the world. For a time, in the fall of 1918, fifty deaths a day from flu were reported in the city of Montreal. All public places were closed, and finally, Archbishop Bruchési, to protect the health of his flock, ordered churches closed too, and no Masses were said in the archdiocese. Nonetheless Brother André kept his office open and people continued to flood his waiting room and he, without fear for his health, ministered to all who presented themselves.

Word was now received that at the school at St.-Césaire there were forty-five children in the infirmary with the flu. Brother André consented to go there to lead a procession. He insisted that all healthy staff and students participate in the procession, which would wind its way through every room in the building except the infirmary (so as not to scare the sick children). It was done and it worked. No one else fell sick — except Brother André, who was indisposed for many days.

By the end of the War, Brother André's routine was fixed. He saw the sick in his bureau from nine to noon and from two to five. At five he was met by a lay assistant who took him home for dinner. Then, armed with a list given him by the superior, Brother André went with his companion for the evening to see some half-dozen sick persons. When he returned to the Oratory at nine-thirty or ten, Brother André invited his driver to join him for an hour of prayer. Lighting a candle, he would kneel in prayer with his companion until the candle went out. That usually took at least an hour. Fridays, as we have seen, he led the office of the Stations of the Cross, adding to the formal written prayers his own extemporaneous petitions. Many who accompanied him on the Stations claimed to experience an infusion of supernatural grace and saw André seemingly transported into the supernatural world. After the Stations, Brother André observed the same hour of prayer with his guests that he observed on other days of the week with his drivers. During these sessions of prayer, some of those with him claimed at times to see the holy man glow with mystical light. All the while, the numbers continued to increase of those who sought comfort and healing from the man now affectionately known to many as "Our Family Physician."

Chapter Seven

The Healer

When the learned Father Henri-Paul Bergeron was researching his 1937 biography of Brother André, he interviewed Father Adolphe Clément. Brother André's "Right Hand" had this to say about André's reputation as a healer: "Brother André made miracles! All I had to do was look at him and he'd make a miracle!"[1]

Typical of Brother André's career is a scene on a Montreal street recalled by Bergeron. "The Miracle Man" was recognized in a car stopped at a light. Before the signal changed someone brought a sick woman to the car. Directing his driver to park the car, Brother André got out and ministered to the woman. By the time he finished with her, the surrounding apartments had spewed forth dozens of invalids, who crowded around Brother André, who patiently spoke with each, anointing some with the holy oil. When, after a long interval, André was able to return to the car, the driver (who is not identified) exclaimed: "How wonderful! It's like a scene from the life of Our Lord! Everybody rushed forth to beg for favors and cures!" The Brother, always somewhat bewildered at his celebrity, mused, "Perhaps so, but God is surely making use of a very vile instrument!"[2]

What can we make of the cures of this "very vile instrument," who, on his rounds through Montreal, oftentimes drew such crowds that the police had to be called to clear the streets? What is a "miracle," and what purpose is served by such a phenomenon? What is the position of Holy Scripture on miracles? Have most Christians throughout the centuries believed in them? Were André's cures really miracles?

A "miracle" is generally perceived as a direct intervention by God in the natural world, an intervention which involves the suspension of the laws of nature, at least as they are commonly understood. *The New Catholic Encyclopedia* isolates three features that must characterize an event if it is to be regarded as miraculous: it must be "extraordinary"; it must be perceptible to the senses (thus excluding such things as conversions); and it must be produced by God in a religious context as evidence of the supernatural.

For example, the Old Testament book of Numbers describes a rebellion against Moses, as a result of which the Lord caused the earth to open and swallow the opponents of the leader He had set over Israel (Num. 16:30). This was certainly extraordinary; it was evident to the senses of all who were present; it was wrought by God as a demonstration of His power and presence, His approval of Moses, and His punishment of those who flaunted the rule of the prophet.

Similarly, miracles recorded in the New Testament are extraordinary, perceptible signs of God's activity and, in particular, of the divinity of Jesus. For example, Jesus healed the paralytic, who had been helped down through the roof, as a demonstration that "the Son of Man has authority on earth to forgive sins" (Mk. 2:10). After He had stilled the seas, the disciples were convinced that Jesus was surely Someone extraordinary and they remarked: "Who is this, that even wind and sea obey him?" (Mk. 4:41). The Lord healed a man born blind, asserting that the affliction was not the result of sin on his part or that of his parents, but occurred so that "the works of God might be made manifest in him" (Jn. 9:1-3). That is, the man was born blind, at least in part, to occasion the opportunity for Jesus to demonstrate His divinity in power.

While Jesus healed "all who were sick" (Mt. 8:16) — at least those willing to approach Him — it seems clear that after Pentecost the Twelve also had complete success in healing the afflicted. Almost all Christians — of all persuasions — if they accept the existence of miracles at all (and if they do not, they can scarcely be said to be truly Christians), would agree that these signs and wonders were prevalent throughout the lifetime of the Twelve Apostles. There is disagreement concerning the occurrence of miracles in later times, however.

The writings of the Early Church Fathers indicate that in the four or five centuries that followed the time of the Apostles, miracles, while not perhaps as numerous or dramatic as those performed by Christ and the Twelve, nonetheless occurred, at least at certain times and in certain places. While the Egyptian writer Origen (c. 185-254) insisted that only "traces" of the signs and wonders which Christ wrought were visible in the Church of his day, his older contemporary, St. Irenaeus (c. 120-202), who ministered in what today is France, wrote that miracles were taking place on a regular basis among his flock, miracles that included even the raising of the dead. St. John Chrysostom (344-407), who ministered in what is now Turkey, in some of his writings seemed to imply that miracles, or at least certain types (such as prophecy and tongues), were no longer common, but his contemporary, St. Ambrose (c. 335-397), Bishop of Milan, reported at least one case of a clear miraculous intervention. St. Augustine (354-430), Bishop of Hippo, in what is now Tunisia, wrote a great deal about miracles.

First of all, Augustine maintained that "miracles" are only *apparent* violations of the laws of nature, as God does not contradict Himself.[3] Miracles, he said, are invitations to faith that call attention to God's greatness. In some of his writings, Augustine implied that the spectacular miracles of Jesus' day no longer occurred, but asserted that there was, at least in his own diocese, an abundance of minor miracles, all of which were "witnesses to that faith which proclaims the supreme miracle of the Resurrection of the flesh into life everlasting."[4] Yet, the miracles that Augustine cited in *The City of God* do not seem minor from a modern point of view.

Augustine referred to the case of a man in Carthage by the name of Innocentius, who had undergone surgery for rectal fistulae. A fistula, which is usually caused by an abscess in the anus, is an abnormal opening to the skin from the lower bowel, through which fecal matter is intermittently discharged. This condition can be corrected only by surgery. Unfortunately, Innocentius' surgeons had overlooked an additional abscess in the rectum which caused the problem to persist. Innocentius was told that a second operation was necessary. The first had been so horrifically painful that Innocentius was terrified at the prospect of a second operation. Summoning his friends the night before the scheduled surgery, he prayed to God "with groans and sobs." Augustine was present that evening. The next morning, when surgeons preparing for the surgery examined the rectum, they found no trace of the abscess, and thus the operation was cancelled![5]

Augustine related the case of a woman named Innocentia (apparently no relation to Innocentius). She was also a resident of Carthage in North Africa. She was suffering from cancer of the breast. In those days, if there were no external indications that the disease had spread, surgeons performed a mastectomy. But if it was apparent that there had been metastasis, the case was written off as hopeless, with no treatment judged useful. Innocentia's cancer was in the second category. She prayed to God and dreamt that she should ask the first woman who came out of the baptistery on Easter Sunday to make the sign of the cross upon her ulcerated breast. She did this and was immediately healed. When her doctor examined her he was enthusiastic, assuming that she had been treated by some physician who had discovered a cure for cancer. When Innocentia told him how she came to be cured, the doctor said, with an air of profound disappointment, "I thought you would make some great discovery to me."[6]

Augustine even wrote of instances in which the dead were raised. For instance, the son of Irenaeus the tax collector had died after an unspecified illness. "While his body was lying lifeless and the last rites were being performed, amidst the weeping and mourning of all, one of the friends who were consoling the father suggested that the body should be anointed with oil." He was referring to oil that burned in the lamps before the shrine of St. Stephen (just as centuries later, the oil burned in lamps before the shrine of St. Joseph would be used by Brother André). The dead boy was anointed with the St. Stephen's oil and was revived.[7]

It is widely known that the existence of miracles was universally believed in during the Middle Ages, which saw a proliferation of shrines, whither the faithful went to touch various relics, both real and counterfeit, in hopes of obtaining some divine favor. This belief in the possibility of miracles persists in the Roman Catholic Church in the twentieth century. The procedure for beatification and canonization established in the eighteenth century by Pope Benedict XIV requires the proof of at least two miracles as a confirmation of the Church's judgment on an individual's sanctity. Some theologians have, however, made a distinction between the miracles recorded in Scripture and those of later days. One such theologian was John Henry Cardinal Newman (1801-1890), who wrote: "The Scripture miracles are for the most part evidence of a Divine Revelation . . . but the miracles which follow have sometimes no discoverable or direct object; they happen for the sake of individuals . . . the miracles of Scripture are undeniably beyond nature; those of ecclesiastical history are often scarcely more than extraordinary accidents or coincidences, or events which seem to betray exaggerations or errors in the statement."[8]

Early Protestants, however, were more sceptical than their Roman brethren. Martin Luther (1483-1546), although he believed that God worked miracles in Biblical times, *at times* seemed sceptical about the existence of miracles in his own day. Although on at least one occasion he approved of an exorcism and he regularly prayed for the sick, Luther, in some of his writings, seemed bitterly critical of miracle stories, denouncing as lies even the lives of saints. "If I should see a priest or monk raise a dead person in the name of St. Ann," wrote the outspoken Saxon priest, "I would say that it was the work of the devil!"[9] Luther admitted that few, if any, miracles of healing were wrought through his followers. "Some fine folk," wrote the good doctor, "to whom all religion is a jest and joke, ridicule us, charging that Lutherans have not even cured a lame horse and lack completely the gift of miracles."[10] Conceding that perhaps Lutherans had not cured so much as a lame horse, Luther called attention to conversions wrought through his reform movement, insisting that such internal miracles are more important than physical ones. "For nowadays the blind receive their sign when minds obsessed with Satan are brought to Christ," the great evangelical reformer wrote. "The deaf hear the Gospel, the lame, who sat in their superstititions, and the idolators, arise with an upright faith and walk about happily." Such signs, Luther wrote, are "no less significant than raising the dead and restoring sight of the blind."[11]

John Wesley (1703-1791) said that miracles stopped when the Roman Empire became Christian, because of "a general corruption both of faith and morals [that] infected the Church."[12] In fact, most of the theologians of the Reformation and those who came later in the Protestant tradition taught that the *charismata* ceased with the Apostolic Age, or, in the words of early-twentieth-century author Benjamin Warfield, "continued for a while in the post-Apostolic period [but] slowly died out like a light fading by increasing distance from its source."[13] In fact, many mainline Protestant churches which are true to the teachings of their founders firmly reject the ideas of the miraculous in the modern world.

Actually, most early Protestants did believe in the power of God over nature, even though they formally rejected the possibility of miracles. While they may have believed that such *charismata* as prophecy and tongues had ceased, many certainly believed in the efficacy of prayer for the recovery of the sick. The response of the celebrated Puritan pastor and scholar Cotton Mather (1663-1728) to the illness of his infant son in 1709 is probably typical of devout Calvinists of his day. Mather, observing that his son Samuel was "taken very sick of a fever which proves very grievous and mortal to our children," decided to set apart May 11 as a day of prayer and fasting before the Lord.

> I bewailed the sins by which the life of my children and of this desirable child had been forfeited. I besought the pardon of them through the blood of the Lamb of God and I pleaded that blood as a family-sacrifice. I resigned the child unto the Lord, submitted unto whatever disposal the infinite sovereignty and faithfulness of God should make of the child. . . . This petition with the child himself I put into the hands of the glorious Advocate whom I by faith saw in the heavens concerned for me. When this faith

came into exercise I found my mind strangely quieted about the child and about the issue of the danger now upon him.[14]

Samuel Mather recovered. While Cotton Mather believed as deeply in supernatural graces as anyone, he, like his Protestant contemporaries, was suspicious of associating "remarkable providences" with specific individuals or places. Certainly he would have been aghast at the thought of using such *sacramentals* as holy oils, medals, and relics, and, probably, at the idea that certain individuals had a special *charism* of healing not given to others.

By the late nineteenth century, with the rise of the Pentecostal movement, some Christians in the Protestant tradition had come to a belief in the possibility of a healing ministry. We have seen that the Rev. Albert Hughes, a Baptist preacher who was contemporary with Brother André, had a well-known ministry of healing in Toronto. In the same breath with Brother André, biographer George Ham describes the healing ministry of the exotic and controversial Pentecostalist Aimee Semple McPherson (1890-1944). However, among most mainline Protestants, the idea of the "miraculous" remained somewhat suspect.

On the other hand, among Roman Catholics, the tradition of the holy man or holy woman gifted with miraculous healing powers was very strong, as was confidence in the cures associated with certain sacred places, such as Lourdes. When Alfred Bessette was a young boy, Father Jean-Marie-Baptiste Vianney (1786-1859) was still active as parish pastor, or *curé,* in the town of Ars in France, and many miracles, including the multiplication of food, were attributed to this holy man who was canonized towards the end of Brother André's life. It was in Brother André's lifetime that the shrine of Lourdes became renowned for the apparitions of the Virgin Mary and for numerous miracles. Similar appearances of the Blessed Virgin were reported in 1917 in Fatima, Portugal. Few of Brother André's contemporaries in the Roman Church would, therefore, have found anything bizarre about his ministry of healing. Moreover, once it was determined that there was nothing theologically, legally, or morally wrong with the Holy Cross Brother, there was no significant objection raised by ecclesiastical authorities to the multitudes who climbed Mount Royal in search of miracles.

Brother André's bureau was located, as we have seen, beside the rectory. The pilgrim mounted a short flight of steps to enter the waiting room, which provided the only access to the office. Despite the large number of crippled and disabled persons, no one in those days thought of constructing ramps to make the building more accessible to wheelchairs. The office was ten feet by eight, the main piece of furniture consisting of a sort of counter behind which André stood. There were two chairs for visitors. The walls of the bureau were paneled in pine. On one wall, directly behind the spot where the Brother stood, there hung a crucifix. Paintings of St. Joseph and Jesus before Pilate were also displayed in the room. Between the office and the waiting room, besides a door, there was a window which was closed except when Brother André was receiving women. As we have seen, Brother André normally started receiving pilgrims at nine — sometimes as early as 8:30, broke for lunch at noon, and returned about two and stayed until five.

In his ministry to the sick, Brother André had recourse to sacramentals whose use is mentioned or implied in Scripture, namely oil and a holy medal. It is written of the Apostles, "They cast out many demons, and anointed with oil many that were sick and healed them" (Mk. 6:13). This and the statement by St. James that the elders of the Church should anoint the sick with oil are the basis of André's use of that sacramental. Although the specific use of the medal is, of course, never mentioned in the Bible, it is recorded that "God did extraordinary miracles by the hands of Paul" with handkerchiefs and aprons and other objects that had touched his person (Acts 19:12). If God made use of handkerchiefs and aprons, it would certainly follow, by implication, that a piece of metal would also be permissible. Brother André frequently cited the waters of the Jordan in which the Prophet Elisha commanded the leper Naaman to bathe and the mud with which the Lord anointed the eyes of a blind man as precedents for the use of the St. Joseph medal.

Brother André, in fact, out of consideration for time, seldom rubbed anyone in his office, but advised his visitors to go to the church to pray before the statue of St. Joseph, and then, anointing the affected part of the body with St. Joseph's oil, to take the medal, wrapped in cloth so as to reduce the possibility of scraping or cutting, and massage until the pain or swelling subsided. "Rub long and hard," he said. "At least an hour. Many more sick would be healed if they would persevere more in these rubbings."[15]

On evening calls or in his apartment over the old chapel, Brother André frequently rubbed the sick. Curiously, he seldom used the medal, but rubbed only with his hand. When Azarias Claude asked why he advised others to use the medal which he himself seldom applied, André responded, "It's because I rub harder!"[16] And, indeed, many of his pilgrims testified to the vigor with which the diminutive Brother rubbed, even as a very old man.

Brother André could never be induced to make a detailed or coherent explanation for his practice of rubbing except to say, "It's a means of proving your faith in St. Joseph."[17] He did make it plain that the oil had no magical properties and that any healing was attributable only to God through St. Joseph. Rubbing seemed simply to be a prayer to St. Joseph expressed through a physical activity rather than a mental or verbal one. According to J. Lionel Lamy, Brother André's physician during the last eight years of his life, there were many physicians at the time who felt that massage, through stimulation of a proper circulation of blood, was the key to the healing of a number of diseases. At least one man who professed a cure through Brother André attributed his healing at least partly to the renewal of the circulation in the limb. Even so, many ailments and injuries cured through Brother André's rubbings were of such a nature that massage could not possibly have had any effect on their cure. Moreover, a number of André's patients were cured without any massage. Thus any benefit accomplished solely through the act of vigorous rubbing would seem to be incidental.

In addition to the medal and the oil, according to Father Albert Cousineau (André's superior during the last year of his life), the Brother sometimes advised such harmless remedies as the drinking of small quantities of St. Joseph's oil or holy water. On one occasion, which we shall examine later, Brother

André insisted on the application of boric acid to an infected leg.[18]

Seeking to divert attention from himself to St. Joseph, Brother André was always exceedingly modest about the healings. "The world is foolish to think that Brother André performs miracles," he told Azarias Claude. When Claude insisted, "But you have your word to say in those things." André objected, "Don't say that. You don't know what you're talking about!"[19] Once, when a visitor told him that he was "even better than St. Joseph," Brother André was so upset that he left his office and took to his bed.

Curiously, Brother André seemed to know which patients were going to be healed and which were not. Archbishop Bruchési once remarked: "Brother André, it's curious, in some cases you tell the sick, 'You're cured,' and it is done. To others you advise to pray to St. Joseph, to make novenas, to others you say to rub with a medal, to use the oil of St. Joseph, to others you say, 'I'm going to pray for you.' What is the reason for the difference?" Brother André replied, "There are times when it is easy to see."[20] To Father Emile Deguire, who put the same question to him, he said, "In some cases it is evident that St. Joseph wants to heal them."[21] Yet another time he explained, "It is according to the will of God. When it is not good for their salvation, the Good God lets me see that it is not His will. I do not want to go against him."[22] On still another occasion, Brother André responded, "When I tell them, 'Let go of your crutches,' it is because it is evident."[23] The Brother observed to yet another inquirer, "I say what I am told to say."[24] Did Brother André have visions or locutions? When pressed directly, he would usually flatly deny that this was the case, as he did when Archbishop Bruchési asked if St. Joseph had told him to build a basilica. Other times, however, he smiled or made a gesture as if to say that he knew more than he was willing to discuss.

At any rate, whenever Brother André announced, "You're not sick!" the pilgrim recovered. Joseph Pichette observed: "Each time Brother André told someone not to be operated upon, if the operation took place, the sick person died. On the other hand, if he said, 'Be operated on,' the operation would always to be successful. Brother André would tell me sometimes that sick people were not cured because they . . . didn't pray enough or did not observe enough the laws of Christian morality. To others . . . he would say, 'It is better to suffer.' "[25] In this vein André once remarked, "I can't obtain the cure of certain sick persons because the eternal salvation of these persons is attached to their infirmity. But people don't understand this."[26]

One of Brother André's younger colleagues, Father Elphège Labonté, claimed to recall the death of a little girl from Hull, Quebec, whose parents Brother André had advised against the surgery that doctors said was necessary to save the child's life. During the investigation of Brother André's life and works, this case was discussed. The facts were hazy. No one remembered the incident except for Father Labonté, who, according to his colleagues, was by then semi-senile. Father Deguire, who was close to Brother André at the time the event allegedly took place, declared, "I never heard that he recommended remedies that made the sick worse."[27] It was determined that the case Father Labonté half-remembered concerned a girl from Hull who had a diseased eye. The doctors insisted that removing the eye was the only way of prolonging the child's life. Relatives of the girl were tracked down, but their testimony made it clear that Brother André indicated only that surgery would cause the girl to suffer longer without being cured. Brother André never promised the child's cure, with or without surgery.[28]

There exists a strange anecdote concerning a cure that lasted only a day because the father of the young patient refused to leave her crutches at the Oratory. A wealthy Jew took his crippled daughter to specialists in Vienna, Berlin, and Paris in a vain search for a cure and then went to the Oratory as a last resort.

"Get up and walk!" Brother André commanded the fifteen year old. The girl, who was dependent on crutches refused. "It's useless to come to see me if you do not do what I tell you. Now get up and walk!" insisted André. This time the girl did rise, and she walked.

Brother André insisted that she leave her crutches, but the father insisted on keeping them as a souvenir. The next morning the Oratory received a frantic call from the father in New

York. The day after their arrival, his daughter awoke crippled as before. When Brother André came to the phone, he is said to have rebuked the man, saying, "St. Joseph wanted the crutches left at the Oratory. You didn't want to do it! You wanted to keep them as a souvenir! Very well, then, if you want to keep them as a souvenir, keep them!"[29]

By no means was everyone who came to Brother André physically cured. A scholar who studied the correspondence from Brother André's time estimates that only seven to eleven percent of those who came to the Oratory actually professed a cure (although, of course, people came seeking favors other than cures). Although Brother André insisted that many were not cured because of a lack of faith, he also felt, as we have seen, that sometimes healing was not God's will. At any rate, his chief mission was to save men's souls and to inspire them to righteous living. Bodily cures were sometimes a way of impressing an individual with the power of the Living God. For strong Christians, especially religious, Brother André felt that it was better to bear one's pain as an offering to God in union with the sufferings of Christ in the redemption of the world. "If it is God's will that you are sick," he was known to say, "why would you refuse to accomplish God's will?"[30]

What is most important is that nearly everyone who visited Brother André went away, if not cured, at least content, able to understand and endure his sufferings more patiently. Pichette remarked that although many pilgrims died shortly after they visited Brother André, they died at peace with God and with themselves.

The number of reported cures attributed to Brother André between 1910 and his death is tremendous. The best estimate is that there were about 400 cures a year, more than one for each day of the calendar. This would make for well over 10,000 cures over a twenty-seven year period. The documentation of most of these is scanty and in many cases even the name of the person cured is unrecorded. In a few, however, the facts are well-investigated and well-substantiated.

The authority for many of the cures comes from Brother André's friends and colleagues. Father Bergeron interviewed a number of these people shortly after Brother André's death and was able to record some remarkable depositions. For example, there was "the unfortunate victim of an accident," whose gangrenous legs looked "like meat boiled to shreds." The physician told the patient, "It is impossible to save you without amputation, as impossible as it would be for the St. Lawrence River to flow upstream." The injured man insisted on seeing Brother André, who delicately massaged the mutilated flesh, while someone murmured, "Surely St. Joseph is not going to make new legs grow. There is nothing left." Brother André continued, the man said he felt better, refused the amputation, and recovered completely.[31] Unfortunately, the name of the man, the date, and the exact nature of his injury were not specified by Bergeron's sources.

In his book, *Brother André: The Wonder Man of Mount Royal,* Father Bergeron recounted the disappearance of a tumor:

> An operation had been pronounced necessary for a woman with a very large tumor in her back. Before undergoing it, she came to the Oratory, where all trace of her trouble disappeared. On the day appointed for the operation, she came to the hospital and asked to be examined once more. The doctor, to his great amazement, could discover no trace of the growth and finally asked in a bewildered way, 'On which side was the tumor?'[32]

Another case came from Brother André's own recollections, and it concerned a man who had been injured in a hunting accident. He recounted to one of his associates, "The lead pellet remaining in the flesh had caused poisoning, and the doctors decided to cut off his hand. I rubbed him, and the infected flesh trickled down to the floor like melted wax. He went away perfectly cured."[33]

In 1945, Adélard Fabre, a custodian at the Oratory, related a healing to which he was himself a witness during the 1920s:

> I was gathering up papers, cleaning, near Brother André's office. I saw a woman enter the office. She was . . . heavy, about forty. Two men were carrying her. The driver of the car that brought her followed with two crutches. I don't know her name. She lived at Lac Nominingue,

more than one hundred miles from Montreal. She stayed about a half hour in Brother André's office. I saw her come out walking without support. Brother André walked behind her, saying, 'Don't be afraid. Walk!' I saw her go to the car, about twenty-five feet from the office. The driver told me that her limbs were as dead and that she hadn't walked in four years. The driver was very nervous and had to wait to calm down before driving away. He said he was sorry he hadn't brought this lady, who was poor, to the Oratory sooner, for she had been insisting for three months that she be brought. I never heard any more about her. Brother Ludger . . . said on that occasion to Brother André, 'You've done a lot of good this morning.' Brother André answered, 'It is not I. It is God.'[34]

Arthur Ganz recalled the cure of the three children of one Monsieur Desgroseilliers, a butcher in Côte-des-Neiges. All three girls were victims of polio and none of them could walk. "Stop giving your money to the doctors," Brother André told the father. "Take the children to the beach. Rub them with the oil of St. Joseph and the medal of St. Joseph." Two weeks later Ganz saw the eldest girl, who was eight years old, leave her house, walking normally. On inquiry, he learned that not only she, but her two younger sisters also were totally cured.[35]

Ganz had an acquaintance by the name of Monsieur Bruhlmann. Bruhlmann told him about his wife, who had been suffering for three years from cancer and was now near death, her digestion so compromised that one beaten egg was the only nourishment that she could receive in a twenty-four hour period. When Ganz spoke to the husband about Brother André, Bruhlmann, who was not a Catholic, "showed little confidence" in the healer of Mount Royal. Nonetheless, Ganz asked to meet Madame Bruhlmann. When he did, he learned, to his amazement, that despite her husband's lack of enthusiasm she had visited Brother André, who had advised her to rub herself with the oil and the medal. Already she was able to keep three eggs down instead of one. After two weeks Ganz testified that Madame Bruhlmann could eat anything she pleased and was "definitively cured." When he recounted the incident some twenty years after the cure, Madame Bruhlmann was still alive and well.[36]

The archdiocesan committee which conducted dozens of interviews during the 1940s in its examination of Brother André's life and works received numerous letters from individuals professing longstanding favors received through the ministry of Brother André. In one of these, a woman described the healing of her sister, Madame Mathilde Levesque, who, in 1908, on a visit to the Oratory, suffered a spontaneous fracture of the knee. She was diagnosed as suffering from tuberculosis of the bone and told that immediate amputation was the only means of saving her life. She insisted on going back to the Oratory before submitting to the knife. She made, in fact, several visits, with no improvement in her condition before Brother André suddenly commanded her, "Well, walk, then, walk!" Madame Levesque discarded the two canes with which she had been hobbling about, and, leaving them with Brother André, called a taxi to take her home. At home she still walked with great difficulty, holding onto furniture and people to keep from falling. Yet, every day she grew a little better until, finally, without any further medical intervention, she could walk normally and without pain. After a time she was able to return to her job as a supervisor in a factory. She was never again troubled by the leg and her death, on July 5, 1925 — seventeen years, almost to the day of her cure — was due to a heart attack.[37]

In 1944 Lucie Drolet wrote the committee about an event that occurred in 1909, when she was four. She was brought to the Oratory by an aunt. "What's wrong with her?" asked André.

"She doesn't walk."

"Well, put her down," insisted the good Brother. "You don't carry a child who has all her limbs."

When Lucie was put down, she crumbled to the floor, but Brother André insisted that she be placed in a standing position on the bench in his office. He stood a few feet away from the child and extended a medal as if it were a piece of candy. "Come and get the medal," coaxed the "Miracle Man." It was then that Lucie took her first steps and walked to the old man, who gave her the medal. "Bring it back when you're seven," he bade her. When she returned, Brother André told her to wear the medal around her neck and pray regularly to St. Joseph. Her cure had not been immediate, for it was "with time" that her legs "straightened out."[38] Exactly what her problem had been, Drolet did not indicate in her letter.

Ernest Belanger was fifty-seven on February 11, 1944 when he wrote, testifying to a cure that occurred in 1906 or 1907. While he was working as a lumberjack, his foot was nearly severed by a misplaced stroke of his companion's axe. Unconscious and bleeding heavily, Belanger was taken to a hospital and remained there four months. Although surgeons succeeded in saving the foot, Belanger was dismayed, when he was discharged, that his injured limb was three inches shorter than his sound one and he was still so lame that he could not work. So he went to Brother André, who told him, "Pray to St. Joseph and it will come back." Belanger returned later to tell André that his leg was still crippled. On a third visit, the woodcutter grabbed the Brother's soutane and pleaded, "I need my leg!"

"Well, go buy some ordinary shoes and go to work!" said André.

Belanger, who had been wearing a shoe with a built-up sole, did as bidden and returned to work. "I never felt any fatigue or lost time because of the leg," he wrote. In his 1944 letter Belanger did not indicate whether the leg returned to its normal length. Interestingly, he recounted that two years after his cure, back at his old trade, he accidentally chopped his right hand completely off! "I thought then, I have a cross to bear. I'll bear it." So Ernest Belanger, resigned that his days as a lumberjack had ended, went to work as a telephone operator for International Pulp and Paper.[39]

Madame Armand Grothé of Montreal wrote, also in 1944, concerning her son who, at eight months of age in April, 1910, was suffering from a deadly combination of pneumonia and meningitis. The child was paralyzed on the right side but his head kept moving convulsively. The 1923 edition of *The Principles and Practice of Medicine* stated "there are no remedies which in any way control the course of acute meningitis." In fact, the doctor predicted that the child would not survive the night, but one of the nurses at the hospital went to the Oratory, after her shift, to tell Brother André about the sick child. André advised, "Rub everything that hurts with the St. Joseph's medal." The nurse did this, and immediately the baby's head ceased its incessant movement, and the next day the paralysis had left. Thirty-four years later the mother declared that her son had recovered to live a normal life.[40]

Miss Marguerite LeRoux wrote of her late father, Antonio LeRoux of Montreal, who in 1911 had a 90% vision loss in both eyes from causes that were not specified. When he visited the Oratory, Brother André made little crosses on his eyes with St. Joseph oil and bade him return for this treatment every day for two months. At the end of that time, LeRoux could see perfectly. Two months later, however, he returned, complaining of excruciating pains in his back. Brother André said, "You were accustomed to wearing glasses, weren't you? Well, wear them all the time and your backache will disappear. You must believe that it is God's will, since He wants it like that." LeRoux put on his spectacles and was immediately relieved of his back pains, which, according to his daughter, did not recur until two years before his death in June, 1940. His vision, however, never deteriorated.

This was not the only cure by which the LeRoux family was graced. Marguerite and her sister Gabrielle (little girls at the time of their father's cure) were both victims of polio, paralyzed and unable to walk. After his own physical problems were alleviated, LeRoux spoke to Brother André about the crippled children. "Bring me one of your little girls one evening, after Vespers, when the weather is good," André bade him. So LeRoux brought Marguerite. At the time she was a quadraplegic, unable to use any of her limbs. Brother André made several little crosses with his fingers on the child's legs, invoking St. Joseph all the while. Nothing happened, and LeRoux returned home with Marguerite still paralyzed. A few months later, Marguerite was taken back to the Oratory by her grandmother. This time Brother André ordered Marguerite to walk. Without anyone's help, she immediately began to do so, as the grandmother and Brother André both prostrated themselves in thanksgiving before the statue of St. Joseph in the church. Marguerite returned from the church able to walk, but with her arms still paralyzed. Over a period of time she gained the use of her upper limbs. Two weeks after Marguerite walked, the mother and grandmother made little crosses with their fingers on Gabrielle's paralyzed limbs, and she, too, was healed.[41]

Fred Hogan, a molder in a Montreal factory, wrote in 1943 that some twenty years earlier he had dragged himself on crutches to the Oratory, a sufferer from "inflammatory rheumatism," from which he had been suffering violently for three months. Hogan had to wait several days for a five-minute interview with Brother André, but left the office perfectly cured, stamping his feet with joy. He returned to work the next day and in the intervening two decades was never again troubled by rheumatism or arthritis.[42]

In December, 1939, Madame Albert Cardinal wrote:

> In 1914 my son Henry was seized with a pain in his eyes. The doctor at the hospital told me to have him operated on without delay. 'Are you going to guarantee his sight?' my husband asked the doctor. 'No, his eyes are finished.' I take my poor little boy in my arms. He was two and a half and I had a three-week-old baby. I take my poor little one and I leave with him in my arms. I was so confident, I put him in the arms of Brother André and he took him in his arms and said there was nothing wrong with him. Oh, he has his eyes and never has had better eyes. He is living. I can show him to you. He has never had an eye problem and has good eyes. I sincerely thank St. Joseph and Brother André. I know that it is he who healed him.[43]

A Rhode Island man named Lionel Maynard testified to a remarkable cure that occurred at the home of Brother André's nephew, John Boulet, of Arctic, Rhode Island. Boulet had died in 1936, but his sister, Suzanne Boulet Paine, offered corroborating testimony. She recalled that in the mid 1920s Lionel Maynard was suffering from tuberculosis of the bone, "and walked with extreme difficulty, using crutches," when he called on Brother André at her brother's home. Maynard himself declared:

> I was afflicted with caries of the bone of the vertebral column. This was in 1926. My brother-in-law, Dr. Fulgence Archambault, diagnosed this malady and sent me to a specialist, Dr. Maria Danforth of Providence. She sent me to the hospital for four weeks where they kept me

> without effect. When I left the hospital I walked with the
> aid of crutches and I had to wear a corset of plaster, rein-
> forced by a corset of iron.

His illness, "caries of the bone," is a malady unfamiliar in
the latter twentieth century. The condition, according to the
compilers of the 1923 edition of *The Principles and Practice
of Medicine,* was officially known as Pott's Disease, and was,
as Mrs. Paine said, a form of tuberculosis. It was characterized by an inflammation of the vertebrae, or the bones around
the spinal cord. The inflammation tended to squeeze the spinal
cord — the sheaf of nerves enclosed within the vertebrae —
causing severe pain, and often, varying degrees of paralysis. In
addition, in many patients, the diseased vertebrae collapsed,
causing a hunched back. By the 1920s caries of the spine was
considered a curable condition. Extensive bedrest and sometimes traction were the treatment of choice. In Maynard's
case, however, the hospital treatment and the corset in which
he was encased, so as to ensure the immobility of his spinal
column, were not working. Maynard was partially paralyzed
and in agonizing pain when he went to see Brother André on
November 29, 1926 at the Boulet home. Maynard was seated in
the large parlor, which was crowded with more than a hundred
people, when Brother André walked over to him and told him
to get up. The simple effort of rising to his feet caused the sick
man excruciating pain, but Maynard, with the aid of his
crutches, struggled to an upright position. Brother André then
told him to walk about the room. Slowly and painfully, Maynard hobbled about. Brother André insisted that he walk faster
and yet faster. Soon Maynard was literally running around the
Boulet parlor — without pain. The guests who were gathered in
the house were in tears. Maynard recalled that he gave his
crutches and corset to Brother André, who took them back to
the Oratory that very night. Mrs. Paine's recollection was that
Maynard came to her house the next day with the crutches and
told her to give them to Brother André.

At any rate, Maynard visited Dr. Archambault three days
later. The physician "turned white" at seeing him without
pain, walking normally. When he examined him, he found in
Maynard's back a large depression caused by the disintegra-

tion of decaying vertebrae, and warned the patient that despite the relief of his pain and paralysis, he was far from cured and needed to continue the prescribed treatments. Against Archambault's orders, Maynard went to Montreal, where Brother André rubbed his back, over his clothing, and asked him to stay in the apartment over the old chapel for two days. Maynard ended up staying six weeks. At the beginning of his stay, Maynard told André that a doctor would have to be consulted concerning the necessity of changing the dressing on his back. André told him that he would like to remove the dressing himself. Maynard consented. Previously this procedure had proven painful and time-consuming, but Brother André removed the dressing with one motion of the hand, "without causing the slightest pain." He then told the sick man to rub himself daily with the St. Joseph medal. Maynard recounted that during the six weeks he stayed with Brother André, "the depression in the spinal column became smaller and smaller until all that remained was a small mark." When he returned to Rhode Island, he went again to see his physician, who confessed himself "baffled" by the cure. Maynard, who had been certified as "an incurable invalid" by both the Metropolitan Life and Prudential Life insurance companies was never again — or at least for the next twenty years — troubled by Pott's Disease or by any pain or disability associated with it.[44]

Of the Maynard cure, several things can be observed. It was not the case of a sudden and complete disappearance of an untreatable distemper. Although the medical texts of the day claimed "caries of the spine" or Pott's Disease, was treatable, Maynard had not responded well to the prescribed medical treatments. Brother André's ministrations on November 29, 1926 accomplished an instantaneous remission of pain and partial paralysis, but the disease itself, without further medical treatment, disappeared gradually during the stay at the Oratory.

Colonel George Ham, Director for Publicity with the Canadian Pacific Railroad in the 1920s, wrote one of the first books on Brother André in 1922. Much to the consternation of the Brother (who was a personal friend), Ham was a non-believer, (he said that if he embraced any religion, it would be Brother André's) but was fascinated by all kinds of parapsychological phenomena, and considered André a "medium." In his book he recounted a number of cures which are fairly well-documented.

One of these involved a nameless "British lady, wife of a former member of Parliament," who visited Montreal in 1920 and met Brother André. Upon her return to England, she wrote Ham:

I have a little story you may like to tell Brother André. When I came home in November, I found a letter from a young friend I had not seen since he was in a perambulator. It was to ask my prayers for his mother who was dying from the effects of an accident. Her foot caught as she was going down a very steep flight of stairs to the Underground Railway at Baker Street, London, England, and she fell the whole length of it, hitting her head . . . very badly. When she was conscious she was taken home and suddenly she went clean out of her senses and knew no one and raved about people dead long ago and called me in my maiden name, as she used to know me when I was a girl. It was this that put it into her son's head to write to me that she was not supposed to live very long and that the doctors held out very little hope for her life. I was told that she was in a mental hospital and that she did not recognize even her son when he went to see her. I asked permission to go there . . . they told me that she could utter nothing but gibberish and was very weak. When I came to her bedside, I would not have known her, but I looked straight into her eyes and told her I was Alice. Then she caught my hand and held it convulsively, and her poor tongue and lips were uttering an incomprehensible jumble over and over again. At last I hit upon it, she was repeating a prayer in Polish that her mother had taught her as a child . . . I told the nurse that she was saying a prayer in Polish and that she appeared unable to say anything else.

At this point Alice asked the sick woman in French if she were in pain. In French the patient replied, "Not at all." Then she began to pray in Polish again. While the nurse was not looking, Alice made the sign of the cross with the St. Joseph's oil she had been given by Brother André, and, with a medal of St. Joseph in her hand, prayed, "If there is any merit in Brother André's prayers and in good works, may this poor woman be restored to health for her own and for her son's sake." Then Alice left and went on vacation for three weeks. When she returned she called the injured woman's son, expecting to hear that her friend had died. Instead, she was told that she had recovered completely.[45]

Colonel Ham recounted the cure of Joseph L'Heureux. On November 13, 1910, Ephrem L'Heureux of 391 St. Joseph Street in Quebec wrote the Oratory to give thanks for the cure of his fifteen-year-old son Joseph who

> had suffered for six years with bone disease, and for more than a year had been compelled to walk with crutches. A novena, which was begun at Quebec and terminated at the Oratory of St. Joseph . . . obtained for him a perfect cure, insomuch that the patient left his crutches at the Oratory. . . .

In 1922 Colonel Ham found Joseph L'Heureux in the Montreal City Directory and wrote to him. L'Heureux, now twenty-seven, responded:

> For upwards of two years I had to walk with the aid of crutches and was unable to use my right leg. Then, having heard of the wonderful miracles performed by St. Joseph through the intercession of Brother André, I made a novena in honor of St. Joseph, in the hope of obtaining a cure of my malady. At the conclusion of the novena I went to Montreal to see Brother André. On arrival there I had a talk with him and told him that I had the utmost confidence in his prayers to our patron saint, St. Joseph. At that same instant I allowed my crutches to drop to the ground and I walked on my own two legs, just as I walk today, without difficulty. And I assure you, Monsieur, that from that time until now I have never suffered from the hip disease. I carry myself very well today, just as on the day when I was first cured.[46]

Dr. Arthur St.-Pierre of Montreal did substantial research in the 1920s on some of the cures of the Oratory. One of the cases in which he was able to obtain a fair amount of documentation was that of Martin Hannon, whose sudden ability to walk without crutches in early 1910 was one of the first cures at the Oratory to attract the attention of the press.

Hannon, a freight handler with the Canadian Pacific Railroad, was forty-nine years old when, in October, 1908, a block of marble weighing more than a ton fell on him, pinning his legs. At the Hospital of the Precious Blood in Quebec it was determined that he had suffered double compound fractures of both legs. After five months of treatment, he was discharged. After several months, Hannon was still badly crippled, in pain, and able to walk only with the assistance of crutches. A very devout Irish Catholic, he first made a pilgrimage to Canada's traditional miraculous shrine of Ste.-Anne de Beaupré, near Quebec. Unimproved, he decided to pray at St. Joseph's Oratory, and there, on January 9, 1910, he experienced a sudden improvement and discarded his crutches.

Nearly three years after his cure, Father Clément wrote to Hannon, inviting him to prepare an account of his cure for publication in the *Annals of St. Joseph.* On December 23, 1912, Hannon replied:

Reverend Father,

I received your postal card with which I am honored, the more so because it gives me the occasion to help you propagate devotion to St. Joseph. Never since I had the honor of leaving my two crutches at the . . . foot of the altar of the Sacred Heart of Jesus have I had the occasion to use any [crutches] again, not even a cane, a stick, or anything else to help me walk. I went down that hill where the chapel is located, in the middle of the road, January 9, 1910, without the help of any living soul. I put myself in the hands of Jesus, Mary, and Joseph, and I asked for their help to walk down the hill on foot, and I felt, Reverend Father, as though I were carried to the end of it where I began to run to catch the streetcar that was coming. Evidently I couldn't walk in the streetcar as easily as people who have the perfect use of their legs, but thanks to God and St. Joseph my friends opened their eyes when they saw me return home without my crutches. The next day, after hearing two Masses at Notre-Dame de Bonsecours, I took the streetcar to Côte-des-Neiges . . . Before starting I prayed to Jesus, Mary, and Joseph to carry me up to the top, to the door of the Oratory, where, inside, I offered thanks to our Blessed Mother, to the Sacred Heart of Jesus, and to Blessed St. Joseph. Since that time my condition has stayed the same each day, and now, thanks to God, I can stand all day and do work that would tire young people, walking all the time without any opportunity to sit down.

Hannon sent Father Clément another letter, signed by twenty-seven co-workers, family, and friends, declaring:

We, the undersigned, certify with great pleasure the miraculous healing of Martin Hannon, after a novena at the sanctuary of St. Joseph, Côte-des-Neiges, January 9, 1910. The wounds he received October 27, 1908 were frightful. He was literally crushed under a block of marble weighing 3,200 pounds, which suddenly fell on him, making of his extremities a mixture of bruised flesh and broken bones. In these circumstances, because of this deplorable accident, he was in a desperate condition and had only the hope of a miracle to be cured. This, fortunately, happened January 9, 1910 in the sanctuary of St. Joseph after fervent prayers, when he was able to dispense with his crutches and to walk to take the train to Quebec. Since then he has continued to enjoy good health. He is even able to fill the arduous job of freight checker, which has him continually on his feet for twelve hours a day without respite.

Around this same time the Oratory received a "touching letter" from a Jesuit missionary who described Hannon's deportment at the shrine of Ste.-Anne de Beaupré, where he "spent long hours before the statue of the Glorious Thaumaturge, mixing tears and sobs with ardent prayers" before leaving crippled as before. The Jesuit therefore noted with delight the news "that the good St. Joseph granted him, in the sanctuary you've erected to his glory, the favor that this pious petition solicited of St. Anne with such great confidence and burning devotion."

Dr. St.-Pierre decided to investigate the healing of Hannon in 1921, because, in reading Hannon's letter and the old newspaper accounts, he was struck by the account of "the instantaneous healing of a fracture of the legs which could be considered as incurable, since it had resisted the most intelligent medical treatment." St.-Pierre wanted first to know how serious the injuries had been so he wrote to Dr. P.C. Dagneau, Professor at Laval University at Quebec, who had been one of the doctors who treated Hannon during his hospitalization. Dagneau was rather negative:

> I received today your letter of the 6th about what you call the apparently miraculous healing of Martin Hannon.
>
> I recall perfectly the history of this Mr. Hannon and I'm going to tell you immediately that in my opinion, there is nothing miraculous in what happened to him.
>
> After six months in the hospital, Martin Hannon got up, and although miserably at first, could walk for some weeks with the help of a cane before making his pilgrimage to Montreal.
>
> On the occasion of this pilgrimage he momentarily abandoned his support, which he had to take up again later.
>
> Martin Hannon limped on both legs for the rest of his life, invalidating any idea of a miraculous healing. I give you these details and this opinion in the most Catholic spirit there is and with the firm idea that the publication of a 'miracle' like this can only raise criticisms and expose to ridicule a religion that, like you, I practice and respect.
>
> Very truly yours,
P. Calixte Dagneau

Thus Dr. Dagneau, in contradiction to other witnesses who maintained that Hannon came to the Oratory on crutches, abandoned them there, and walked normally and unassisted after that, insists that by the time of his visit to the Oratory Hannon used only a cane, which he continued to use as a support for the rest of his life as he limped around on two permanently disabled legs.

Having ascertained that both Hannon and his wife were now dead, St.-Pierre wrote Hannon's daughter Kathleen, as well as a surviving brother and sister, mailing them a long questionnaire. The replies from all three confirmed that 1) Hannon's legs were "literally crushed" by a 3,200-pound marble block while at work on October 27, 1908; 2) he spent six months in the hospital, and after that could walk only with crutches. ("The doctor told him that he had saved his legs but could do nothing more," stated Kathleen Hannon); 3) he went to the shrine of Ste.-Anne de Beaupré in July, 1909, without obtaining any improvement; 4) he went to Montreal the following January, still on crutches; and 5) after January 9, 1910, Hannon never used crutches or cane, and he continued to work as a freight checker, twelve hours a day, on his feet constantly without fatigue.

Next St.-Pierre checked Hannon's work record. This showed that Hannon began work for the Canadian Pacific in May, 1906, that he left in October, 1908 because of an accident, but returned in April, 1910, continuing in the position of freight checker until his death at sixty-two from a heart attack in February, 1921.

St.-Pierre wrote again to Dr. Dagneau, who once more insisted that there was nothing unusual about the Hannon case. Any version of it but his own was "gossip," Dagneau maintained, stressing that Hannon had experienced "a normal, but incomplete" healing of "a double fracture of the legs" and that there was no miracle. St.-Pierre could not ascertain from Dagneau whether he had examined or even seen him after he left the hospital in 1909.

St.-Pierre then wrote to Joseph Lacroix, who had been with Hannon on his visit to the Oratory in January, 1910. Lacroix stated that even before their arrival at the Oratory, Hannon was convinced that he would not need crutches when they returned home. Lacroix confirmed that Hannon indeed "never needed crutches" after his healing. He did not say whether he ever used a cane or whether he limped. The Hotel-Dieu du Precieux Sang in Quebec, where Hannon had been a patient, offered St.-Pierre the extent records: "Martin Hannon, 49, married, day laborer, Quebec, fracture of legs, healed, Dr. Dagneau. Entered October 27, 1908. Left April 3, 1909." The hospital administrator interviewed all personnel still with the institution who remembered the Hannon case, all of whom testified that Hannon had left the hospital not with a cane but under two crutches, and that he had returned later, insisting that he was completely cured.

St.-Pierre, despite the statements of Dr. Dagneau to the contrary, was confident enough to conclude: 1) Hannon's injury was serious; 2) Hannon was not healed when he left the hospital; 3) Hannon could walk only with crutches at the time; and 4) after his visit to the Oratory in January, 1910, Hannon walked without cane or crutch for the balance of his days. Concluding, St.-Pierre said:

> It is my absolute conviction that Martin Hannon was radically healed from his infirmity for all practical purposes on January 9, 1910, at the Oratory of St. Joseph of Montreal. It is also my conviction that no human power, no natural agent, could heal that suddenly such a serious and long-term condition as that suffered by Hannon. A supernatural intervention, a miracle, is the only logical and intelligent explanation of a healing of which the reality alone, not the extraordinary character, could be doubted.[47]

Dr. St.-Pierre, in 1927, published in his book, *St. Joseph's Oratory of Montreal (A Descriptive and Historical Account)*, a section on "The Miracles of the Oratory," in which a number of cases are carefully analyzed. Among these are two cases cited by Dr. Henri Dufresne of 262 Roy Street, Montreal. The first was described in a certificate written December 14, 1911 and concerned the doctor's own brother, J. O. Dufresne, who had "been cured of tuberculosis in a very far advanced stage after a pilgrimage to the Oratory of St. Joseph on Mount Royal." The second certificate described the cure of Mademoiselle Alponsine St.-Martin, who had been Dufresne's patient for four years and also suffered from advanced tuberculosis. She too experienced a sudden and complete cure after visiting the Oratory. In 1922 St.-Pierre contacted Dr. Dufresne and questioned him, ascertaining that both patients were still alive and free from tuberculosis.[48]

St.-Pierre recounts the cure of Charles Eugene Veilleux of Rivière du Loup. The cure occurred at the Oratory on October 3, 1910 and was described in a certificate written by his physician, Dr. L. J. Piuze of Fraserville, Quebec:

> I, the undersigned, medical practitioner at Fraserville, certify that, in company with the late Dr. F. G. Gilbert, I examined young Veilleux, son of Mr. Eugene Vellieux of this place, about August 30, 1910. We found that the youth was suffering from tuberculosis of the spinal column, in the cervical region. We put him in a plaster cast. Several weeks later the boy went to Montreal with his mother and came back completely cured. On different occasions since then I have examined the boy and have never been able to discover the slightest trace of the terrible disease from which he had suffered, a disease the treatment for which usually takes more than three years.[49]

Veilleux was suffering from the same medical problem that would afflict Lionel Maynard a decade later — tuberculosis of the spine — a malady which, though curable, required lengthy therapy. The extraordinary aspect of the cure was its quickness. St.-Pierre seems, however, to have made no effort to follow up on the permanence of the cure when he was engaged in his study in the 1920s.

We will recall that in about 1911, Joseph Pichette, then beset with various health problems, was encouraged to visit Brother André by a salesman whose father had been cured of cancer at the Oratory. The healed man's name was Louis Bertrand, about whom Dr. E. C. Campeau of 829 Notre-Dame Street West, Montreal, wrote the Oratory on May 6, 1911:

> Mr. Louis Bertrand, of No. 74A St. Margaret Street, St.-Henri (a suburb of Montreal) was suffering from a cancer on the right arm. Already the ganglions of the [armpit] and the arm had been attacked. The wound caused by the cancer increased in size rapidly, the cancerous infection making daily progress. I had not the slightest doubt as to

the diagnosis of the case; it was really a cancer in the malignant stage.

I certify that today Mr. Bertrand is completely cured. That the ganglions have disappeared, and that there is no trace of the cancerous infection. As Mr. Bertrand assures me that he has had no recourse to medical remedies — remedies which, for that matter, had previously proved ineffective so far as he was previously concerned — I conclude that his cure is certainly the affect of a miracle, due to the intercession of St. Joseph, in whom Mr. Bertrand placed his hope.[50]

St.-Pierre evidently did not track Bertrand down, but Colonel Ham found the former cancer patient alive and completely well in 1922, eleven years after his cure.

Another case examined by both Ham and St.-Pierre was that of Mrs. Joseph Marcoux, whose Christian name was never recorded in any of the documentation. A resident of Quebec, in early 1921 she was suffering from heart disease. Her husband wrote the editor of the *Annals* in July, 1921:

Mrs. Marcoux was dying. She had been constantly watched for five days. She had frequent weak spells and the doctor said that she would pass away in one of these crises.

Learning that the founder of the Oratory [Brother André] was passing through Quebec, Mr. Marcoux sought him out at the residence of the Holy Cross Fathers, Sainte-Famille St., and induced him to return home with him. At the very moment when the husband was requesting the favor of Frere André at the residence of the Fathers, Mrs. Marcoux suddenly felt her strength return, and, getting up, dressed herself and went into another room where, on his arrival, Mr. Marcoux, much to his astonishment, found her sitting. The happiness of the family may be easily imagined.

In addition, the physician of Madame Marcoux issued a certificate in which he testified:

I, the undersigned, solemnly certify that Mrs. Joseph Marcoux has been under my medical care since December 27, 1920; that she was afflicted with heart disease of a very serious nature; that her legs were swollen; and that she was succumbing to progressive feebleness. I looked upon her case as hopeless. She is at present quite well, her heart beats regularly, her pulse is good, and her legs have resumed their normal condition. I consider her cure to be a wonderful grace obtained by Frere André, of St. Joseph's Oratory.

M.A. Falardeau, M.D.[51]

On March 3, 1911, Arthur Rochette, a 23-year-old brakeman on the Grand Trunk Railway, working at Richmond, Quebec, slipped and fell under a moving freight train. He scrambled or was pulled to safety, but not until two wheels passed over his right foot and left ankle. Rushed to the General Hospital at Montreal, it was determined that both feet had been crushed. After two operations, the right foot began to heal, but the left one, infected, remained "in a pitiable state." Surgeons advised a third operation and, if that proved unsuccessful, amputation. Rochette refused the operation to the dismay of the medical staff who warned that his life was endangered without it. He called his father to pick him up and seven weeks after the accident he left the hospital. At that time, according to Rochette's testimony, the foot "was held to [the] leg only by the skin and some soft flesh. At the least movement it swung like a bit of lead at the end of a line, and could be turned halfway round without the slightest difficulty. The bones and muscles were reduced to a pulp." After he returned home, Rochette's doctors' fears were realized, as the entire leg became infected and swelled to four times its normal size. When general blood poisoning set in, his father called a priest to their Princeville home, so that the injured man might receive the last blessings of the Church. Rochette was also visited by Arthur Gilbert, a family friend who was also a member of the Canadian Parliament. Gilbert urged Rochette's parents to pray to St. Joseph and to write to Brother André at the Oratory. After a short time a medal of St. Joseph and a vial of oil arrived from the Oratory. Rochette applied the oil and the medal to his mangled limb and professed at once to feel relief. The entire Rochette family made a novena to St. Joseph, and the blood poisoning readily abated. Concerning this development, Dr. St.-Pierre commented, "In view . . . of the fact that he was being treated for blood-poisoning while having recourse to St. Joseph, it is difficult to say how much of the improvement was due to natural and how much to supernatural causes."

Although his blood poisoning was cured, Rochette was still badly disabled. He could walk only with crutches and had to wear a special boot to keep his left foot motionless. When he was examined in August, five months after the accident, the doctors noted that the foot "still swung at the end of the leg. Within the leg itself there had been formed a sort of cavity which communicated with the exterior by seven gaping holes. The flesh around these holes was putrefied . . . [and] insensible to the touch; and the suppuration from the open wounds emitted a strongly offensive smell." The surgeons told Rochette to enter the Hotel-Dieu of Victoriaville and submit to immediate amputation. "Whoever can cure your foot," insisted one of the physicians, "can just as easily pick a church up from its foundations and turn it end for end!"

Again Rochette defied his doctors, and, along with a friend, went to the Oratory, where Brother André agreed that he should refuse amputation. He returned to Princeville, where he refused all medical treatment, even antiseptics, merely following Brother André's advice to wash the leg with lukewarm water and apply the oil of St. Joseph. Slowly the leg began to improve.

In late September Rochette returned to the Oratory and made a novena there. When he departed, he offered to leave his crutches at the Oratory, but Brother André warned him that it was too soon to abandon them. Within a few weeks, however, Rochette felt so well that he began to walk unassisted, and by the end of October, he felt totally cured.

St.-Pierre met Rochette in February, 1922, more than a decade after the cure. The doctor described Rochette as a tallish, square-shouldered man with "every appearance of physical vigor." He displayed no sign of lameness. But strangely, when St.-Pierre requested a medical certificate from the doctor who had said that it would be easier for a man to pick up a church than for Rochette's leg to mend, the physician now insisted that there had been nothing supernatural about the cure. St.-Pierre was also unable to locate the records of the hospital where Rochette had been treated. He did collect depositions from the mother and brother of Rochette and from four others who corroborated the testimony of the former cripple. For his part, Rochette stated that he never had any doubts as to the supernatural character of his healing.[52]

On June 3, 1909, 13-year-old Marie-Antoinette Mercier of Quebec City was struck with an oar in the right eye by a belligerent playmate. Dr. Wilfred Beaupré examined her eye with an ophthalmoscope and noted that he was unable to see the interior of the eye "because of the disturbance of the vitreous humor."[53] He saw evidence of hemorrhaging, but did not venture a definitive diagnosis. However, the fact that the eye did not respond to light suggested irreparable damage to the optic nerve.

Marie-Antoinette returned to school that fall, but could not see well enough to do her lessons. The nuns (and in those days nearly all public schools in Quebec were run by religious orders) obtained a medal of St. Joseph from the Oratory and began a novena in behalf of the partially blinded girl, applying the medal to the sightless eye each day. For eight days there was no improvement, but, on the last day of the novena, in chapel, Marie-Antoinette suddenly cried out, "I see!" With her bad eye she had looked in the direction of the statue of St. Joseph — and had seen it. The Sisters, after chapel, handed Marie-Antoinette a book printed in very small type and directed her to close her good eye. When she was able to read this without difficulty, the Sisters assembled the entire student body to sign a hymn of thanksgiving.

On February 15, 1910, six days after Marie-Antoinette regained the sight in her injured eye, she was examined by Dr. L. O. Gauthier, who was one of the physicians who examined her eye after the injury of the previous June. He recalled that the eye was rendered blind by hemorrhaging in the optic nerve. Yet:

> Today, February 15, 1910, I have again examined Mlle. Mercier and find that the sight of her right eye is about

111

normal, a circumstance which would indicate that a complete revolution of the nerve has taken place. I am not prepared to admit that the sight of this eye has been restored through purely natural means.

Marie-Antoinette Mercier was also re-examined by Dr. Beaupré, who declared:

On June 19, 1909 I examined at my office, with all due care, the eyesight of Mlle. Marie-Antoinette Mercier, thirteen years of age and residing at No. 20 Laval St., Quebec. Her mother, who accompanied her, told me that the girl had received, a fortnight before, full on the right eye, a blow from an oar in the hands of a little girl who, apparently, was somewhat malicious; and that, since then, the daughter had lost the sight of the eye. . . .

I had no hesitation, accordingly, in assuring the mother that the eye would eventually be lost, and that no human means could bring back its sight. Such was my sincere conviction. At the same time I told the mother that if the child were mine, I would have her undergo a new treatment which had already produced successful results in certain ocular troubles. The mother decided that the treatment in question should be given, and accordingly, during some weeks the girl was submitted to this 'special treatment,' but without the slightest result, as was proved by an examination of the eye on August 26, 1909. I then advised that it be discontinued.

Beaupré went on to say that in September he filled out a certificate, which Marie-Antoinette's parents needed in order to sue the parents of the attacking child. In the certificate the physician confirmed "the total and permanent loss of the eye's sight." However, on February 9, 1910

Mlle. Mercier again came to my office for a new consultation. The religious who accompanied her, the Rev. Mother St. Ephrem of St. Joseph's Convent at Levis, informed me to my great astonishment that Marie-Antoinette Mercier, who that very morning had finished a novena to St. Joseph, had suddenly during Mass recovered her sight. I made, not without considerable emotion, another examination of her right eye and found that for the first time I could see into the depths of the eye, and that, moreover, the sight of the eye was absolutely perfect and in every respect equal to that of the left eye, which was perfectly normal.

It is needless to dwell on my astonishment or on the girl's happiness. If the finger of God is not manifest in this cure, then I know not whose finger has been working.

In February, 1922, Marie-Antoinette's sister Jeanne, in response to St.-Pierre's inquiry, wrote: "My sister has been perfectly well since her cure . . . Her right eye is thoroughly sound, just like the other one."[54]

Alfred Stanhope (sometimes spelled Standhope), a tall, heavy fireman in his mid-twenties, was on duty in the Westmount Fire Station in Montreal on April 5, 1916 when, descending on the brass pole from the second story, he lost his grip and fell thirty feet to the cement floor below. In his own words, "the fall was so severe, especially on the foot that first struck the floor, that the bones of [the] leg, reduced to splinters, protruded through the skin near the ankle. That the veins had burst was clear from the quantity of blood that soon covered the floor."

Stanhope spent six weeks in Western Hospital, and when discharged could walk only with crutches. After some months he was able to discard his crutches, but he suffered from osteomyelitis, a chronic inflammation of the bone, in the injured leg, which remained so stiff and painful that he was forced to give up his job as a firefighter for a position as a watchman which allowed him to perform his duties seated.[55]

Stanhope, who came from an English Protestant background, was himself a member of no church and characterized himself as a "skeptic" who did not believe in miracles. However, his pain grew so extreme that he heeded the advice of a Roman Catholic friend and decided to visit Brother André. Thus, in June, 1917, Stanhope painfully toiled up the steps of the Oratory. It took him a half-hour to reach the top. "I was crying with pain when I got to the top," Stanhope recounted.

"Do you think I can help you?" Brother André asked.

"If I didn't, I wouldn't be here," replied the cripple.

André removed the steel brace encasing Stanhope's bad foot. "Immediately the pain left my right ankle," Stanhope told a reporter. "I left the Brother and without the steel brace on my foot I ran down the steps it had taken so long to climb." Fourteen years after the cure he insisted, "I have never had a pain since and I have never worn the brace." He took a job as a watchman in a factory, a job which involved "walking, standing, and climbing stairs." He was still employed in this capacity as late as 1954 — thirty-seven years after his cure. Although Stanhope seems never to have gone back to visit Brother André, his encounter and cure may have led to his union with the Church of Rome in the late 1920s. "I never went to Church," he told an interviewer in 1931. "I felt it would be a good idea to join. My wife is a Catholic. Now I go to church every Sunday and one of these days I'll go back and see Brother André. I must go back and see the old man. He certainly helped me. Sure, you got to have faith. Noah had faith and it saved him. You got to have faith."[56] Interestingly enough, when Dr. St.-Pierre, having interviewed Stanhope, questioned Brother André and Father Clément, he was amazed to learn that neither remembered the man or the cure![57]

Frederick Griffin, a Canadian reporter, interviewed Sam Chagnon, another firefighter, in 1931. Chagnon recounted that on November 30, 1922, when he was twenty-four, he was en route to a fire when the engine on which he was riding overturned, coming to rest against a steel-link fence, pinning him between and ripping one of his legs out of its socket. Chagnon underwent surgery to repair the limb and after a hospital stay of sixty-eight days, went home for twenty days of bed rest. At the end of that time he was still badly crippled, suffering from phlebitis (the inflammation of one or more veins) in the injured limb, which remained swollen, painful, and "stiff as a stovepipe." When his doctors told him that there was nothing more to be done and that he should expect no more improvement, he decided to go to Brother André.

> I began to go once a week to the shrine. I had a big confidence in Brother André and St. Joseph. I went to the shrine weekly for three months. I made a novena . . . with

Brother André. We were there maybe fifteen minutes making the prayer.

Then, on June 16, 1923

I stood in front of Brother André. He started to feel up and down my leg. He did that for about ten minutes. Then I felt kind of warm. Suddenly it was warm all over. The circulation of the blood was running again. I could feel the bandage kind of loose. It was coming down. I told Brother André. 'You feel better?' he said. I said, 'Yes, better.' We went to the chapel. We went there together. And I went down on my knees for fifteen minutes. It was the first time. Before, my leg was too big. It would not bend. But now it bent easy. I was crying, crying like a baby. Brother André looked at me with large eyes. He said, 'It doesn't hurt too much, eh?' I could scarcely imagine it true. After that I gave him my cane. I did not use it since.[58]

Strangely enough, several years later, Chagnon was in another accident. The same leg that had been injured nine years earlier was again pinned under an overturned truck, an eight-ton "pump." "My leg should have been made into a pulp and mince meat," Chagnon declared. "Everyone thought I was finished, but when they take me to the hospital and make X-ray, the leg is not broken, the bone is not hurt. For nine weeks I couldn't walk, but then I went to the shrine and I could."[59]

Another cure recounted by Dr. St.-Pierre was that of Germaine Doyon of Augusta, Maine. This healing was reported by the Montreal *La Presse* of May 21, 1924:

An event which happened yesterday about 3 p.m. at Saint Joseph's Oratory, Mount Royal, made a deep impression on the thousands of pilgrims who assisted at the ceremony of the Tercentenary of the proclamation of St. Joseph as patron of Canada.

A young girl declared that she was cured. Hundreds of persons were witnesses of the alleged cure, and the news spread quickly among the assembled multitude. A loud shout was heard, 'A Miracle!' and invocations to St. Joseph ascended from all sides.

Our representative had the privilege of speaking to

Miss Doyon, 21 years of age, of 61 Washington Street, Augusta, Maine.

Miss Doyon could not walk without the aid of crutches for two years, and after going to see Frere André she began to walk normally and without pain. She related her history most simply and with great joy:

'Eight years ago I fell on my left knee and was ill for some time. I was cured, however, and two years ago I entered the novitiate of the Sisters of Bon-Pasteur, Montreal. Unfortunately, I fell a second time on the same knee, and this time I dislocated the kneecap. I consulted several doctors without obtaining any relief. Pus formed in my knee and my limb remained bent. Consequently I was obliged to leave the Convent.

'After medical treatment at the Hotel Dieu I returned home a year ago, having lost confidence in medical skill. Moreover, I did not receive any assurance of a possible cure. Three weeks ago I made a last attempt by consulting a doctor, but he told me to be resigned to my lot as I was condemned to remain lame the rest of my life. It was then that I resolved to go on a pilgrimage to Ste.-Anne de Beaupré. Arriving in Montreal I was advised by my cousin, Mr. Edgar Doyon, to visit Saint Joseph's Shrine on Mount Royal. Last Sunday I visited the Shrine, and Father Theoret applied Saint Joseph's medal to my sore knee, but I returned without receiving any relief.

'As I was to leave on the next Tuesday for Ste.-Anne de Beaupré, I returned today to the Oratory, and climbed the hill with great difficulty. I visited Father Clément, and he advised me to see Frere André. The latter ordered me to drop my crutches, and at that very moment I was cured. As you see, I walk very well, and the curvature of the spine from which I suffered has also disappeared.

'A radiograph of my affected limb was taken several times. I now intend to see several doctors in order that they may be able to certify my cure, which I consider miraculous. There is no question of a nervous disease, and the cure was instantaneous. I am deeply impressed by this cure; I thank Saint Joseph and I will keep my promise of going to Ste.-Anne de Beaupré.'

La Presse recounted that Miss Doyon attended all the evening services and was seen to genuflect without effort. She made her trip to the Shrine of St. Anne, then returned home to Maine. In July she was back in Montreal, where she announced to Oratory officials:

> Since May 11, I have enjoyed very good health and I feel no fatigue although I walk a great deal. I have had no respite on account of the great number of persons who came to inquire about my illness, and this fact retarded my return home for four weeks.

That October, Dr. Howard S. Williams of Augusta wrote to the Oratory:

> I hereby certify that on October 15, 1923 I was called to the home of Miss Germaine Doyon, 93 Northern Avenue, Augusta, Me. She was unable to walk without the aid of crutches, an impossibility due to a disease of her left knee, which, on account of the fracture of the kneecap of four years' standing, caused the knee to increase in volume one half greater than normal. On June 9, 1924, Miss Doyon visited me, and gave ample proof that she could walk normally with both limbs, on level ground, up and down stairs, and in every possible manner. Both knees have the same volume and appear normal in every respect.

A similar certificate was prepared by Dr. Adolphe J. Gingras, also of Augusta:

> I hereby certify that I examined the case of Miss Doyon last January and found that the left knee had increased considerably in volume, and that there was an abnormal displacement in the kneecap, and that the sick person complained of suffering pain at the slightest movement she made. She made use of crutches during the past year.
>
> Since her return from a pilgrimage to Saint Joseph's Oratory, I find that her knee has diminished in size and that the articulation now appears to be normal in every respect. All the movements of her limbs are without pain and she walks without the aid of crutches. The cure appears to me to be complete.[60]

Another interesting account is from Dr. J. Lionel Lamy, who was Brother André's personal physician from 1928 until the end of the holy man's life. In 1930, when he was forty-three, Lamy was confined to bed for twenty-four hours with a high temperature and sore throat.

> I thought I had the flu or tonsillitis . . . In the afternoon, the doorman of the Oratory asked me to go visit Father Grou. Mrs. Lamy answered that I was in bed. Then the doorman of the Oratory told Brother André that I was sick. Dr. Bordeaux, after his office hours, came to examine me. The analysis was made in the laboratory that evening at the Hotel-Dieu. That evening, about 9 p.m., Brother André came to the house, 3496 Laval, to see me. On seeing me, he told me that it wasn't serious. Then, for about five or six minutes, Brother André rubbed my throat. I spent a good night and the next day, about 5 o'clock, I woke up, needing to clear my throat to spit. To my great surprise, I saw the elimination of a large grey membrane. I thought of diphtheria [of which this is a symptom]. I went back to bed and Dr. Bordeaux came to visit me about 9, after having received the lab report that said: 'very positive diphtheria bacilli.' Dr. Bordeaux, when he came, told me not to say a word but to show him my throat. To his surprise, the throat was clear and he couldn't understand the sudden change that took place in twelve hours. He wanted to inject anti-diphtheria serum in my children and servants. There wasn't any reaction and everything was normal. Some days later, Dr. Bordeaux told me about the case of a young lawyer from Ottawa who died in spite of all the serum he was given against diphtheria. Usually diphtheria takes more time than that to be cured, but I can't affirm that it was a miracle. It was certainly a very great favor.[61]

The only person whom I (the author) have met personally who professes a cure through Brother André's ministry is Father Henri-Paul Bergeron, an immensely learned and erudite theologian who (as of 1987) has been teaching for many years in Haiti while spending his summers at the Oratory. He was twenty-five when he recovered, in February, 1936, from an infection which his physicians expected to cause his death. He recalled in an interview:

> I was ordained February 2, 1936. Already I was very sick. I had been to the doctor but he could not diagnose my illness. On February 5, I was taken to the Hotel-Dieu in Montreal, where my illness was diagnosed as mastoiditis, and I had an operation. I forget the name of the surgeon. The operation was performed under local anesthesia. I was awake while they were hammering. I developed penumonia and for several days I was deathly ill. Brother André came to see me. He was accompanied by Monsieur Pichette. Brother André said, 'You're just a young priest. You're supposed to work. It's too soon for you to go to heaven.' He came twice. I was too sick to remember much of the conversation. But improvement came a few days later and I was out of the hospital by the end of February. I later learned that the nurses had been told that I would not recover. Dr. Lamy had told them, 'It's no use. He's finished!'

When asked if he believed his cure was a miracle, Father Bergeron, seated at his desk, surrounded by his books and papers one hot and steamy August night, shrugged his shoulders and said, "It's difficult to say. . . ."[62]

The dozens of cures relating to Brother André's ministry which are well-documented are impressive. A great many relate to orthopaedic problems, as the multitude of canes, crutches, and braces in the votive chapel behind the Crypt Church testify. Most of the cures are not of the earth-shaking sort. There is vague mention in some accounts of the raising of a woman from the dead, but substantial evidence of the type amassed by St.-Pierre and Ham seems to be absent. There seem to be no instance as of the multiplication of physical substances (such as bread or wine) or the restoration of lost body parts. With regard to the latter, there is recorded a remark Brother André made to Azarias Claude when he saw a legless man wheeling towards his office: "I hope that fellow isn't coming to ask us to give him a pair of legs!"[63]

There are instances, such as the case of Madame Marcoux, Marie-Antoinette Mercier, Alfred Stanhope, Germaine Doyon, and Sam Chagnon, of instantaneous healings, but most of the cures consisted either in the gradual healing of conditions diagnosed as incurable (such as the cancers of Madame Bruhlmann and Louis Bertrand) or the rapid amelioration of conditions that would normally require more time to mend (as in the case of Lionel Maynard). It seems true in most of the thoroughly documented instances that the cures took place only after the sick person sought medical treatment which proved unsuccessful.

Dr. Lamy stated in 1962, "For ten years, from 1944 to 1954, I was director of the Medical Bureau which was composed of ten specialists. We studied all that had been gathered as favors for years . . . I prepared a brief on each case and I had authorization to consult the medical dossiers of the sick." When he was pressed as to whether he believed that the cures which he studied were in fact *miracles,* Lamy carefully responded, "I know that they were favors . . . In my opinion those favors that we studied were not miracles."[64]

What is important, however, is that innumerable persons went to the Oratory afflicted in body and left satisfied. Many insisted that ailments and disabilities, unresponsive to medical treatment, disappeared. Others, while experiencing no physical relief, professed the grace to better bear their infirmities. However the graces or favors or miracles are defined or described, however they are analyzed by physicians and scientists, thousands of people were sincerely convinced that they were healed, not only physically, but also mentally and spiritually, by St. Joseph and his servant, Brother André, through the ministry of the Oratory.

Brother André's role as a miracle worker, however, is certainly not the only reason, or even the major reason, for his beatification. The most striking characteristic, according to all who knew him well, was not his prowess as a worker of wonders, but his godly life. Nearly all his friends and associates stated emphatically that the trait in Brother André that impressed them the most was his holiness of life and mind.

Chapter Eight

'A Humble, Pious and Jolly Man'

S anctity is proved, not by signs and wonders, but by holiness of life and character. We can learn a great deal about the character of certain historical figures through published writings, letters and diaries, but about Brother André, who wrote nothing save a handful of dictated notes, we cannot expand our knowledge in this manner. It is only through the testimony of those who knew him well that a reasonably clear picture of the character and personality of this man, celebrated for his goodness and piety, can be established.

Brother André had detractors, to be sure. In 1987 one of the senior religious at Notre-Dame College recalled that when Brother André was still alive, there lived in the College an ancient working Brother, Léon by name, who was even older than André, who had nothing good to say about his famous confrere. To tease the old man, some of the younger brothers used to say to him, "Brother André is a saint!" "No! No!" piped the ninety-eight year old, "Brother André is no more saint than I am!"[1] Just why he felt this way Brother Léon apparently never said. Another religious, whose association with the Oratory extends back into the lifetime of Brother André likewise recalled "some narrow-minded Brothers" who seemed ill-disposed toward the founder of the Oratory. By 1941, when the diocese came to interview those who had been closely associated with

André, the detractors had either died, changed their minds, or fallen silent. Father Albert Cousineau, who was superior at the time, found not a single objection in the community to the introduction of Brother André's cause. Nearly everyone interviewed during the 1940s portrayed the founder of the Oratory in the most positive of terms. But it is curious that when Brother Abundius Piché, at eighty-six perhaps the oldest person interviewed, was called upon to give his testimony, he recounted the construction of the first chapel, but then cut short his deposition, declaring, somewhat enigmatically, "On the subject of Brother André I have nothing else to say,"[2] — this concerning a man with whom he had been associated for four decades. Yet, since Brother Abundius chose to say nothing, it is scarcely legitimate to interpret his silence to necessarily infer any disapproval.

The descriptions of Brother André by those who knew him are sometimes different, but they fit together like pieces of a puzzle, to form a picture in harmony with the description of him by Father Emile Deguire, as "a man of obedience and prayer and sacrifice."[3] They also concur with the more human portrait of "Blessed Uncle Brother André" by his grandniece, Aurore Snow Lawrence (granddaughter of Léocadie). André frequently stayed with Mrs. Lawrence at her home on Summit Street in West Warwick, Rhode Island during his trips to New England. Mrs. Lawrence characterized him as "a very jolly and humble man, very pious," lively, down-to-earth, and warm, who "always wanted to box with my dad."[4] He impressed most of those he met as happy, cheerful, and confident. "Happiness comes from the Good God, sadness from the devil," he had a habit of saying.[5] "It's not necessary to be sad," he once told Pichette. "You have to laugh a little."[6]

Yet, to many, Brother André's most obvious characteristic was not his warmth nor his joy, but his reticence. Dr. Lionel Lamy spoke of this reserve, recalling that Brother André "did not talk much," and when he did, it was only "of God." Nor did he enter into discussions, "but listened to the conversations of others, smiling." Never speaking of himself, "he continually effaced himself," always attributing healings and other favors to St. Joseph.[7] Fellow religious likewise observed that at "recreation," when the priests and brothers socialized, Brother André, while listening and smiling, never ventured an opinion, insisting, when pressed to join a conversation, that such a humble brother as he had nothing of consequence to add to the discourse of such learned spiritual men.

Brother André's reluctance to confide seems partly the result of a painful experience early in life, when a "friend" had hurt him badly by revealing confidences. When Azarias Claude asked him why he was not more open, Brother André told him, "I have spoken before of some things and I was betrayed, now I keep these things to myself"[8] Pichette similarly admitted, "He never said if he had any interior difficulties, temptations, or spiritual discouragements."[9]

Brother André's reserve was also the result of his deep humility. He sincerely did not think himself of any consequence. So completely did his concern center on others, he seldom even thought of himself. Pichette recalled "a complete forgetfulness of self"[10] and Father Deguire a single-minded desire "to do good to others."[11] Brother André could never understand his fame and popularity and was always surprised when people recognized him. According to one religious, he never could quite grasp "that he was *the* Brother André, the ... well-known celebrity."[12] Steadfastly he refused to accept credit for the cures, insisting that they were the work of St. Joseph. When anyone suggested that he had a hand in the favors as well, André protested, "You don't know what you're talking about!"[13] If he were complimented, André quickly changed the subject, typically declaring, "How good God is! See how St. Joseph loves us!" And if his own role in the ministry were pointed out, he often replied, "The Good God often uses cheap instruments!"[14] No one who ever knew Brother André ever believed that there was anything artificial in his self-effacement, convinced as they were that he was without vanity or guile.

Another striking characteristic was a disinclination toward complaint and resentment. Attaria Lafleur, one of Léocadie's daughters, affirmed that her uncle was "always happy" and never complained,[15] and niece Suzanne Paine, Alphonsine's daughter, recalled that he never talked about the faults of others nor engaged in any kind of gossip.[16] André once told Pichette that he felt sorry for people who complained about the weather, "For they don't understand God's will."[17] When frustrated or disappointed, Brother André typically remarked, "This is a trial that the Good God is sending me. I've got to bear it and I offer it to the Good God."[18] Once, when a trip which he had been eagerly awaiting was suddenly cancelled by his superiors, he uttered not a word of dissatisfaction, observing to Arthur Ganz, who had come to pick him up, that although he dearly wanted to make the trip, "the Good God had judged otherwise."[19] His health was never the subject of his complaint, nor were the long hours he worked. One day, when Brother André was very old and feeble, Azarias Claude expressed concern at his obvious exhaustion. Admitting to deep weariness, the old man said: "It's good to suffer. It makes you think. You feel better after suffering."[20] When insulted, he offered the abuse to St. Joseph, declaring: "We must pardon others if we want to be pardoned by the Good God. We must suffer because Our Lord suffered. We must suffer in gratitude and love for Him. The servant is not above the Master. These sufferings are little things compared to those Our Lord endured upon the cross."[21]

An example of a typical response to abuse is an incident that occurred while Brother André was visiting the sick in a Montreal hospital. A patient, observing his clerical garb, began to shout, cursing and railing, "You shouldn't be allowed in a government hospital!" He was ranting so violently that André went to him and asked quietly: "Are you very sick, my friend? Do you want me to pray for you?" At once the angry man calmed down, sinking into his bed in total silence as the Brother offered his petition to Heaven.[22]

A religious, who characterized Brother André as completely "without rancor," declared that he was "all kindness, exquisite softness" towards those who abused him. Those who had offended him and expressed their regret he "loved more than before."[23]

Nonetheless, Brother André was fond of saying, "I am a man, just like you are." Just as all human beings have, he had more than one side to his personality. He was not *always* kindness and softness, nor did he *always* react to frustration with equanimity. He had bad days. In fact, towards the end of his life, many people were appalled at the old man's irascibility. One poor lady, bewildered by an outburst of temper, left Brother André's office, saying in confusion: "But he *can't* be angry. He's a saint."[24] Yet, while they walk the earth and wear the flesh, even saints lose their temper, and certainly Brother André was no exception. In fact, Azarias Claude, while affirming that Brother André was usually amiable, had to concede that he did have a "violent" temper.[25] Cousineau too admitted that André could be "rather violent."[26] When Father Bergeron was conducting interviews for his 1937 biography he was told by some intimates that Brother André could at times be so touchy that "a mere trifle was enough to break the ties of friendship,"[27] and so morbidly sensitive that he often "interpreted the reserved deference of his confreres as cold indifference."[28] Yet these instances were rarer in Brother André than in persons less spiritually advanced. The same Father Bergeron, in August, 1986 related that in his own limited contact with Brother André, he himself saw none of this touchiness or ill-humor. André was invariably "pleasant," with "no signs of irritability," and even in his nineties was given to cracking jokes.

Brother André himself realized that his temper was a problem. In his eighties he told a reporter, "Impatience is my great besetting sin."[29] Yet most of the time he was able to control his impatience along with other unsociable inclinations. In extreme old age, loss of control became more frequent. Pichette stated that until the last five years Brother André was almost always "happy and in good humor,"[30] but at the end he grew somewhat crotchety, occasionally intimidating pilgrims with displays of pique. Yet, when the causes of such incidents are recalled, Brother André's bad temper is more understandable, if not excusable.

Brother André's blow-ups usually resulted from an unreasonable attitude on the part of his visitors. In later years the austere ascetic was especially disgusted by immodesty in feminine attire. After the First World War, he claimed, it was impossible to distinguish a virtuous woman from a "disreputable" one by her apparel. Increasingy confronted with scantily-clad ladies, he was increasingly given to remarks such as he made to the woman who introduced her heavily-painted daughter as "a good child." "Is she your daughter? If I were you, I shouldn't boast of it!"[31] he groused. Another time a woman came to him complaining of a "compression of the chest." Only to be put down with the sarcasm, "It surely isn't because of excess of clothing!"

Frivolous, silly requests irritated Brother André, as when his friend, Sister Leblanc came to him when he was suffering from a heavy cold, inquiring about her sister, who had visited him a few days earlier. "Yes, yes, I told her she wouldn't faint any more. What more does she want?" he asked. When Sister Leblanc told him that the sister was now complaining that she could not bear to wear her false teeth, Brother André exploded, "Tell her to wear her dentures! I surely can't wear them for her!"[32]

What irked Brother André the most was the insistence with which some people demanded that he heal them. "Do you think that I'm God?" he cried. "*I* don't perform miracles! I only pray!" One particularly outrageous demand prompted the sardonic response, "I'm going to pray to the Good God to grant you the gift of intelligence."[33]

Though usually indifferent to abuse, there were times when Brother André was unnerved by insults. When a man coldly asked: "What is your procedure as healer? Do you use magic or hypnotism?" André, probably taken off guard, snapped, "Get out of here!" ordering Claude to physically expel the man. Trembling with rage and horror, it took him two weeks to regain his composure.[34]

Perhaps the difference between an ordinary man and a saintly one is not a matter of whether imperfections exist but rather with how imperfections are dealt. Brother André, far from trying to justify his impatience, was always deeply grieved whenever he lost his temper. Many times he was found weeping bitterly in his room, because, "I made somebody cry today."[35] Sometimes, after a bad day, he would ask one of the priests whether he might still receive Communion after carrying on so sinfully.[36]

Despite occasional lapses, the thousands of pages of depositions made after his death leave an overwhelming impression of Brother André as a joyful and patient Christian. Deguire maintained that "Brother André seemed . . . in a state of incomparable joy. His face was illuminated with a smile that seemed to be the reflection of his soul."[37] "Never give way to sadness," he told Father Bergeron. "Always be cheerful and avoid giving pain to anyone."[38] Deguire further remarked that "constantly animated by the love of God," Brother André was overflowing with love towards others"[39] and "to the end of his life had only one preoccupation, [namely] to relieve the miseries of his fellow men and to bring them to love God better."[40]

Brother André was thus a happy, quiet, reserved, humble, loving man animated by an extraordinary faith in God, a man who, like everybody else, had occasional lapses. Brother André's physical appearance, however, was as unprepossessing as his character was impressive. By all accounts he was a tiny man. Many newspaper reporters described him as "dwarfish" or "gnome-like." He stood five feet three inches tall when young, but by the time he achieved celebrity, Brother André had shrunk to less than five feet and his wiry frame, which had never carried more than 110 pounds, was twisted into a swaybacked posture with hunched shoulders, protuberant abdomen, and a chin almost resting on the hollowed chest. Notwithstanding, Brother André's step remained quick and sprightly almost to the end of his days. Father Bergeron recalled that at ninety Brother André walked slowly but steadily, without the straddle-legged, tottering gait that characterizes many very old men. In fact a reporter, doubtless exaggerating, described him at ninety-one as "agile as a monkey." Another noted that although André's hands shook with palsy, his step was "sturdy."

Brother André's voice has been described as "thin," "rasping," "low," "weak" and "squeaky." Especially towards the end, he could be understood only with difficulty. This, coupled with the deafness that overtook him in later years, made it very hard for him to communicate, another factor contributing to his irascibility in old age.

Many described his face, at least at rest, as severe, ascetic, and austere, but also testified that the impression of harshness vanished when he smiled. As early as his late fifties, Brother André's face was leathered and furrowed with deep wrinkles, but these lines, like the impression of sternness, also disappeared, it was noted, when his face was illuminated with mirth.

Photographs taken early in life show wavy brown or black

hair, but by the time Brother André became famous his thinning hair (not enough, he said, "to make a pillow") was snow-white. His most impressive features were his eyes, which, shortly before his death, were described as "dark, deep, and bright, filled with a luminous intensity that defies description," eyes which reflected his faith with "unmistakable strength."[41] J.J. Delara, writing in *Columbia* in 1921, noted that "translucent" quality of the eyes, while another reporter wrote of their "bright and birdlike" appearance. Interestingly, although most people were struck by the piercing and luminous intensity of Brother André's eyes, there is some disagreement on their color. Delara described them as grey, but most reporters noted brown or black eyes, one of them, in fact, remarking on their "inky blackness."

In his personal habits, Brother André was, of course, given to great austerity as a result of the ascetical philosophy in which he was nurtured, a philosophy which holds that the closer a man would draw to God, the more he must shut off the world and the things of the world. Not only did Brother André continue to wear a leather belt studded with large nailheads, he also felt it useful to limit severely such normally innocuous things as eating, sleeping and talking.

Brother André refused to read newspapers, use alcohol or tobacco products, or, when it became available, listen to the radio. His most conspicuous austerities, however, related to his diet. Dr. Lamy recalled that when Brother André prepared his own meals, in the little room above the old chapel, his meals consisted of "little balls of flour which he cooked in bouillon or even water."[42] Pichette observed that Brother André generally took "barely one good meal" a day. In the morning he had a cup of coffee and a piece of bread, then in the evening, if he were in his little apartment, "a kind of stew" consisting of milk and water boiled together, which he gulped standing up because he felt that life was too brief to be wasted by such useless things as eating.[43] Father Deguire spoke of a diet consisting of warm milk with bread crumbled into it.[44]

When Brother André was a guest at a private home, however, he did not insist on his usual disgusting concoctions, but ate whatever was placed in front of him — even desserts — out of humility. Pichette recalled: "When they asked him what he would like to eat he answered, 'Anything,' and it was impossible to know what he wanted. He would even eat things that disagreed with him to please his host."[45] Mrs. Lawrence, however, recalled that when "Uncle Brother André" visited her, he always asked for "johnnycake" (a cake made with corn meal, milk, and eggs), which he ate sparingly.[46] Jules Cayer said that at his home, at midnight, Brother André asked for a plate of baked beans.[47] However, Mrs. Frank Comeau, daughter of André's brother Claude, declared at her house, André ate "little more than a piece of dry bread with a cup of coffee, and no butter on the bread or sugar in the coffee."[48]

It has been suggested that the bread dunked in milk or water and the coffee were eaten at times (and these were many) when Brother André's digestion was extremely slow and he was having stomach pains, but that under normal circumstances his diet, while "austere" or "extremely moderate," was more normal. When asked directly about his dietary habits by a reporter, Brother André at eighty-six replied: "I eat very little. A little bread. A little tea. Meat, no, very seldom meat. Just sometimes a little."[49]

What was the reason for such a diet? More than once Brother André was known to remark that it was to one's physical as well as spiritual advantage to "eat as little as possible and work as much as possible."[50] Attaria Lafleur said that Brother André told her that he ate foods he least enjoyed in meager quantities as a penance to help the impenitent. "I have to do penance for sinners because they don't."[51] Others believed that Brother André's apparent asceticism was largely the result of his chronic indigestion.

Indeed, it was clear that Brother André suffered from headache, intestinal cramps, stomach pains, heartburn, constipation, and assorted other digestive ills. Whether these resulted from his austerities or whether his evident austerity was a result of the physical problems is a matter of debate. André's sister Léocadia insisted that the stomach problems were the direct result of the austerities practiced even in childhood.[52] Dr. Lamy suggested that at the time he knew Brother André "his stomach had become intolerant for lack of food," *perhaps* because of a lifetime of mortifications.[53]

It is also uncertain how early in life Brother André's

digestive troubles began. Father Labonté (considered an unreliable witness) insisted that Brother André told him that while attending a funeral as a little boy, "My mother told me that the wooden box in front of me contained a dead body, and after that I had stomach trouble."[54] Others remembered Brother André tracing his stomach trouble to his days as a shoemaker when he worked bent almost onto all fours. In 1931 Brother André told Frederick Griffin that his stomach problems went back only forty years (to his forties).[55]

No one has ever been able to identify precisely Brother André's digestive problem. He himself never consulted a physician to diagnose his problem and never even prayed to obtain relief. Father Deguire was of the opinion that Brother André suffered from ulcers, citing the fact that he sometimes vomited blood. When Brother André was hospitalized at the end of his life it was noted that he suffered from lactose intolerance — the inability to digest milk products, a problem common in older persons. It is not clear whether this afflicted André in his younger days, much less whether it was responsible for all his digestive afflictions. Brother André himself characterized his affliction as "dyspepsia," defined by the 1923 edition of *The Principles and Practice of Medicine* as "a condition of disturbed digestion associated with increased mucous formation, qualitative or quantitative changes in the gastric juice, enfeeblement of the muscular coats, so that food is retained for an abnormal time in the stomach." This accords with other descriptions of "slow digestion."

Whatever the precise cause of Brother André's poor digestion, he made light of it most of his life and insisted that he was in good health. By his mid-eighties, however, he had to concede that he was no longer in good health. "I am never well," he told a reporter. "Always the pain here and here," he said, indicating his chest and abdomen.[56] The pains of which he spoke at this time may have been the result of the heart condition from which he had begun to suffer, however. One thing is certain: Brother André never asked for healing. When a confrere asked why he never besought St. Joseph on his own behalf, André said that Christians should desire to endure their sufferings "for the love of God, without complaining."[57]

Brother André was as noted for his austerity with regard to

sleep as he was for his ascetic diet. Just how much (or how little) he slept seems to have varied throughout his lifetime, but it was always less than that allowed to the community. Sometimes he spent entire nights in prayer. Jules Cayer recalled that when "Uncle Fred" was his guest, he insisted that sleep was really not necessary and never allowed himself much more than an hour of it.[58] Pichette noted that when he was a guest in Brother André's apartment in 1912, André "spent two or three hours in bed and worked twenty hours a day."[59] Father Deguire, observing him late in life, noted that Brother André slept "six hours a night or less, on an iron bed with a very hard mattress."[60] Claude stated, "I couldn't say how many hours Brother André gave to sleep, but I know he slept little."[61] Dr. Lamy noted that "he went to bed late and got up early."[62] As André grew more feeble, Deguire urged him to take more rest, assuring him, "Your sleep would be as agreeable to God as your prayers." His ascetical confrere responded, "If you knew the needs of the souls who come to me, you wouldn't be talking like that."[63]

Brother André's austerity extended to his clothing. Although the CSC was not one of the most rigorous Orders, in André's day Canadian religious still wore the flowing black robe known as the soutane. Nonetheless, even within the dress code of his Order, Brother André still found room to practice mortification, in that he insisted on wearing his soutane until it was shiny with age and literally coming apart. Pichette claimed that André wore the same soutane, every day, for ten years. One day Azarias Claude, noting that Brother André's overcoat, once black, was turning red with age, decided to buy him a new coat. André told him that he was allowed to accept no gift without the permission of his superior. When Claude obtained this permission, Brother André said that he would accept only a cheap, worn-out coat. Claude recounted:

> I took him to a tailor. I chose good material. Brother André objected, saying it was too nice and too expensive for him. I had to get the permission of the superior and threaten him with refusing to go out with him if he didn't accept it. Brother André resigned himself to it. Then he wore [the coat] for about fifteen years.[64]

Although Brother André never wore underwear and usually slept in his soutane, all accounts hold that he was physically very clean. His modesty bordered on prudery, even by the standards of his day. When he had overnight guests in his apartment, he slept and dressed separated from them by a curtain. When he stayed in a private home, he usually did not enter the bathroom until everybody else in the house had retired for the night.[65] Even at ninety, when he was very weak, Brother André refused to allow anyone to see him disrobed or help him dress, insisting on "taking care of all his most intimate needs."[66]

Brother André's chastity was unquestioned. All his colleagues were convinced that despite his comparatively late vocation and his years as a factory worker and farm hand, he had preserved his "angelic purity." One of his confreres said that he once found Brother André in tears because he had, earlier in the day, seen from his window a beautiful woman and "had temptations."[67] So straitlaced was he that when, during the Stations of the Cross, he read a prayer that contained the word "concupiscence" (a theological word referring to the condition of loving created things more than God) he refused to speak the word aloud because he associated it with sex!

André's modesty with women was legendary. Following to the limit a practice common among religious before Vatican II, he never looked a woman in the eye nor sat on the same seat with a woman on a train. Nor would he ride in a car alone with a woman. When he received female visitors in his office, he opened the window that overlooked the waiting room, a window he closed when his visitors were male. In the early days he sometimes performed rubbings on women, although (according to Father Cousineau) he "never, never" touched the "intimate parts of the body."[68] After 1906, when his superior, Father Dion, forbade the practice, André advised ladies to rub themselves or have the office performed by female relatives or friends.

Brother André insisted that Azarias Claude keep a supply of women's coats in the office wherewith to cover visitors who had the ignorance or temerity to enter his presence revealing the flesh of arm, ankle, or neck. If somehow a pilgrim managed to gain access to his office immodestly attired, she could expect snide remarks, just as: "You have the wrong address. Go dress and come back,"[69] or, "Say, aren't you afraid you'll entangle yourself in your skirt?"[70] He even disapproved of short sleeves worn in the privacy of the home. Aurore Snow Lawrence recalled, "On his last tour in the summer of 1936 he came to visit me. I was doing laundry on a scrub board. He touched my arm and said in French for me to hide my big arms."[71] Immodesty in dress was to Brother André a symptom of the "abyss into which Christian civilization" had plunged.[72]

As might well be imagined, Brother André never laughed at a dirty story. If anyone was crazy enough to tell an off-color joke in his presence, he said nothing, but showed clearly his discomfort and said something to change the subject.[73]

In Brother André's day, unquestioning obedience to the superior was a virtue by which all good religious wished to be characterized. "The voice of the superior is the voice of God," was the typical saying of the day. Unless a superior issued an order commanding what was clearly evil, the religious was bound to obey. Padre Pio (a Capuchin priest whose cause for beatification has begun) once remarked, "If my superior told me to jump out of the window, I wouldn't argue, I'd jump." Brother André felt just as strongly the need to submit to authority unconditionally. His relationship to his superiors was characterized by "practically blind obedience."[74] "Whoever does not want to obey his superiors," Brother André said, "cannot succeed in anything."[75] An example of his obedience to religious authority occurred during an illness André had while visiting at the home of Joseph and Albertine Pichette. Dr. Lamy begged Brother André to consent to hospitalization, but the sick man refused until Lamy called the superior, who ordered him to go; whereupon André immediately complied.[76]

Brother André interpreted his vow of poverty as strictly as he did his vows of chastity and obedience. Although it was through his efforts that one of the largest churches in the world came to be constructed, he was never aggressive about raising funds, trusting that if St. Joseph wanted a basilica, he would provide. Whenever he traveled, special collections for the Oratory were taken during the services in which he was a speaker or participant, but the "miracle man" engaged in no hard-sell tactics. If someone felt led by God to offer him money, he took it, saying, "This is for the Oratory. May the Good God reward you."[77] However, if he were asked, in return for his ministrations, "What do I owe you," André's invariable response was, "You owe me nothing."

Brother André seldom even looked at the cash or check that he was given, simply stuffing it into his pocket or dumping it into his valise. Once Ganz pointed out that the envelope that he was stuffing nonchalantly in his pocket contained $500. Looking up at the man who had just given it to him, André said simply, "I'm happy since I need to build the Oratory."[78] Once André and Ganz were on their way back to Montreal from Ottawa when Ganz suggested that they count the money donated during the tour. "No, it's not necessary," objected Brother André. "The Father Superior will arrange to have that done."[79] Upon his return to Montreal, André, without comment, handed the contributions to the superior.

The good Brother, in fact, hated to have money on his person. He once commented that he felt that he would have no right to burial in the community's cemetery if a single penny were found on his person at death. When he returned with his pocket bulging with cash donations, he was known to joke with Father Clément, then his superior, punning on the words *cent* (money) and *sangue* (blood) (which sound alike in French), "Operate on me. I have an abscess of money."[80]

In his handling of contributions, Brother André never lost sight of the true priority of his work. Presented with handsome donations by wealthy benefactors, he was known to warn them: "It's not enough just to give money. You must also give your heart."[81] Having spent his secular life in poverty, he had a great sympathy with and love for the poor. Although he had many well-to-do friends, such as Pichette, Claude, and Ganz, he seemed most comfortable with the poor in whom he clearly saw the image of Christ. His concern was not limited to words or even prayers, and whenever he was physically able to benefit a needy person directly, he would. For instance, once he and Ganz were on a sick call to the apartment of a Montreal woman who had four seriously ill children. The two men were horrified to find that the only furniture in the flat consisted of some cast-off wooden boxes turned upside down to serve as tables and chairs. When the mother offered a few pennies for the

Oratory, Brother André was stupefied. "What you're doing is criminal, Ma'am!" he protested. "You're offering alms when you yourself have nothing." When he and his companion were outside, André insisted, "We have got to do something for this family!" So he persuaded some wealthy friends to aid the woman and her children. When, two days later, he returned to the apartment, not only did he find food on the table and furniture in the house, but four healthy children as well.[82] Incidents such as this one were not uncommon in the ministry of Brother André, nor was it unheard of for him to reach into his valise to give a sum of money from the donations to the Oratory to a person in real need. He had, of course, standing approval from his superior to do this.

Inasmuch as the vows of poverty, chastity, and obedience were practiced to the limit, and even rest and nourishment were severely limited as Brother André strove to serve his fellow man and his God, one is led to wonder whether he allowed himself any pleasures. The testimony of his friends and family indicates that Brother André in fact seemed to enjoy nature, contemplating with delight fields, flowers, trees, mountains, meadows and sky, and other wonders of the creation of the Good God. He enjoyed the company and fellowship of family and friends. Yet his chief delight seemed to be in prayer and in communion with his Lord. Indeed, people found themselves wonderfully edified when they saw Brother André in prayer. Moreover, many found it "really beautiful" to see him receive Holy Communion. "His face was different from that of the others," recalled Pichette, groping for words to explain that which language is inadequate to convey.[83]

Prayer was the axis around which Brother André's existence turned. Throughout the day, even when he was riding in a car, he prayed the Rosary, usually dedicating each decade for the intention of someone who had asked an interest in his prayers. Pichette and others were certain that André completed at least thirty Rosaries each day.

After his sick calls, even after the departure of his companion of the evening, Brother André was not done with his orisons. When Adélard Fabre lived at the Oratory as a custodian, André liked to pray with him late at night. After they prayed, they would often repair to Brother André's room to talk. As always the subject was spiritual. "Brother André would read me the Gospels, then talk to me about the Lord, up to eleven or later," Fabre recalled. "No matter how tired he was at the end of the day, he said his evening prayers in the chapel and made the Stations of the Cross."[84] Fabre remembered times when he observed André motionless for hours in prayer.

Although everyone who knew Brother André perceived him as an intelligent, witty and nimble-minded man, because of his lack of education, he could scarcely sign his name and read with great difficulty. He was known to peruse newspaper obituaries in search of names of persons for whose souls he might pray, but, other than that, Brother André's reading was confined to the Bible and three books of devotion, all of which he had virtually memorized. These included *The Imitation of Christ*; *The Herald of God's Loving Kindness* by St. Gertrude of Helfta, a 13-century Saxon nun; and a book of meditations on the Holy Wounds of Christ by Sister Marie-Marthé Chambon (1841-1907), a Visitation sister who was almost an exact contemporary.

Brother André urged his disciples to regular Bible study as well as meditation on the wounds of Jesus. Insisting on prayer to Mary and Joseph as well as to Jesus, he explained, "We must never separate devotion to the Holy Virgin from that of St. Joseph, and devotion to Our Lord from devotion to the Holy Family." On the other hand, he commented, "I do not like devotion to the saints that does not lead to the worship of God."[85] Father Bergeron explained that for Brother André, prayer to the saints was simply another way of praying to God: "It's all the same." Brother André, moreover, recommended "ejaculatory prayer" — for example, the utterance of such short phrases as, "My Jesus, mercy," and "Lord, have mercy on me, a sinner." "You don't have time to be distracted when you say them," he said.[86] Brother André did not confine himself to prepared prayers, but prayed freely, from the heart, during his public and private devotions, whenever he felt it appropriate. He also recommended to the faithful the practice of climbing the stairs to the Oratory on the knees.

Communion he recommended as frequently as possible, even daily. "If you eat only one meal a week, would you live?" he asked. "It's the same with your soul. Nourish it with the Holy Eucharist if you want to live."[87] Again, he asked, "When you have an intimate friend, you do not let whole weeks, whole months go by without going to see him, without giving him [indications] of affection? . . . What sacrifices do you make for Jesus, Who died on the cross for your salvation?"[88] Mrs. Comeau, André's niece, recalled:

> Brother André showed a great devotion to the Holy Eucharist . . . because each time he came to pay us a visit he would ask me if each member of our family had gone to Mass and whether each had received Communion. Brother André always asked that each of us receive it as frequently as possible, at least once a week. He had a habit of telling us how God died on the cross to save us. 'But remember,' he said, 'God expects you to do something for Him. He died because He has a need of souls, and this is what He expects of you.'[89]

Mrs. Comeau furthermore remembered how once, on a visit, Brother André brought as a gift a statue of the Holy Virgin, urging the family to use the short prayer inscribed on the pedestal. "She will help you obtain from God the graces you really need, and she will be with you at the hour of death," he promised.[90]

Brother André would describe heaven so vividly that it would seem to his listeners that he actually must have seen it.[91] Ganz recalled, "Brother André spoke often of heaven and how heaven is the great reward we await from the Good God in return for our merits, and that heaven is perfect happiness."[92] To an objection oft expressed that "one has to be so holy to go to heaven," André responded: "When we do the best we can, we must have confidence in the Good God. It would be an insult to Him if we believed that we would not go to heaven after we did our best."[93] To those in the agony of their last sickness, Brother André typically said, "Offer your life with a generous heart and you will not pass through the flames of Purgatory."[94] Once he was trying to assuage a sick woman's fear of death by telling her about the beauties of the world to come. She listened to him, but said, "All the same, Brother, we all fear death." André replied, "When one has led a good life, death is not a thing to fear, for it is the gate of heaven." The woman raised the objection, "Of course, and yet heaven is very far away." Thereupon Brother André whispered the Our Father. Then he told her, "You know the Good God heard me — and that shows that we are very close to heaven."[95] Oftentimes he remarked that the Christian, even in the world, is separated from heaven by only a narrow veil.

Devoted as he was to traditional Catholic teaching and practice, Brother André has nonetheless been described as one of the first modern ecumenists. Some of his acquaintances claimed, perhaps with some exaggeration, that he helped more Protestants than Roman Catholics. Certainly anyone who sought his aid was welcomed to the mountain without any pressure to "convert." Brother André's attitude towards Protestant Christians lacked the insulting approach, common in his day, that relegated them almost to the state of unbelievers. Never was he known to withhold aid or counsel even to those who had no religion at all.

Some people criticized his lack of a hard-line approach towards those who failed to toe the line of the Church's doctrine. For instance, a Freemason came to Brother André one day, suffering from cancer. After André prayed with him, the receptionist at the rectory expressed his horror that "you are curing Freemasons!" André replied, "The man came to the Oratory from a great distance. It took him six days and six nights. His masonic insignia is just a little piece of tin, but there is a great confidence in his heart."[96]

Several years after Brother André's death, one of his confreres attempted a door-to-door survey in a predominantly Protestant neighborhood in Montreal, for the purpose of determining the miracle worker's reputation among non-Catholics. In an enclave of the militantly anti-Roman sect of Jehovah's Witnesses, the priest, clad in his soutane, found one door after another slammed in his face until, finally, he identified himself as a colleague of Brother André. The word went out, and from that moment on the priest was welcomed into the homes of the Witnesses, where he heard Brother André praised with great love and enthusiasm — by folk whose religion held the Church of Rome in deep and utter opprobrium. Many of these people, as well as Protestants and other non-

Catholics, frequently displayed pictures of Brother André on their walls and had wonderful stories to relate concerning favors obtained through his prayers.

The story of Mrs. A. H. Anthony, a Canadian Methodist, is typical of Brother André's approach to Christians who were not Roman Catholic. Mrs. Anthony wrote to the Oratory in 1944, when she was seventy-one years old, relating that many years ago she had gone to see Brother André when she was ill with cancer. The first thing André had asked her was, "Do you know St. Joseph?" When Mrs. Anthony replied that she did not, he insisted: "Well, I can't help you unless you pray to St. Joseph. Take this holy cord. Tie it around your waist. Take also a bottle of holy oil and rub yourself with this medal, and wear it. And go to the church to receive the blessing."

Mrs. Anthony was confused. Methodists regarded holy cords, blessed oil, and sacred medals, not as beneficial sacramentals, but as appalling objects of superstition, useless, if not downright dangerous for people saved by grace alone. Mrs. Anthony's companion, an agnostic, encouraged her, however, saying, "Come, dear, let's go to the church. Perhaps something will begin to make itself felt."

"I entered," wrote Mrs. Anthony, "and I knelt down before the statue and said, weeping, 'Saint Joseph, if you want to cure me, I will learn all your prayers and recite them every night, if necessary. I will honor your statue, without . . . any shame preventing me. I will climb the steps for any favor I ask you. I will never fail to follow you.' I was suddenly overwhelmed with the feeling of so much happiness that I began to cry."

The companion thought that Mrs. Anthony was weeping in pain and asked her if she were too sick to stay. The cancer patient, who now felt a "physical lightness" and "a sense of being freed from illness," answered, "No, I'm happy. I want to sing." In fact, she wrote, "I was stupefied." From that moment on she was cured of the cancer. Later she attributed her escape from serious injury in a motorcycle crash to Brother André's prayers. Although she continued to practice the devotions that Brother André taught her, Mrs. Anthony remained a devout Methodist.[97] Despite his insistence on certain devotional practices typical of Roman Catholic piety, Brother André never insisted that the lady change her church affiliation.

So extraordinary was the faith of Brother André that most people assumed that its basis lay in extraordinary revelations — in apparitions, locutions, and other mystical phenomena. This may not have been the case, but, in fact, we know very little about Brother André's mystical life, much less than about some of his contemporaries. For instance, a great deal is known of the mystical experiences of Padre Pio of Pietrelcina — not because Pio was any less reticent about his interior life, but because, for a time, the superiors of the Italian priest ordered him to write about his experiences with the invisible world. Brother André's superiors could not issue a similar command to the founder of the Oratory, even had they been so disposed, for the good reason that Brother André could not write! So one must rely on the testimony of others, and this testimony is not always clear or consistent.

There is disagreement as to the extent of Brother André's mystical gifts. Father Deguire declared that as far as he knew, Brother André's only mystical gift was the gift of healing. His life was apparently "without those extraordinary manifestations that some saints had," he said.[98] Azarias Claude testified, "I was never witness to events showing that Brother André might be favored with supernatural gifts, such as ecstasies, stigmata, etc."[99] Yet Claude admitted that Brother André apparently "read consciences":

> Some people who came out of the office were surprised to find that Brother André had spoken to them as if he knew their past. Brother André corrected things, saying, 'But didn't such a thing happen like this?' And the people involved were forced to note that this was indeed the case![100]

Father Labonté insisted that Brother André had many visions. Asked why he alone seemed to be privy to the knowledge, Labonté replied, "[Brother André] spoke to me of apparitions because I asked him a lot about it."[101] But, as stated earlier, some insist that at the time of his testimony Labonté was a rambling old man, given to telling far-fetched stories and no longer capable of remembering accurately. In contrast to Father Labonté, Father Deguire observed, "Whenever I questioned [Brother André] about any visions he might have had, he smiled, but did not answer.''[102]

Father Deguire knew of but one instance of a mystical charism other than healing. This was an incident recounted to him by "an employee of the Oratory, now deceased." This man was in the Crypt Church where Brother André was praying and was startled to see "a very bright light" emanate from the statue of St. Joseph and envelop Brother André, who was meditating beneath it. Later the employee questioned Brother André and was forbidden to speak of it.[103]

The man to whom Deguire was referring when he made his deposition in the early 1960s was Adélard Fabre, who, around 1945, recounted:

> I saw Brother André kneeling on the floor of the nave of the Oratory, at the foot of the Holy Table, enveloped in light, a light coming in a trail from the statue of St. Joseph on the altar. [Fabre stated that he was standing parallel to Brother André, approximately six feet away.] It was 8:30 in the evening. Brother André was completely illuminated. I was not. The trail of light stopped at Brother André and covered a length of about twenty-five feet. There was only the sanctuary light in the Oratory. The statue of St. Joseph was in darkness but the luminous rays seemed to come from the statue. I had the impression then that the statue was going to fall in the direction of Brother André. I went up to Brother André and touched his arm to warn him and pull him away. Brother André said nary a word nor moved. Then I went, very frightened, into the sacristy, hoping to find Brother Ludger, who was usually there preparing the wine and water cruets for the first Masses. Brother Ludger had already gone to his room. Leaving the sanctuary to go to Brother Ludger's room, I looked again through the sacristy door at Brother André, who had gone to the altar of the Holy Virgin, next to the main altar. He was still enveloped in light.
>
> Brother Ludger came with me to the Oratory. When we arrived, Brother André was leaving the altar of the Holy Virgin to go to his room, but the light had disappeared. Brother Ludger and I looked to see if the moon could have made that light, but there was no moon that night. I never

spoke of it to Brother André nor did he speak of it to me. Father Clément advised me not to speak of it to Brother André.

Three weeks later I saw above Brother André's head a light fifteen feet by two feet in circumference and about the same in height. It lasted three to four minutes. Brother André wanted to turn on the electric lights of the sanctuary to see if the effect resembled what I had seen, but it was not the same.[104]

There is evidence that Brother André, at times, may have been accorded the gift of prophecy. Joseph Pichette recalled in 1941 how Brother André predicted the death of one of Pichette's brothers while the doomed man was in apparent good health:

It was in April and my brother died in June. My brother was sixty-five and he seemed very well at the time. Brother André was having dinner with us and asked about the health of members of our family. I had to go out of the dining room for a moment, and Brother André said to my wife, 'One who is going to die soon is the doctor.' I heard the word 'die.' When I was alone with my wife, I asked her if Brother André had not spoke of one of my sisters, who was sick. My wife answered that it was concerning my brother the doctor. I was very surprised and called my wife's attention to how well he seemed. Yet the following June 6 my brother died suddenly.[105]

Father Labonté recounted an incident in which Brother André predicted the exact day of a man's death. Labonté took André to visit the priest's 21-year-old brother, who lay dying of tuberculosis. The young man had previously been unwilling to accept death, but after Brother André's visit he became peaceful and was resigned to die. But what was unusual was that Brother André told the parents, "In nine days there will be a change." The sick man did in fact die exactly nine days after the conversation.[106]

Arthur Ganz, testifying around 1945, related another incident in which Brother André accurately foretold a death. Ganz had forgotten the child's name but recalled that she lived on Rue

Jeanne Mance in Montreal and that she was a patient at the Hotel-Dieu when he accompanied Brother André on his visit to her bedside.

"How are you?" asked the Brother.

The child, who seemed in terrible pain, did not respond. The physician, Dr. Letendre, whispered, "The child has meningitis."

Brother André startled the doctor by insisting, "The child no longer has a fever and she is no longer suffering."

Letendre protested, "Brother André, I just took the patient's temperature and it is higher than the child can stand."

"Doctor, I don't believe you."

"Permit me, Brother André, to take the patient's temperature in front of you," insisted the physician.

To his amazement, Letendre found that the little girl's temperature was suddenly normal. All signs of suffering disappeared from her face. The mother, who had been witnessing the dialogue, was delirious with joy and shouted, "Brother André, you've saved my child."

Brother André again shocked his hearers. "Madame, your child is going to die tomorrow, between eight and half past eight," he said. "But she will not suffer."

"Brother André, save my child!" screamed the frantic mother.

"Madame, God alone knows this child's destiny," rasped the old man, who added, "Don't oppose the will of the Good God."

The next day Brother André was informed that the child had died at 8:22 in the morning, quite unexpectedly, since she seemed well on the road to recovery. There was no apparent suffering, however, and the mother, on receiving the news, was calm and resigned. "I knew it," said André when he heard the news, and that was the extent of his comment.[107]

In 1936, Monsignor George Gauthier, Archbishop of Tarona, who functioned as Archbishop of Montreal (in behalf of the aged, senile incumbent, Paul Bruchési), was hospitalized, in critical condition, after a massive heart attack. Brother André confided to Arthur Ganz that the archbishop would survive *this* attack. "But when the second one comes, he's finished." Four years passed. Brother André had gone to his reward and Gauthier had just become Archbishop of Montreal. Ganz and his wife were reading the morning paper and noted that Gauthier had been hospitalized with another heart attack. "You're going to see that Gauthier is going to die this time!" Ganz remarked. And he was right.[108]

An example of an apparent ability to discern spirits has been related by Azarias Claude. A 20-year-old unmarried woman went to Brother André's office in behalf of her foster mother, who had eye problems, but said nothing about the sexual abuse to which she had been habitually subjected to by her foster father. After listening to the girl, Brother André dryly remarked, "The lady is blind." When the girl insisted that, despite her eye problems, her mother was by no means blind, André maintained, "She is blind. Otherwise she would see how her husband conducts himself with you." Thereupon the girl wept hysterically. Brother André told her that she had to change her life. It is not recorded whether the foster mother obtained relief, but Claude learned that from then on the girl successfully resisted her foster father's advances.[109]

One night Pichette told Brother André that the wife of a Monsieur Brosseau, one of his salesmen was critically ill after major surgery. "She is dead," said André. When Pichette insisted that, Madame Brousseau was still alive, André repeated, "She is dead." Pichette looked at his watch. It was 8:40 p.m. Sure enough, the next day M. Brosseau arrived at the store in tears with the news that the previous evening, at nine o'clock, he had gone to the hospital to see his wife, only to learn that she had just died. Pichette asked Brosseau if he had phoned Brother André. The widower replied that he had not.[110]

Pichette is the source of yet another story about Brother André's apparent gift of discernment. A blind man from America came to see Brother André, accompanied by a woman whom everyone assumed to be his wife. When they visited André in his office, they were directed to pray in the chapel. Later that day Pichette met the blind man and found him weeping bitterly. "I came from far away and I am returning not healed," he lamented. Pichette suggested that the man and his wife visit Brother André again. The merchant was not privy to the conversation, but watched the couple leave the office, still in tears, the man still very much blind.

"Your blind man isn't healed, Brother André," Pichette remarked the next time that he saw his friend.

"Do you know him?"

"No. I met him outside. He was weeping because he wasn't cured."

"It's not very good luck to come asking for miracles from St. Joseph," André observed, "when you come with the wife of another!"

"What! Did he tell you that?" asked Pichette.

"Oh, no, there's no great danger that he did."[111]

Now, some devout persons, such as the Curé of Ars and Padre Pio, have suffered apparent physical attacks by infernal powers in the form of "hauntings" and poltergeist activity which was sometimes visible and audible to others. Pichette recounted several instances of this in relationship to Brother André. For instance, when he was a patient in Brother André's room above the chapel in 1912:

> Sometimes, at least three or four times, it happened that during the winter when I went to sleep in Brother André's room above the little chapel, I heard some noises, like someone who was dragging sheet iron or chains on the floor of the chapel. One night when it was the loudest, I was afraid and awakened Brother André, who told me, 'It's nothing. It's nothing.' Other nights when I heard those same noises, trusting in the word of Brother André . . . I didn't start up.[112]

Pichette recollected how a priest once came to see Brother André in the room above the chapel.

> The priest went there and was surprised, on arriving near the room, to hear a noise, as of two people who were arguing and fighting. He turned to see Father Clément and told him what he had heard. Father Clément said that he was sure that Brother André was alone. The priest returned to the room, heard the same noises and approached the door to listen. He heard Brother André's voice. 'Leave me! Leave me alone! Go away!' Then the priest knocked on the door and entered with Father Clément. On entering, they saw indeed that Brother André was alone.[113]

Pichette related still another incident involving apparent demonic molestation.

> When they enlarged the rectory [in 1929], we had gone, Brother André and I, to pray in the Crypt. On our return, we passed by a room where they had taken up all the old floor and at each end of the room they had left a piece of flooring a foot or a foot and a half wide. Between the [uncovered] beams and the ground there must have been two or three feet of depth. The room was probably about fifteen feet long and ten feet wide. Brother André explained to me how that room was to be changed. We were then leaning against the wall as he told me [about the building plans]. He added, 'How good the Good God is.!' He didn't have time to end his sentence. He leapt as if he wanted to jump over the gaping hole in front of us. He hit his head on the part of the floor that remained on the other side of the room, and he lay there, his legs dangling, for the time it took me to rush to help him. I think that jump appeared to me to be a dozen feet and I don't know any man who can jump twelve feet like that. Brother André had made a standing jump without any running. Brother André had a lump on his forehead. He passed his hand over his forehead and the lump disappeared. He had also hurt his legs. I had remained convinced that Brother André had tried to make an unwise jump and did not speak of it to anyone.

A year later, while Pichette was sitting in Brother André's room, waiting for him to return from an errand, he decided to look over the meager library and picked up the book by Sister Marie-Marthé Chambon. Brother André, on his return, noticed that Pichette was looking at the book, and turned to a page where an illustration showed a nun being snatched off her feet by a devil. André made no comment, but from that time on Pichette was convinced that "the leap that Brother André had made the preceding year must have come from the devil."[114]

Pichette also claimed to be aware of other extraordinary phenomena that were witnessed by few, if any, of the other persons who knew Brother André. When Canon Etiènne Catta was compiling his exhaustive biography (in French) of Brother

André in the 1950s, he interviewed the aging Pichette, who told him amazing stories that he had omitted in his testimony a decade earlier. He claimed, for instance, that Brother André spoke of frequent visits from his dead mother, who, he said, "looks at me and smiles." The retired merchant told Catta of an occasion when, as a guest at his home, André casually remarked, "I saw St. Frances of Rome," and was about to recount what she had told him when, noticing Madame Pichette searching for a pen and a paper, he cut short his narrative and said, "I think I'm going to bed. It's rather late."[115]

Pichette told of two instances of bilocation (the facility to seemingly be in two places at one time). Pichette, ill, had gone to the Oratory, only to be told that Brother André was on vacation. As he passed the sacristy, however, Pichette, looking through the open door, saw Brother André alone inside. André noticed Pichette and motioned him to enter the room. When Pichette described his physical complaints, André massaged him "with a very firm touch." Yet, when Pichette left the Oratory, he was again told by members of the community that Brother André had left town two or three days before and was not expected back for two weeks! Another time Pichette was taken ill in his store and was about to go home. Just then Brother André entered the store and suggested that the two of them retire to the back room. There André bade Pichette take off his coat, and proceeded to massage the merchant over his heart and arms. "Aren't you supposed to be in the States?" Pichette asked. Brother André said nothing, but, when he finished the rubbing, he strolled out of the door and started walking in a direction opposite to the Oratory.[116] Pichette was convinced that both of these incidents constituted instances of bilocation in which Brother André was both in America and Montreal at the same time.

Pichette seemed to have been aware of more mystical phenomena than anyone else. The older he grew the more unusual incidents he recounted. Still fresh in the memory of many religious at the Oratory in the late 1980s, Pichette, who was still alive in the late 1960s, is remembered as a kind, friendly, devout old man who seemed to be very alert. However, many of his reports of alleged supernatural activity can possibly be explained in a natural way. For instance, Pichette may have been mistaken about the absence of Brother André from Montreal in the alleged instances of bilocation. Perhaps André's confreres at the Oratory were giving out misinformation to keep the public away and allow the old man some rest. In speaking of his mother and St. Frances, Brother André may have been recounting dreams. Old though he was at the time, Brother André may indeed have been attempting to jump over the unfinished area of the floor when he fell. Perhaps, with the years, Pichette had unconsciously magnified in his mind the actual distance of the leap and fall.

An example of how the natural and supernatural can be confused comes from Brother André himself, who recounted to an undertaker named Hébert an incident which took place around 1903. A terrible electrical storm had broken out, and André moved to close the window. Just then he heard a mysterious tapping on the pane, but no one was in sight. One of his confreres was dying, and André came to the conclusion that the man had just then passed away and that his spirit was tapping on the window to apprise him of the need to prepare his body for burial. "I took off," recounted André, "barefoot down the hall, trembling, before I discovered the real reason for the tapping — the cat!" — a very real, very wet cat![117]

Mystical phenomena of any sort are, of course, no proof of sanctity, or anything else, for that matter. The lives of many evil persons or morally neutral ones have been characterized by parapsychological phenomena, and many individuals of the highest sanctity have experienced no paranormal encounters whatsoever. Brother André attained his reputation for holiness through his character and his success in drawing people closer to God. The healings and whatever other private mystical phenomena that may have characterized his life were but a means of enabling him to carry out his mission of saving and enlightening souls. Most of his associates firmly believed that more miracles were wrought through Brother André in men's souls than in their bodies. Since spiritual enlightenment and conversion are less spectacular, harder to describe and harder to document, there were few recorded interesting incidents, except innumerable statements by individuals claiming that Brother André changed their life and led them to God.

His manner of dealing with sinners was strange, yet simple.

Whenever a visitor came to see Brother André whom the Brother judged to be lacking in faith or commitment or living in sin, he often spent an hour or more with such a pilgrim, in contrast to the minute or two he spent with visitors in search of a physical cure. Typically he produced from a drawer in his desk a statue of a scourged and bloody Jesus.

For example, reporter Frederick Griffin of the *Toronto Star,* after a five-minute interview with Brother André, decided to wait in line for another opportunity to talk to him. The second time, an hour after the first visit, Brother André, who had earlier answered some of the reporter's questions, was silent.

> He was alone, a little old man with very tired eyes. He did not seem to recognize me. I tried to explain. There was no response. He got down from the stool, came in front of me, opened a drawer and from it took a foot-high figurine of the Christ, stripped to the waist, with the arms and chest covered with bleeding wounds. 'That is what I show to those who are bad,' he said. And he looked at me from underneath those drooping lids, his mouth querulous. I did not understand. Even now, I do not understand. I looked at him. He looked at me, his head bent back. Slowly he put the bleeding Christ back in the drawer and closed it. I bowed and left him.[118]

Although the gesture seems to have been lost on Griffin, other visitors were moved to tears of repentance by the sight of the statue of the scourged Christ and by Brother André's expression. "Rarely could a sinner resist the authority of the frail old man who, with tears in his eyes, talked about the Passion of the Lord," Father Bergeron wrote in 1937. He continued:

> Much could be written about his ways of drawing hardened sinners to God. Ordinarily he took a crucifix from a drawer in his desk and began to speak about the Passion of Christ. He would relate all the details concerning the lashes and the pain of each wound, describing the lacerated flesh and the bones crushed by the nails. He would recall the ignominious insults of the Jews and the Roman soldiers and would end his exhortation by expatiating on

the infinite mercy of God. So earnest and sincere was he that he seemed to talk from heavenly inspiration. At times he struck his audiences with awe. At other times he insinuated his ideas gently and persuasively into their minds. When he had moved his listeners to tears, he spoke of God's infinite goodness . . . He delighted in showing the artful and gentle way in which God's grace allures the sinner. He was most convincing when trying to awaken hope in sinners by recalling the conversion of some great sinner who . . . grew to be a great saint.[119]

Although Brother André could be severe towards those who openly defied God's laws — and knew that they were doing so — he is remembered for his tenderness and compassion toward the penitent. "It is through ignorance, rather than malice that most people offend God," he often said.[120]

If there was one problem upon which Brother André focused most, it was the problem of suffering. If he is remembered best for his healings, his greatest gift, perhaps, was that of enabling individuals to understand, endure, and rise above their suffering. Although thousands of people claimed cures, the majority of pilgrims were not healed in body. Testimony is overwhelming, however, that most of Brother André's visitors were healed in mind and soul. In fact, one of André's confreres wrote, "Those who are healed quickly are either those who do not have faith or those who have little faith — so that they might have faith; while those who already have a firm faith are not healed quickly, since the Good God would rather test them and make them suffer in order to sanctify them more."[121]

Brother André believed that St. Joseph bestowed upon the faithful the capacity to imitate Jesus in holiness and in suffering. St. Paul has written, "Now I rejoice in my sufferings for your sake, and in my flesh I complete what is lacking in Christ's afflictions for the sake of his body, that is, the Church" (Col. 1:24). In other words, suffering endured for God has a deep redemptive value, because it is incorporated into the Passion of Christ through which the world is redeemed. Through holy suffering the Christian, moreover, procures an eternal reward, over and above the fact of his salvation. "The people who think they are the most unhappy are the happiest,"

Brother André said. "Those who suffer something have something to offer God . . . And when they manage to endure successfully, that is a miracle that keeps repeating."[122] For this reason, when the construction of the basilica was far enough underway to permit the installation of escalators, Brother André was not happy. "They should never have been installed. People would achieve more faith by climbing and they would obtain more favors."[123]

If Brother André believed in the benefits of suffering, he was always compassionate and sympathetic toward the sufferer. "God will have eternity to console you," he frequently said. "If you knew what reward awaits in heaven for the smallest suffering well borne, you would ask on your knees to suffer."[124] Suffering, he said, "is a deposit in your account in heaven. After this life, you can claim it and benefit from it."[125] Urging sufferers to identify with the Passion of Christ, he encouraged those beset with headaches to think of Christ crowned with thorns, those with leg problems to identify with Christ carrying the cross, and those afflicted with heart disease to consider the Sacred Heart pierced by the lance.[126] "Don't try to have your trials removed. Ask rather for the grace to bear them well," he said, "for the fruit of our suffering is the reward of heaven."[127]

Such then, was the counsel of Brother André, the humble man of prayer, sacrifice and obedience, who was much more than a "faith healer." He was a man whose life was wholly dedicated to the worship of God and the service of mankind. If there was one thing upon which his ministry was founded, it was the love of Christ through love of St. Joseph. The instrument of his ministry was confident prayer. The fruit of his ministry was the release of men and women, through the assistance of heaven, from suffering, either by the removal of physical ills, or better, by the enabling of the sufferer to rise above his trials through the offering of these sorrows as a sacrifice to the throne of the suffering yet triumphant Christ.

Chapter Nine

A Miracle a Day

B y the end of World War I the Oratory of St. Joseph at Côte-des-Neiges (which had recently been incorporated into the City of Montreal), was a major pilgrimage resort, rivaling in popularity the Shrine of Ste.-Anne de Beaupré (twenty miles northeast of Quebec, which had been the site of miraculous favors since the 1600s). Thousands of pilgrims were making their way up Mount Royal, many of them mounting the stairs to the Crypt Church on their knees. Growing crowds queued up outside Brother André's office, necessitating, at times, a wait of two or three days. Archbishop Bruchési remarked that whenever he was in the United States he was best known, not as Archbishop of Montreal, but as "Brother André's Bishop."

By 1920 the volume of mail had reached 150 letters a day. By the decade's end, more than 400 pieces of mail were arriving daily and the total was still growing. Sometimes letters arrived addressed merely, "Brother André, Montreal." These not only bore requests for healing from afflictions of body or mind, but frequently contained expressions of thanksgiving, not only for cures, but for such other favors as the deliverance of a family from fire, the conversion of a "heretic," the obtaining of a job, the successful adjustment to an artificial limb, the attainment of an academic degree, an easy childbirth, a good grade on a school paper, a profit on the sale of a property. The letters were technically the responsibility of the superior, who, in turn, usually delegated the responsibility to one of the teaching brothers. During the 1920s Brother Hyacinth served unofficially as Brother André's secretary, reading all the letters and answering as many as he could, signing them "Brother André." He did pass the requests on to Brother André, who dedicated to each person who sought his prayers a decade of the Rosaries which he prayed almost continuously.

How many people were cured? Some claim as many as 15,000 a year. The best estimate is that there were normally more than 400 claims of *major* cures each year — more than one for each day.

Father Dion had died at seventy, of a heart attack, during the fall of 1918 and had been replaced by Father Alfred Roy, a gentle, deeply spiritual ascetic of sixty-seven who had long been an enthusiastic supporter of Brother André and the Oratory. Confident that the money for the construction of the basilica would continue to accumulate, as it had in the past, "not by princely gifts, but by the accumulation of the little alms of the people," Father Roy set to work beautifying the land on which the edifice was to rise, terracing the ground around the Crypt and planting it in lawns and gardens. In 1922 a huge bronze statue of St. Joseph with the Christ Child in his arms was erected at the entrance to the Oratory grounds.

News of miraculous cures continued to appear in newspapers not only in Canada but also in America. Screaming headlines in a number of New England papers in the fall of 1919 proclaimed one of Brother André's most striking cures. CANCER CURED BY MIRACLE declared one paper. MIRACULOUS CURE trumpeted another. CANCERS DISAPPEAR FROM THROAT AND TONGUE OF PLATTSBURGH WOMAN declared a third. Concerning this remarkable providence the Burlington [Vermont] *Free Press and Times* reported on September 10: "There is probably not a happier woman in Plattsburgh today than Mrs. Albert Sharron, whose sublime faith has made her well and strong almost in the twinkling of an eye, after five years of most intense suffering from a disease claimed to be incurable."[1]

Marie Julia Valley Sharron, the 56-year-old wife of a department store owner and sometime mayor, and the mother of eight, was one of the best known citizens in Plattsburgh, a town of about 15,000 on the shores of Lake Champlain. A gentle, self-effacing woman, she was widely known for her "great faith" and her charitable works. She would later be described as "never far away in the hours of perplexity and need, when [her] gentle counsel and words of comfort and encouragement seemed like a balm to wounded spirits."[2] She was also celebrated for her beautiful voice with which she led the choir of St. Peter's Catholic Church. By 1919, it was "well known to almost everyone in Plattsburgh," that Mrs. Sharron was dying of cancer.[3] Five years earlier, unable to swallow properly, she submitted to a medical examination and received the unwelcome diagnosis of cancer of the throat. Surgery achieved a temporary success. When the cancer returned several years later, Mrs. Sharron, who had met Brother André through a cabdriver named Wilson (at whose home the holy man was frequently a guest), went to Montreal. Six weeks after her visit with Brother André the cancer was again in remission. By the spring of 1919, the disease had reappeared, affecting her tongue as well as her throat, and was so widely spread that surgeons declared it inoperable and terminal. Mrs. Sharron, in "almost unbearable" pain, decided to visit Brother André again. On a Sunday in late August or early September, in the only recorded instance in which he physically touched a woman since he had been forbidden to do so in 1906, André laid his hands on Mrs. Sharron's head, declaring: "There is nothing wrong with your throat. You are well."[4]

Marie Sharron later declared: "The pain, which was like a ball of fire in my throat, ceased. I walked out of the building as well as I ever was in my life."[5] Her physicians, in Plattsburgh, upon examining her, found no evidence of cancer in her mouth or tongue or throat. Later she would attribute the sudden cure of her son Roswell, from osteomyelitis in an arm, to Brother André's prayers. Frequently she would pick up her phone and call Brother André, informing him about crises among her family and friends. "I'll start praying and you do likewise," she would say in English, before repeating her telephone prayers in French.[6] On September 23, 1932, Marie Sharron and her husband Albert, had just returned from the movies and she was regaling her family with stories of a recent trip through

New England, when, instantaneously, she died from a heart attack. She was sixty-nine and had not known a day of sickness since her cure from cancer thirteen years before.

In 1920, the papers were full of the news of the cure of Onézime Joncas of Buckingham, Quebec, who had been crippled for ten years with rheumatoid arthritis. One leg was totally immobilized and he suffered "atrocious pain." In July, Joncas and his parish priest visited Brother André at the Oratory and he was cured as instantly as Marie Sharron had been. Several weeks later, Joncas, requesting a Mass of Thanksgiving, declared that he was fully mobile and had not suffered a single pain since his trip to the Oratory.[7]

During Brother André's fall trip to New York State in 1920, more cures were reported by the papers. In October he was the guest of a Father Valois at Morrisonville when two dramatic cures were reported by the local paper. The recipients of these favors refused to identify themselves, but the paper recounted their cure at St. Alexander's Church. "Hundreds of people stood in amazement as they watched a man who had been bedridden for years arise from his cot and walk from the church. There is not the slightest possibility of doubting the condition the man was in, as it was well known to his neighbors, none of whom ever hoped to see him walk again." A blind girl was healed when Brother André told her, "Never mind, my girl, I think you shall see." At those words the child "turned and walked down the aisle . . . and today sees as well as she ever did." Although the girl and the former cripple did not give their names, a Methodist named Seth Baker, formerly a great sufferer from arthritis, willingly identified himself and told reporters how, just a few months earlier, he had to be carried up the steps of the Oratory, but now was perfectly well, was able to drive and "haven't an ache or a pain."[8]

There was one cure that year that drew an angry response from a noted Montreal physician. Dr. Leo Parizeau, a well-known medical man of Montreal, was treating at the Hotel-Dieu a 15-year-old high school soccer player who had injured his leg and developed blood poisoning. Parizeau ordered amputation. Brother André, who had been summoned by the parents of the young athlete, insisted that they refuse to sign the papers and directed them to apply to the damaged leg a compress soaked in St. Joseph's oil and boric acid, while beginning a novena to St. Joseph. Immediately the boy was healed, but Parizeau was beside himself with rage. Admitting to no miracle, he attributed the cure to "natural curative forces that got the better of the doctors."[9] Since no individual can know when this force will come into play and to what extent, in Parizeau's opinion, Brother André was recklessly endangering the life of his patient. In November, 1920, the doctor gave an angry talk before a group of physicians, a talk quoted in part by the magazine *Le Nationaliste,* in which he reviled Brother André as "a frustrated and ignorant creature" and characterized those who attributed cures to his ministry as "hysterics" and "pseudosick healed by suggestion."[10]

Parizeau's blast prompted a discussion of Brother André's cures by a number of Montreal's most eminent physicians and psychiatrists at a meeting at City Hall on November 23. Present was Lionel Lamy, a young physician favorable to Brother André, who was later to become his physician. Although he took notes, out of professional courtesy Lamy omitted the names of the participants when he reported the discussion to André's friends at the Oratory.

One surgeon argued that "unforeseen facts, when they are completely indifferent to use, are called 'phenomena of chance'; when they are harmful to us, they become 'fatality'; and when they are favorable, they are called 'miracles.' " Brother André's healings were therefore merely unforeseen facts with a favorable outcome. While devotees of the "miracle man" might explain the cures as "the action of God," this physician made no attempt to explain them, but looked forward to the day when science could furnish him with the means to understand them naturally.

A second physician insisted that describing inexplicable cures as "miracles" was "contrary to the scientific spirit." He argued, "Where would science be if everything inexplicable was considered to occur because of the intervention of St. Joseph or some other saint? The doctor must practice medicine. It is not for him to decree that a healing is miraculous. That is for the theologians. We must be satisfied with deciding whether, medically, there is a healing." He went on to catalogue various diseases which occasionally disappear or go into re mission without medical intervention. But, he insisted, such events were not miracles, for "there are no miracles."

Other physicians emphasized the unknown effect of mind over matter, one of them going so far as to claim "rare are the cases when the neuropathic agent does not play a role." In other words, an individual's will and mind are sometimes capable of influencing almost any medical conditions.

Still other participants, like Dr. Lamy, had no hesitation in attributing to supernatural intervention the cures of some of their patients. All that the doctors agreed upon, however, was the recommendation that the Oratory set up "an objective medical commission," similar to that at Lourdes in France, in which all those professing a cure would be invited to submit to an examination by a medical team responsible for determining what, if anything, was wrong with the individual and whether the disease or injury, if it existed, was in fact cured.[11]

Such a Bureau, first recommended by the Bruchési Commission of 1911, was never established at the Oratory. Parizeau, criticized by other physicians not so much for what he said, but for the way in which he said it, made no more public complaints. People kept going to the Oratory. And cures and other graces continued to abound, both there and in the towns Brother André visited on his travels.

Not all the "miracles" involved cures. For example, Azarias Claude had given up his business to serve as Brother André's full-time receptionist. By the early 1920s he was in terrible financial straits. Brother André prayed, but nothing turned up to ease Claude's monetary crisis. Finally, one evening, Brother André was at table with the Claudes, preparatory to his sick calls. It was snowing as Claude lamented that he was on the verge of losing his house since he could not keep up with the mortgage payments. Just then there was a knock on the door. Brother André opened the door to a stranger who said, "This package is for the man with the financial problems," and then "disappeared in the snow." André and the Claudes took the package to the table, opened it, and in it found the exact amount of money needed to pay Claude's debts.[12]

The Oratory drew increasing numbers of pilgrims. A Montreal newspaper in the 1920s described the scene: "Cars, sightseeing buses, and taxis ascended the slope to the Oratory all day long, each depositing still more visitors eager to see Brother André. A long queue formed in the little frame building in which his office is located and extended onto the asphalt pavement outside."[13] More and more Brother André was on the road. In 1920 he was appointed by his superiors as a delegate to the General Chapter of the Congregation of Holy Cross. The Chapter, which constitutes the governing body for the CSC in America and Canada, met at Notre Dame University in Indiana. There is no record of anything that Brother André did or said there. Occasionally he left the Oratory to attend such events as the consecration of a bishop, but most frequently and regularly, his journeys took him to New England, where he spent his "vacations" talking about the Oratory and ministering to the sick in local homes and parishes.

When Brother André was in his seventh decade, Father Roy would occasionally send him off to a retreat house so he could escape the press of humanity for a few days. The pious frequently discovered the hideaway despite the best efforts of André's community to keep his temporary whereabouts a secret. For example, in April, 1921, he was sent for a few days of rest to the CSC theological seminary in Quebec City. The priests and brothers at the Oratory were ordered to reveal Brother André's whereabouts under no circumstances whatsoever. Within days, however, there was a leak and a newspaper reported: "Brother André is resting in Quebec in a religious institution, the name of which, at his request, has not been given out. But the doorkeeper at the seminary admits André is there."[14] That same day the seminary was besieged with throngs of desperate folk. For once, however, Brother André refused visitors. With a grin, he told the doorkeeper, "Tell them I am with the Superior General."[15] He said this with his finger pointed heavenward.

In the autumn of that same year, John Doran, a wealthy businessman from Sudbury, Ontario, approached Father Roy and asked his permission to take Brother André with him to his winter home in Pasadena, California. Despite André's protest that "I don't have the right to such a privilege," Roy ordered him to go.[16] And so, Brother André, clad, uncharacteristically, in civilian apparel, joined Doran on the four-day automobile journey, passing most of the time meditating and praying the

Rosary, until their arrival at the fashionable Victoria Apartments at Pasadena on November 22. Within three days Brother André's presence was discovered, as an article from the *Pasadena Star-News* related:

> Attempting to keep his presence in Pasadena a profound secret from all except those whom he felt it might benefit, it has just been learned that the Rev. Brother André of Montreal, asserted to be one of the most successful healers in the Catholic Church, has been quietly going about his mission here. It has been said that he has been working in Pasadena for the last three days, healing the sick, sending people away without crutches, despite the desire of those arranging Brother André's trip to be kept secret.[17]

The *Los Angeles Examiner* reported that Brother André, "a very aged man devoting most of his time to prayer," had held forth the evening before at St. Andrew's Church, ministering to 500 persons, of whom seven professed miraculous cures.[18] After only five days of "vacation," Brother André asked to be driven back to the Oratory, where he arrived December 1. Wherever he went, he could not avoid the multitudes.

Many wondered whether such a schedule was too much for this "very aged man." A reporter asked this question of him when he was seventy-five. "Old? I'm not old!" he retorted. "Look you, seven and five makes twelve, which is to say I am twelve years old! Tired? Is ever one tired in the service of the Master?"[19] Brother Placide Vermandère, who played the organ in the Crypt Church during these years, described Brother André as "very jolly" and lively enough to "shadow-box" with his younger friends.[20]

The largest crowd ever to assemble at the Oratory to date gathered in and around the Crypt Church on August 31, 1924, when 35,000 persons witnessed the blessing of the cornerstone of the basilica by the Apostolic Delegate to Canada, Pietro di Maria. Insisting that he was never much of a mason, Brother André spread the first mortar with a trowel. The next summer another massive congregation marked a triple celebration — the fiftieth anniversary of Father Roy's ordination, the twenty-fifth anniversary of the priesthood of Father Clément, and

Brother André's eightieth birthday. The Mass was celebrated by Bishop Michael Fallon of London, Ontario. The *Montreal Daily Star* reported:

> It was a simple service which marked the anniversaries. Originally it had been the intention to make it a family affair, but so anxious were thankful people to show their appreciation of the devotion of those who serve their Lord at the shrine that arrangements were made for a celebration of High Mass in which a number of distinguished clergy should have a part. First-comers arrived at 6 o'clock, and long before the service was scheduled to begin, crowded cars had unloaded their freight of humanity at the foot of the long flight of steps. By the time St. Joseph's Guard, smartly uniformed, had played its way to the shrine, there was standing room only in the church, and at 9 o'clock when Mass was to begin, even the corridors were jammed and many waited outside.[21]

By 1926 more than a million pilgrims were visiting the mountain a year. Groups such as the Knights of Columbus were making annual pilgrimages, and church dignitaries like Di Maria, Fallon, and George Cardinal Mundelein of Chicago made appearances before crowded congregations. (The latter agreed with André in his denunciation of the "spiritual pestilence" of modern female attire.) Another frequent visitor was Monsignor Georges Gauthier, who was now acting Archbishop of Montreal. Archbishop Bruchési's mental faculties were now failing, and, although he was allowed to retain his formal title, he was relieved of his duties.

Work began in earnest on the basilica in 1927. There were problems from time to time, such as a bomb scare which sent hundreds of firefighters searching every corner of the mountain and the growing complex of buildings that stood thereon, only to find nothing, and two robberies, which outraged Brother André because the stolen goods were the property of St. Joseph. Nonetheless, he retained his humor in the face of such untoward incidents. When a reporter asked him what had been stolen in the robberies, he replied, "A bag full of miracles."[22]

What truly irked Brother André, however, was the insane adulation of the Little Sisters of the Holy Family. The nuns lived in a separate wing of the rectory, cooked the meals, did the laundry and performed other similar services for the male religious. The Little Sisters cut tassels off his soutane and pieces from whatever article of clothing he gave them to launder. They even saved his nail and hair cuttings to give away, along with the snippets of clothing, to give to pilgrims as "relics." This infuriated Brother André, who, when he learned of the consistency with which the nuns committed such abuses, insisted that his clothing no longer be attended to by these "thieves," but instead by the reliable wife of his friend, the sexton Adélard Fabre. "Tell me," André fumed to Father Roy, "what can they do with my hair? I don't even have enough to make a pillow.!"[23]

Chapter Ten

The Traveler

For many years, Brother André's semi-annual excursions had been an integral part of his ministry. He usually took two "vacations" of several weeks, one in the spring and one in the fall. In the spring, he sometimes visited other Canadian cities and towns, such as Ottawa, Toronto, and Sudbury, where he had friends and admirers. Other years he went south into New York State, visiting Plattsburgh, Keeseville, Glens Falls, Schenectady, Troy, Albany, and occasionally New York City and northern New Jersey. In the fall, he nearly always traveled into the States by a more easterly route, first visiting friends in Granby, Quebec, just outside of Montreal, then proceeding south to Sutton, on the Vermont border; then on to Burlington, Vermont; Holyoke and Springfield, Massachusetts; and Moosup, Sterling, and Thompson, Connecticut; then north through West Warwick, Rhode Island and Fall River and New Bedford, Massachusetts.

Many of Brother André's hosts were priests who had first met him years before, when they were boys studying at Notre-Dame in Montreal. Often he was hosted by his relatives, who were now scattered multitudinously about the New England states. He took special delight in visiting his surviving brothers, Napoleon and Claude, who lived in Sterling, Connecticut. These venerable men, who, with their flowing white beards resembled Old Testament patriarchs, have been described as "beautiful," "wonderful," "sweet," and "loving" Christians of great sanctity and holiness. "I can't begin to describe what beautiful and holy men Uncle Claude and Uncle Napoleon were," a nephew recalled. Wherever Brother André stayed, there was usually a tacit understanding that he, on "vacation," would minister to the sick of the host's community.

Brother André sometimes traveled by train and sometimes by car. Although air travel began in his very last years, there is no record of his utilizing this new development in transportation. Railroad officials allowed him to travel free and often made unscheduled stops so that he could board or alight where convenient. Sometimes André traveled alone, sometimes he had a companion, sometimes he sat in the coach, sometimes he used a roommette. A traveling companion once recalled how he and Brother André knelt side by side at their berth for their evening prayers. After what seemed an interminable interval, Brother André bade his nodding companion turn out the light, promising to retire within a few minutes. Hours later, when the companion awoke, he found that André was still kneeling in the dark. When day broke, he found the old gentleman awake, bright and alert, with his face lathered for shaving. Aghast at the sight of the ancient straight-razor with which Brother André was preparing to shave, the companion expressed fear that the lurching and swaying of the train would cause him to lose his balance and cut himself. André laughed and said, "I can shave anywhere, and without a mirror, too!"[1]

Once, returning alone to Montreal, Brother André was carrying, as was his wont, a collection of discarded crutches. He was in the coach, occupying the seat next to the window, with the crutches in the seat next to the aisle. As he dozed, the crutches slipped off and clattered onto the floor, causing a terrible racket. This was one of the rare occasions when Brother André was in civilian attire, and the conductor gazed at the seedy old man in his threadbare overcoat and battered black bowler hat, and, taking him for a salesman down on his luck, asked if he sold orthopaedic devices. When the old man identified himself as "Brother André" the conductor was stupefied, and, in front of the other gawking occupants of the car, got down on his knees, sobbing, recounting how he had written him in the past and obtained a cure. Not having ever seen him, the conductor apologized for not recognizing him. By this time the other passengers, realizing that they were in the company of the "Miracle Man of Montreal," pressed about him, begging for divine favors. It was because of scenes like this that Brother André preferred to travel by car.

When he motored to the States, Brother André was often driven by Dominique Cormier, who was a relative of Joseph Pichette. Cormier was an auto mechanic in the service department of a Cadillac dealer in Montreal. The proprietor, a devout Protestant by the name of Walsh, not only allowed Cormier extended leave when his services were requested by Brother André, but also granted him the use, free of charge, of the finest Cadillacs he had in stock. It was not that Brother André was fond of fine cars, though, Ganz (who frequently drove him about in Canada) insisted that André was "content with the oldest of cars and those of the worst appearance." "So long as it has four wheels and runs, it's enough for me," Brother André insisted.[2]

Before he left the Oratory, Brother André always went to the old chapel, where he knelt and prayed that God would bless the journey that he was about to undertake, that it might prove an occasion of comfort and succor for the many souls whom he would encounter. Usually he wore his black soutane and wide-brimmed hat. By this time many religious, especially in the States, were abandoning the soutane for a clerical shirt, coat, and trousers. Some of André's friends suggested that he might be more comfortable if he journeyed dressed in the modern style. One of them joked, "I know why you always wear your soutane! You're bow-legged!" Cackling with laughter, Brother André explained that he dressed in the old style because it attracted respect. Occasionally, as we have seen above, he was persuaded to travel in civilian dress to preserve his anonymity. Whatever he wore, he always carried a big battered leather valise full of medals. According to grandnephew Jules Cayer, "he gave out those medals like Rockefeller gave out dimes."

A trip of several hundred miles with Brother André was not necessarily a pleasant experience, for the old man did not believe in stopping, either to eat or for any reason other than to adore the Blessed Sacrament at a wayside church. He carried a bread roll and a thermos full of coffee and could not understand why such ample provisions were not as sufficient for the driver as they were for him. For a while he would chat with his companion, mostly about religious matters, but then he would announce, "We're going to pray to the Holy Virgin," producing his rosary. At times he read a bit from his Bible or *The Imitation of Christ.* At times he prayed silently or dozed. He always insisted that his driver go as fast as possible. One of his drivers, in fact, insisted that the old man never liked to go less than ninety. Brother André never worried about accidents and was never involved in any, although someone once put sugar in the car's gas tank. "Your car has diabetes!"[3] he cracked when he was told the cause of the problem.

At length he descended — without warning — on relative or friend. Aurore Snow Lawrence recalled "Blessed Uncle Brother André" visiting her parents' home in West Warwick, Rhode Island. She wrote: "We never knew when he was coming. We would either see him walking up the hill or someone would give him a ride. He would always ask my mother to bake him some johnny cake, with milk and watermelon rind preserves. People from the streets would come in as soon as they learned he was here."[4] Jules Cayer, a grandnephew, had similar recollections about the visits of "Uncle Fred" to his home in New Beford, Massachusetts: "We never knew in advance when Uncle Fred was going to come. He always came unannounced . . . He wasn't in the house one hour before there were 100 people outside the door. I still don't understand how they knew. We never understood."[5]

Whenever Brother André stayed at the home of his brother Claude in Sterling, Connecticut:

> He bowed his head whenever he passed a pious statue or a crucifix. Every time he came to our home . . . he would . . . teach us about the Passion of Our Lord, showing us how He suffered and died on the cross for us and how most people are ungrateful to Him after all He did for us.[6]

Attaria Lafleur, Léocadie's daughter, who lived in Moosup, Connecticut, recalled that during visits, her uncle made the Stations of the Cross with her family every Friday and spent a good deal of his time alone in his room. He was given to the utterance of such pious platitudes as: "Pray to St. Joseph and he will always be your father and your guide"; and "Pray to your Guardian Angel, because he is your best defense in danger"; and "If the Good God should put you to the test, it is perhaps because He wants you to love Him more."[7]

Mrs. Lawrence recalled a happy, jolly man who liked to shadow box with her father. Mrs. Lafleur described him as "always happy" and never remembered him complaining or discouraged.[8] Suzanne Paine of Natick, Rhode Island, daughter of André's sister Alphonsine, recalled a quiet, dignified man who, except for family news, never spoke of worldly affairs and spent most of his time praying or ministering to the sick. In 1988, Mrs. Albert Sharron III of Plattsburgh likewise recalled a quiet, reserved man. Henry Bessette of Moosup, Claude's son, remembered a friendly man of "sincere reserve," who, on his two- or three-day visits, rose at four or five to pray, went to Mass at seven, and spent the rest of the day ministering to others. In 1987, Jules Cayer said: "I can't describe how humble and beautiful he was. He always wore a long soutane and a pot-pie hat. Whenever he met a stranger, he held up his hands like he wanted to box. He never talked about miracles to us. He just talked about the family. Sometimes, though, he talked about the difficulty he'd had entering the Order. But Uncle Fred loved to be with his family. He usually stayed one day and one night with us. His chauffeur would go to a hotel. My Dad was his favorite nephew. Uncle Fred would sit aside Dad and hold my father's hand, just like he was a little boy."[9]

Brother André's relatives preserved varied memories of his eating and sleeping habits. Mrs. Comeau, Claude's daughter, said that her uncle ate "little more than a piece of dry bread with a cup of coffee — no butter on his bread, no sugar in his tea. Sometimes he took hot water with a couple sips of milk."[10] Attaria Lafleur remembered similar austerities. Aurore Lawrence recalled André's fondness for johnny cake, milk, and watermelon rind preserves, but added, "he could not eat too much, as he had a sensitive stomach."[11] Cayer, however, related that before he retired for the night, about midnight, when asked what he wanted to eat, Uncle Fred frequently requested baked beans. "We thought that would kill him at his age, but he said, 'If you crush them they'll be all right.' "[12] Mrs. Comeau and Mrs. Paine believed that Brother André spent most of the night in prayer and Mrs. Lawrence said that the bed in his room "was never used."[13] Cayer stated that André retired at midnight, but by two he was up dressed in his long-johns. "You're going to be tired, Uncle Fred," Cayer's wife warned. "I don't have to sleep," insisted Brother André. "Sleep is just a habit." He would spend the next few hours walking the floor, praying and reading the Bible.[14] Henry Bessette remembered Brother André sleeping until four or five.

On vacation Brother André began his day with Mass in a local church. "I never observed anything remarkable," declared Attaria Lafleur, "except that he heard the entire Mass on his knees and went to church early and remained long after the Mass was over."[15] Sometimes Brother André spent the morning visiting with the parish priest and his staff, sometimes he spent it visiting relatives and friends. The second day of a stay in New Bedford, for example, Brother André usually spent the morning visiting with his nephew Joseph Lefebvre, Léocadie's son, a widower who called on him at the Cayer home. After a meager noonday repast, he usually spent the afternoon visiting the sick in local hospitals. "Once he asked me to take him to see the manager of a department store in New Bedford," Cayer recalled. "He had his chauffeur, but since I knew the town, it was easier for me to take him. The man came out of the store to see Uncle Fred at the car. It would have created a big stir for Uncle Fred to go into the store. So they spent an hour talking at the car. Then the businessman reached in his pocket and gave my uncle something."[16]

At night Brother André received the sick. Both Aurore Lawrence and Jules Cayer were amazed how people would, without any prior announcement of Brother André's visit, walk in off the street. Cayer said most of these visitors were French-speaking and that they were allowed to see Brother André one at a time, with the others remaining queued up outside. "We never knew what he said to them, for the meeting was private. Many people left so happily. Some left crying. He never discussed what was said."[17] At other homes he saw people in groups. Attaria Lafleur said that at such times he would give a brief, pious talk, urging his visitors to pray to St. Joseph and have confidence in him. He also distributed medals. "This touched the hearts of his listeners and made a profound impression."[18] Often he saw more than 200 people a night. According to Suzanne Paine, "He received people until midnight and didn't send anyone away, even if it was late. At quarter to twelve one night a man arrived and Brother André said, 'Let him in.' "[19]

Brother André was not always happy about the influx of visitors. "He didn't always feel too comfortable," said Cayer, "because these visits interfered with his time with his family. And some of these customers, as I call them, made comments and as a result he got a little rough."[20] As we have seen, people often learned of Brother André's presence without any public announcement. When his hosts placed an advertisement in a local paper or on a radio station the result was a crowd so large as to prove scarcely manageable. Once André's hostess, having notified all the radio stations in town of the holy man's visit, found a line a mile long queued up outside her door that night. "What's this?" demanded Brother André as he scanned the sea of humanity. "I can't see them all! I came here to rest!" Yet he received all of the visitors anyway. When he left town the road was sometimes so jammed with supplicants and well-wishers that an auto trip that should have taken thirty minutes was prolonged to three hours!

Brother André was bewildered by all this adulation. In June, 1927 when he was the guest of Father Roger McGinely (a former student at Notre-Dame who was now pastor of St. Aedan's in Jersey City, New Jersey), the newspapers reported the visit in advance, and to some it seemed as though the entire city on the Hudson turned out to welcome him. When he returned to Montreal he remarked to Father Clément (now superior), "Jersey City was all decked out in honor of somebody or other."[21] He said this with an entirely straight face, for he was never able to grasp why multitudes should run after an elderly, illiterate working brother who could do no more than pray to St. Joseph.

Although usually jolly and warm, Brother André could be abrupt with people who wasted his time, or, as Cayer has recounted, came to him "with problems that they could work out themselves." He grew upset when people called him a "saint," and blew up at one priest in New Bedford who had the imprudence to ask the means by which he performed miracles. "All I do is to pray to St. Joseph," he retorted. "You would receive graces, too, if you had confidence in him!"[22]

With women, Brother André was very reserved. "He was brief with women," remarked Henry Bessette, "but always polite and sensitive, never rude nor brusque."[23]

At times Brother André could be demanding of his hosts, especially if they were clergy. For instance, the first time he visited Father Frank Cornish, pastor in the village of Keeseville in upstate New York, he was met at the train station by the priest. It was dusk as the two men walked up the steep hill to the rectory. Brother André asked which day was reserved for the Holy Hour and was informed that, due to a lack of interest, Holy Hour was offered but once a month. Brother André pointed, from the crest of the hill, to the lighted houses in the village, illuminating the darkening valley. "Shouldn't God's house be lighted, too?" he asked. "People are coming and going between their homes. Don't you think they would come to visit God?" Holy Hour only once a month did not satisfy Brother André, who insisted that Father Cornish schedule it on a weekly basis. "I won't move until you promise me to have a Holy Hour every week," he declared. Cornish agreed and announced a Holy Hour during the time Brother André was with him. Cornish attributed the massive turnout that first evening to the presence of the renowned visitor. But even after André's departure, the weekly Holy Hour continued to attract a large congregation, with the faithful coming from Keeseville, and from neighboring villages as well. The next year, when Brother André returned, Father Cornish expressed his amazement at the continuing popularity of the Holy Hour.[24]

During his travels, Brother André encountered many unusual people, but none stranger than a young, French-Canadian woman living in Woonsocket, Rhode Island by the name of Marie Rose Ferron, who, hailed as a saint by some, was scorned by others as a hysteric. According to her biographer, the Rev. Onesimus Boyer, the life of "Little Rose," who died at thirty-three in 1936, was a continuous martyrdom of suffering from a gruesome combination of unidentified ailments. Almost totally paralyzed since childhood, the unfortunate woman was able to move only her mouth and the tips of two fingers. One of her hands was clenched in such a position that her long nails were embedded in the palm, and, according to Boyer, if anyone tried to loosen the grip, the finger joints came apart. "When they dressed her," Father Boyer wrote, "and fixed her bed, much care was used, for when she was untied she rolled back like a hoop and it required the strength of more than one person to straighten her out again.[25] In addition, she threw up nearly everything she ate or drank. She developed wounds suggestive of those of Christ's Passion, but unlike the stigmata of her contemporaries Padre Pio and Therese Neumann, which usually oozed, Miss Ferron's wounds "streamed" with blood. In fact, she was covered with "red blotches all over her body . . . all discharging blood." Even her eyes, eventually blind, poured blood that "bubbled like boiling water."[26] The tortured woman was known to declare, "The more the body is tortured, lacerated, and soiled, the more the soul becomes pure, healthy, and holy."[27] At any rate, on one of his visits to Woonsocket, where one of his nieces lived, Brother André was invited to visit Little Rose. At first very positive, he went, but upon his return, he refused to discuss the lady or his visit. "If my superior general tells me to go again, I'll go, but not otherwise."[28]

As one might well expect, numerous healings were attributed to Brother André on his American journeys. When Jules Cayer first met his Uncle Fred in the fall of 1916, he had the opportunity to chat a few minutes with the driver, an Irishman whose name he forgot. "Do you believe in miracles?" the driver asked. When Cayer told him that he did, the Irishman, leading him to his Cadillac, asked, "Do you want to see something curious?" In the back seat were about a dozen orthopaedic devices — crutches, trusses, and braces — all discarded by persons with no further need of them after their encounter with Brother André. "I must say," recalled Cayer more than seventy years later, "it struck me an awful lot!"[29]

Cayer remembered no dramatic cures during Brother André's visits to his home, but Aurore Lawrence recalled a Mrs. Provost who came to her house. "Two men crossed their arms to make a chair and carried her in the house. When it came her turn to speak with Uncle Brother André, he gave her a St. Joseph medal and told her to rub herself with St. Joseph oil. Then he told her to stand up. She did. He told her to put one foot on the spoke of the chair. She did. He told her to walk. She did. She walked out by herself."[30]

Mrs. Lawrence related the healing of Henry Paine, fiancé of her cousin Suzanne Boulet. Paine had accidentally pierced his hand with ice-tongs and it was now so badly infected that his doctors were threatening amputation. Paine promised Brother André that he would "turn Catholic" if he were healed. As soon as Brother André touched the hand, there was no more pain, and the infection cleared up almost immediately. Paine immediately united with the Church of Rome and married Suzanne.[31]

Mr. and Mrs. Eusebe Viau, of Central Falls, Rhode Island, testified in 1942 concerning the cure in 1917 of their nineteen-year-old adopted daughter Agnes, who was suffering gruesomely from "uncontrollable eczema," which had progressed to the point that the girl was almost totally blind and deaf. She had been at Rhode Island General Hospital, but had been discharged without improvement after three weeks. When Brother André visited the Viau home he announced that the young girl would "see clearly again." Agnes began to slowly regain her sight until, after a year, her vision was normal. Her parents did not say whatever became of her "eczema."[32]

Visiting Sudbury, Ontario, Brother André met Camille Gravette and his wife, whose toddling daughter had swallowed a cup of bleach six months before, severely burning her esophagus. The little girl could swallow nothing solid and only a few drops of liquid at a time. Brother André announced the child would be healed and within a short time the toddler was able to eat and drink normally.[33]

Brother André once stayed with the family of an alcoholic. The husband and wife fought constantly. Right in front of André the drunkard poured himself a glass of whiskey. "You won't drink that!" screamed the wife. "Oh, yes I will!" bellowed the husband, cursing gruesomely. Brother André just looked at him. The glass shattered in the tippler's hand before it touched his lips. With a terrible oath, the drunkard filled another glass. Again André gazed at it and the glass shattered in his hand. When the third glass broke as well, André's besotted friend vowed to never again touch alcoholic beverages.[34]

In October, 1927 Brother André was staying with a cousin in Springfield, Massachusetts when he was called upon by a crippled man, fifty-nine-year-old Francis Xavier Gelineau of Willamansett. Several years earlier, Gelineau the father of nine, had fallen from a ladder and broken a hip. Even after four operations he hobbled about painfully with a cane. When the injured man told his story, Brother André declared, "You don't feel any pain!" and bade him arise. When Gelineau got up, he had no pain and could walk without his cane.[35]

On that same visit, Brother André was visited by a wealthy businessman, James E. Mullen, of Holyoke. The owner of a hotel, Mullen had been en route to Florida the previous January when he suffered a massive stroke on the train as it sat in a New York station. He spent three months in hospital, and now, nine months after the stroke, his left side was still partially paralyzed and his speech was badly impaired. With the aid of a cane, Mullen shuffled into the room in a private home where Brother André was receiving the sick. The invalid was accompanied by his pastor, Father Hubert. There were a number of others in the house, including a newspaper reporter who recounted: "Less than five minutes later the door was opened and over Mr. Mullen's face was written a smile of triumph. He lifted his left leg with ease and swung it back and fourth as he stood on his right one. He extended his left arm, heretofore practically useless, and wiggled every finger of his left hand." Two doctors, interviewed the next day, declared the case "wonderful."[36]

On his hospital calls the same day, Brother André was taken to see twenty-seven-year-old Felix Morin, who had been ill for several months. A real estate broker, Morin had fallen ill in early July. His physician, Dr. Goodwin, diagnosed a brain tumor and declared the case hopeless. Morin's parents sent him to New York for surgery. A Dr. Elsburg operated and found a benign growth known as an acoustic neuroma on the right side of the brain. He removed all of it, but when Morin regained consciousness, he was totally paralyzed on his left side and unable to speak. After three months there was no change in his condition and the doctors were certain that the paralysis was permanent. When André first visited the young man, Morin could not even move his head, and André succeeded in making him raise it for the first time since his surgery. The following day he got the sick man to sit up. Then, on the third day, according to Philip Erard, who accompanied him: "Frere André found the young man seated and ordered him to walk. The sick man rose and walked, painfully at first, then faster. Finally Frere André requested him to walk alone. His . . . leg was still inflexible and Frere André ordered him to lift the leg and put it on a bench, and this is what the sick man did."[37] Within a few days, Morin was completely recovered.[38] Morin was studying medicine eight years later when he fell ill with a recurrence of the neuroma. He was operated on for a second time October 17, 1935 at Deaconess Hospital in Boston, but two days later developed "post-operative edema of the medulla oblongata" and died on the 22nd.

There were, of course, instances in which Brother André announced that there would be no cure. One of them concerned one of his numerous cousins, a Miss Bessette, who was a few years younger than he and lived in Hull, Quebec. The old lady had become blind and asked her cousin to pray for a cure, only to hear him say: "You have enough faith to bear this infirmity. You must endure it for the love of God. It's your vocation."[39] Miss Bessette accepted her blindness and endured it cheerfully until her death in 1937.

Brother André often pushed himself to the very limits of his strength. Although he was now in his eighth decade he would not slow down. A relative commented, "He's so afraid that he won't do his duty that he puts aside all personal considerations of conserving his own personal health and strength."[40] In the fall of 1927, on that same tour in which Francis Gelineau, James Mullen and Felix Morin regained their health, Brother André collapsed. On October 21, probably on the evening after his last visit to Morin, Brother André was invited to address a gathering of the pious at the Hotel Nonotuck in Holyoke. Before he could say a word, André blacked out and was taken for observation to Mercy Hospital, from whence he was released, after a few hours, to the care of his cousin, Dr. Homer Bessette, a physician. The next day he slept until ten, then went to the monastery of the Passionist Fathers of West Springfield for "absolute quiet and seclusion." After a few days, however, he was on the road again, traveling to see his niece, Marie Lefebvre Villeneuve, in Woonsocket, Rhode Island, and then on to his relatives in eastern Connecticut, before returning at last to the Oratory on December 3. Despite his collapse, the physician who examined him in Holyoke told the press, "I've never seen a stronger man for his years."[41]

Some members of Brother André's community complained about his long absences from the Oratory, questioning whether their famous confrere was participating as fully as he should in the life of the community to which he had vowed himself. However, Brother André had the full support of his superior, Father Clément, who had succeeded Father Roy in 1926. Clément understood that Brother André had a unique mission in spreading the devotion to St. Joseph. Doubtless Clément also realized that now that the construction of the basilica was underway, Brother André's visibility, especially in the United States, was crucial to the attraction of sufficient contributions for its completion. Brother André, conscientious in the discharge of his duties, never had any qualms about his travels. He insisted that he never went on pleasure trips and declared, "It is not forbidden to travel in order to do good to our fellow men."[42]

Chapter Eleven

St. Joseph Finds a Roof

O n November 19, 1929, the Oratory of Saint Joseph celebrated its Silver Anniversary. The Crypt Church was resplendent with roses, carnations, chrysanthemums and palms that day, as well as with the huge silver garlands that bedecked each of the windows. The first Mass of the morning, at six, was celebrated by the current superior, Father Clément. The next was said by former superior Father Louis Geoffrion, now in his nineties, and served by Brother André. Simultaneously, another former superior, Father Lecavalier, said Mass in the little chapel, served by Brother Abundius. Later that morning, Mass was sung by Archbishop Forbes of Ottawa, followed by the Solemn High Mass celebrated by Cardinal Rouleau, Archbishop of Quebec, assisted by Monsignor Gauthier and four other prelates and attended by a multitudinous congregation. Canon Harbour, Archpriest of the Montreal Cathedral, preached, pointing out the connection between the "spirit of popular piety" and the official work of the Church and how these, working together in the growth in Canada of the devotion to St. Joseph, were the perfect answer to the needs of the present day.[1] That evening a banquet was held at Notre-Dame College. Cardinal Rouleau, the speaker, congratulated the religious of Holy Cross "for having been favored by heaven in being chosen to spread the cult of St. Joseph among us." The Lord, to reward the zeal with which the brethren of Holy Cross had prepared generations of youth to be good Christians and good citizens, "chose one of them as the instrument of the diffusion of the cult of St. Joseph in our country, as the founder of His temple on the mountain." Not only did Rouleau cite Brother André, "the propagator of the cult," but also Brother Abundius, "the builder" of the original oratory.[2] The day's festivities were concluded by the veneration of the relic of St. Joseph's cloak and the nocturnal illumination of the Oratory and its surrounding grounds.

Miracles continued to be reported. That same year a woman from Hull, Quebec who had a long history of eye problems, came to the Oratory, suffering from a malignant tumor in her eye. Referring to her healing four years earlier from eczema, she said to Brother André; "You cured my hands. Now heal my eye disease as well, once and for all, if you can." When André insisted that it was not he but St. Joseph who effected cures. He asked her if she had confidence in the saint, and the woman replied, "Yes, and in you, too, because I know that St. Joseph refuses you nothing."

Brother André looked at the woman and bade her take some oil and apply it to her eyes, using the medal of St. Joseph and offering daily prayer to him. "Do that and you're going to be healed," he assured her. Immediately, she felt relief. She went to the altar of St. Joseph to pray, climbed the stairs to the Crypt on her knees and spent the rest of the day in prayer. Within weeks the cancer had disappeared entirely and in August, 1930, a year after the cure, the woman's daughter wrote the Oratory to report that her mother continued in excellent health.[3]

On March 15, 1930 the *Montreal Standard* reported the cure of a man named William Lord from Chicopee, Massachusetts, who had been speechless and without memory for four years. His complete healing was attributed by his family to the prayers of Brother André.[4]

On June 22, 1930 a little boy named Philippe Raymond of Montebello, a little town west of Montreal, fell suddenly and violently ill. It was only after two weeks that he was diagnosed as suffering from cerebrospinal meningitis. When the doctors told the mother that the best hope they could offer her was for the boy's survival as a brain-damaged invalid, she went to the Oratory to obtain some oil, which she applied to the child's head when she returned to his bedside. Despite the warning of the nurse on duty that the remedy would do no good, the mother cried out repeatedly, "St. Joseph, cure my child!" On July 16, at 11 p.m., the child — who, though senseless, had been writhing in pain — grew quiet. The next morning Madame Roland was informed that the boy had regained consciousness and was asking for her. Thinking that little Philippe was about to die, the parents went to the boy's room, sobbing. Philippe, perfectly lucid, insisted: "Don't do that. It upsets me." He seemed, in his mother's words, like someone awakening from a pleasant sleep. The boy returned to school in September and made a full recovery. "He was truly and completely cured without having taken a single remedy," his mother wrote a year later. "Thus, it's easy to see that it was St. Joseph alone who cured him." The physician also wrote to the Oratory, stating, "For my part, I am of the opinion that the child was healed by the intercession of St. Joseph, as the mother affirms."[5]

In 1929, at the age of two, Roland Cyr of the town of Chandler on the Gaspé Peninsula in eastern Quebec was a sickly baby, to say the least. Covered from head to toe with boils resistent to the skill of every physician consulted by his parents, he could neither stand nor walk. In early 1929 the parents took him to the Oratory, where he was suddenly cured of his boils, but he still could not stand. That March the parents besought St. Joseph, at the beginning of the month sacred to him, "to have our child walking by the end of the month." With "great confidence" they made a novena to the saint and went to Mass with their entire family on March 19, the saint's feast day. "We also did not fail to put on his little legs the oil of St. Joseph that had been sent us. The feast day went by without any apparent change but on the very last day of March he began to walk without any help." However the troubles of little Roland were not yet over. A year later, when he was three, he fell so ill with typhoid that the hospital to which he was hurried refused to admit him, since the doctors there were convinced that the child was beyond help. At home Roland was wracked with high fever and intestinal hemorrhages as his parents made "novena after novena." Gradually, however, as the parents wrote in a letter to the Oratory, "St. Joseph brought our child back from the portals of the tomb." By the time Roland was four, he was a happy, normal child.[6]

As for Brother André, as he approached his latter eighties, his meager frame began to suffer increasingly from the insults of nature. He was growing extremely deaf and his voice was now exceedingly feeble. The combination of these two infirmities made it difficult for him to communicate with the pilgrims who continued in great multitudes to seek his counsel, and, as was previously mentioned, this inability to understand or to be understood increased the old man's nervousness and irritability. Dr. Lamy noted frequent episodes of angina pectoris (pains resultant from a decreased blood flow to the heart), severe headache, nausea and dizziness. In 1931 Brother André was severely ill with gastritis, an inflammation of the stomach lining. Later that year he told a reporter that he was in constant pain, both in heart and stomach. Yet he refused to take the medication Dr. Lamy prescribed to quiet the stomach spasms. Although, a lifelong teetotaler, he gave in, with great reluctance, to the counsel of the physician to take a spoonful of cognac a day to stimulate his weakening heart. André found it difficult to heed Lamy's ban on climbing steps, since he often had to negotiate flights of stairs to visit the afflicted on the sick calls that were still a part of his ministry. Since the old man now weighed only ninety-five pounds, the problem was often solved by companions who could carry him up the stairs with little effort. When such help was not available, André, undaunted, insisted on toiling up the steps, in defiance of Lamy's orders and heedless of the pain that crushed his chest with the slightest exertion. Despite his worsening debility, Brother André, according to Dr. Lamy, remained, for the most part, "happy and joyful."

It was in the April of 1932 when the manager of the souvenir store adjacent to Brother André's office expressed her alarm at André's rapid deterioration to Father Emile Deguire, who was now second in command to Father Clément at the Oratory. The venerable Brother was now fainting several times a day. "I'm not lying, Father Deguire," the woman said. "I saw him fall three times in one day. He was stretched out full length between the rectory and his office."[7] Deguire noted that of late André seemed to be short of breath and in pain. He went immediately to the office to check on him and found him barely able to stand on his feet. Refusing Deguire's request that he return to his room to rest, Brother André even resisted Dr. Lamy, insisting that he did not want to disappoint the people waiting for him. By the end of the day, his lips white and his brow feverish, the ancient man was gasping for breath and spitting blood. When Joseph and Albertine Pichette arrived to take him on his evening calls, they were alarmed when he did not respond to their knock. Listening, they heard labored breathing. When they obtained permission from Father Clément to take him to their home, the sick man did not protest.

At the Pichette house, Brother André collapsed onto the bed, fully clothed. That night Madame Pichette heard him moaning, and when Joseph went in to look in on him, André insisted that the devil was strangling him, cutting off his breath. He bade Pichette massage him with the medal and the oil, and passed the rest of the night more easily.

After a few days it was apparent that Brother André was no better, so Dr. Lamy asked Father Clément to order the sick man to the hospital. At Montreal's Hotel-Dieu, Brother André was diagnosed as suffering from double pneumonia as well as stomach and liver problems caused by "poor alimentary hygiene" — or bad diet.[8] As to the prognosis, the doctors were non-commital. Lamy said, "He's eighty-seven, and at that age anything can happen."

Yet he pulled through. During his three weeks in the Hotel-Dieu, Brother André impressed his nurse, Sister Leroyer, with his patience, piety, and sense of humor. She recalled that he recommended that she commit all her troubles to paper and place them at the foot of the statue of St. Joseph in the Oratory. He did show some displeasure when the curious peeked in his room just to gawk at the "holy man," and he questioned why the hospital authorities allowed his privacy to be disturbed in this way. Sister Leroyer was concerned when the old man refused to eat the hospital food, insisting that he would accept nothing but flour soaked in water and seasoned with salt. When she protested that this was glue, André replied, "Yes, it's glue," and demanded it until it was prepared.

It was while a patient at the Montreal Hotel-Dieu that Brother André confided a strange dream or vision to his friend, Abbé Joseph Nelson Duquette, bidding him not to tell anyone about it. Like most of André's confidences, it was quickly broadcast to the world. André had seen on the wall of his room a mysterious eye, "an eye which reminds me of God's eye as shown on pious pictures. What do you think of that?" When Duquette replied, "What do you make of it?" André said, "I conclude that the closer one is to God, the more one suffers."[9] How that statement related to the eye is not clear.

Brother André returned to the Oratory late in the spring of 1932 and began seeing the sick again. Despite the infirmities of four score and seven years, his mind and personality remained intact. Father Deguire recalled, "I've noticed that usually, with old people, many defects show up and make life less tolerable for those who live with [them], it was not the same with [Brother André], who did not show any unreasonableness, but a very great union with God . . . Up to the end he kept his taste for laughter and for making innocent little jokes."[10] For instance, frail and now barely able to walk, André joked with Léopold Lussier, a firefighter who was serving as his driver for the evening, saying, "When we get back to the Oratory, I'll race you up the mountain."[11]

Shortly after his return, he received the sad tidings of the death of his great friend, Chief Gauthier, who, in his early fifties, was killed in the line of duty. On June 17, an oil tanker, the *Cymbeline,* exploded in the harbor, killing several crewmen. Gauthier and several of his men were standing on the deck of the smouldering wreck, pouring foam into the hold, when the hulk resounded with a second explosion which propelled the firefighters into the air, then dashed them down into the flaming waters. Four days later, the bodies of three firemen had been recovered, but searchers had all but given up hope of finding the remains of the Chief. Brother André was driven to the site of the explosion, and taking two medals from his pocket, he threw them into the water. It was five in the afternoon. Twelve hours later, midway between the spot where the two medals landed, Chief Gauthier's body floated to the surface. Although it was badly burned, the features were recognizable and the face bore a beautiful expression of peaceful serenity.[12]

In 1933 Brother André was back on the road, traveling alone

by train to Toronto. On the way back, he got on the wrong train, but the conductor, when he learned the identity of the venerable passenger, escorted him off at the next stop and saw to it that the stationmaster flagged down the express to Montreal. Even though it was not scheduled to stop at that location, an exception was made for Quebec's best-loved citizen.

In 1934 Brother André again traveled to the States, where another remarkable cure was reported. This time it concerned Stephen Johnson, brother-in-law of André's nephew Henry Bessette. On his visit to Connecticut, Brother André found Johnson critically ill with cirrhosis of the liver. He had been sick for more than six months and was now in a coma, swollen from head to toe, with his doctor predicting that he could not last the night. Brother André rubbed his head with the St. Joseph medal and asked the family to pray to St. Joseph. That very day Johnson began to show some improvement, and, over a period of several months, slowly regained his health. Less than two years later, Dr. Gorcha, his physician, admitted that Johnson was "better than ever."[13]

By now nearly all of Brother André's contemporaries had been gathered to their fathers. Father Roy, the former superior, died in the infirmary at the College of St.-Laurent, in March, 1934, at the age of eighty-three. The next month Father Geoffrion quit the world at the age of ninety-seven, declaring, "God has already been too good to me! Look how many years he put up with me."[14] Brother André outlived all his immediate family. Léocadie had died suddenly, at the age of eighty, in the house of her daughter Clothilde Snow on January 5, 1916. Isaïe, long a resident of Vermont, went to be with his Lord in 1920, at eighty-three. Napoleon died at ninety in Sterling, Connecticut on February 2, 1928, followed exactly one year later by Claude, who was eighty-seven. That left only Alphonsine, who, at eighty-seven, was gravely ill and in great suffering with heart and kidney problems in her Natick, Rhode Island home when Brother André visited her on the same trip in which he ministered to Stephen Johnson. She begged him, "Heal me! You know how much I'm suffering. You cure everybody and yet you will not do anything for me!" André bade her resign herself to suffering and death. "It is not I who heal," he said, "it is St. Joseph. But, suffer and accept everything for God's sake, for it is better for us to suffer before death."[15] On October 27, 1934, Alphonsine was finally released from her bodily torments.

That same year Father Clément stepped down as superior of the community, although he continued to be responsible for the services of worship and for receiving groups of pilgrims. Like Father Geoffrion, Brother Abundius, and several other senior members of the community, Father Clément was considered a saint by many, and when Brother André was absent, many pilgrims asked him to rub them with the St. Joseph medal. Several miracles of healing were in this way attributed to him. In later years there had been some misunderstanding between André and Clément. A religious familiar with the situation said that as Brother André grew old and weak, Father Clément "tried to save him from himself."[16] For instance, one day Father Clément was trying to explain one of the old man's bursts of pique to a bewildered and offended pilgrim. In describing how Brother André was old, weak, and deaf, he made a gesture which Brother André observed and at which he took offense. André was convinced that the superior was telling people that he was senile, and he became upset.[17] One of the problems with Father Clément, according to one witness, was that the superior "couldn't give orders"[18] and Brother André could not understand what he wanted. Nevertheless, Father Cousineau, who became superior in 1936, had no doubt that "Brother André loved Father Clément and Father Clément loved him."[19]

Father Clément was replaced by Father Albert Charron, who has been described as cold and aloof. He accepted the "obedience" as the superior of the Oratory only until the Superior General of the Order could find someone "more suitable." Most people who knew him well felt that Father Charron "had a problem" with Brother André's style of ministry and had no aptitude or interest in raising money.

This was not a happy time for Brother André. He felt useless. To a lay friend he confessed that no one consulted him about the basilica anymore. He was deeply hurt when he overheard one young religious remark to another, "Don't ask Brother André about it. He's an old fool. He's irrational." Convinced that he was about to be transferred from the Oratory to a Holy Cross house in New Brunswick, André remarked to one of his friends: "I shall be satisfied, so long as I am of some use to the Congregation. Perhaps God wants that sacrifice of me before I die."[20]

In the summer of 1935 Brother André was taking a rest at the home of his cousin, Ubald Bessette, a physician in the little village of Rawdon, north of Montreal. Some years before, Dr. Bessette attributed his recovery from tuberculosis of the tongue to the prayers of his cousin. Sitting at table with the family and enjoying the company of the little children, Brother André seemed happy. But suddenly, right there at the dinner table, he collapsed into unconsciousness. The doctor brought him around with an injection, but it was the beginning of the end. The old man was never the same again. After his return to the Oratory, André gave up his regular office hours, although he still saw visitors occasionally and still made sick calls when he felt up to it. During the ensuing months he spent comparatively little time at the Oratory and many days at the home of the Pichettes. Father Charron approved of this arrangement, believing that only away from the crowds of the Oratory could a man of ninety obtain the peace required to keep body and soul together. Nonetheless there were some complaints by certain religious that Brother André's lengthy absences were a violation of the spirit of the Rule of Holy Cross.

During the mid-1930s Canada, like the rest of the world, was in the midst of a severe economic depression. As demand fell for Canadian agricultural products, lumber and minerals, thousands of factories, stores and mines closed. Farmers were devastated not only by rapidly falling grain prices, but by the same drought, in the Prairie Provinces, that turned the American Midwest into a "Dust Bowl." Prime Minister Richard Bennett, called "Iron Heel" because of his tough position against labor disturbances, established over two hundred camps for single, unemployed men and committed government funds to aid the needy. Nevertheless, conditions remained bad. The few visitors whom Brother André saw asked him whether the Depression would end soon. "No!" he declared. "God is angry because people do not pray. The Depression is meant to teach the world a lesson. God is forgotten and many blaspheme against Providence and do not pray. Churches are empty of worshippers. Economic conditions will change only when people pray more."[21] To a ruined millionaire from New York who threatened to commit suicide by jumping off a bridge, André said, "If you do, tell me and I'll help you sink. You were interested in the golden calf and God took it away from you. Pray that He will help you bear the test. Money is nothing. You should worry about your soul." When he had gone, André remarked to a companion, "People who have lost money seem more discouraged than those who are paralyzed or have cancer."[22]

In 1936, Brother André told a reporter that he had never heard of fascism, of Hitler, Mussolini, or even Franklin Roosevelt. Yet he knew about communism and was disturbed by its rapid growth. Aware of the civil war raging in Spain, he feared that it would end in a victory for the communists. When he learned that a chapter of the Communist Party had been opened in Montreal, he expressed a desire to be put to death by the communists in order to effect their salvation. "I wouldn't care if they put me to death by cutting me to pieces, provided the people do not suffer."[23]

The only communist Brother André ever met was a dying man whom he visited at the request of a priest-friend. When André and the priest appeared at the door of the communist's home, the wife warned, "If you go in, my husband will knock you down." André decided to take the risk and was insulted by the invalid: "Get out: I'm still strong enough to throw you out the window!"

"That would be funny!" retorted Brother André. "That's never happened to me before." Having failed to break the ice with that remark, André grew serious and told the communist, "I'm asking St. Joseph the special favor of your healing in order to obtain your conversion." When the sick man insisted that he was not interested, André, with nothing more to say, left discouraged. "What can I do?" he shrugged.[24]

In the spring of 1936 Brother André made his usual trip to New York State. On April 22, at the rectory of St. Clement's Church in Saratoga, he met police sergeant Edward J. Kelley, who had been unable to work for two months because of an arthritic foot. André announced, "The foot is all right now. It doesn't pain anymore."

"I tried it then by stepping lightly on the foot," reported

Kelley. "It didn't hurt. The Brother told me, 'Stamp hard with the foot.' I did. The soreness was gone and I walked as well as any man." A year later Sgt. Kelley was still pain-free.[25]

When he returned to Montreal, Brother André found a crisis in the making. It had been several years since any work had been done on the basilica. Because of the Depression, donations had virtually dried up. Architects now warned that if the structure remained in its unfinished condition it would soon sustain such damage from the weather that it would have to be torn down and rebuilt from scratch — that is, if it were rebuilt at all. The Oratory Council was now unable to pay its creditors. The chief creditor, the Silver Granite Company, consented to delay the maturity of the debt (which was supposed to be paid off by May, 1935) for two years and three months, without interest. Even so, the members of the Council realized that they would still have to find the means to pay by August, 1937 if they wanted to avoid declaring bankruptcy. Moreover, the mere payment of this debt would do nothing to ensure that the basilica would be finished. The Council needed to obtain a loan of at least $1.2 million. This the members judged a hopeless proposition. In their spring meeting, the Council concluded, "Financially speaking, it is impossible to continue the work."[26]

When Brother André learned of the situation, he rather ineffectually suggested that the structure be covered by a tarpaulin to minimize damage from the elements. He was told that this would not work. A mood of deep pessimism spread among the members of the Council as well as all those who for so many years had been following the progress of the plans for the basilica.

Father Charron felt the heat of the crisis. He had never considered himself gifted in fund raising and he had never wanted to take responsibility for the basilica. Now he found himself blamed for the apparent collapse of the project. Father James W. Donohue, Superior General of the Order, wrote him that the present condition of the Oratory was "the cause of much just criticism of you and me."[27] He wrote, "I am praying daily that God will help you to make important changes in the organization of the Oratory."[28] By the time the General Chapter met in early July, nearly everyone agreed with what Father Charron had insisted upon when he was appointed superior two years earlier — that he was not the man for the job. Even Brother André, uncharacteristically, asked the Pichettes to pray that there might be a change of superiors. At the General Chapter, Charron tendered his resignation as superior. It was accepted and he was promoted to the position of Father Provincial, supervising all the institutions connected with the order in the Montreal vicinity. The new superior of the Oratory was the dynamic, forty-one-year-old Father Albert Cousineau, who, as Rector of the College of St.-Laurent, had been noted for his skill as an organizer, administrator and businessman, as well as for his deep and sincere piety.

As soon as he took up residence at the Oratory, Father Cousineau sent for Brother André, who was staying with the Pichettes. He was concerned about the "comments" regarding the "absences of Brother André." Cousineau talked to the old man about his long ministry, about his hopes for the Oratory, as well as his sorrows and frustrations. He asked André "to make sure of his presence at the Oratory on certain days." Fully accepting the request of the superior, André told him that he wished to return to live full-time at the Rectory. "I didn't demand that much," recalled Cousineau. "Brother André was now more than ninety years old."[29] It was agreed that Brother André would hold office hours twice a week. After talking to Father Cousineau, Brother André, who in recent months had felt ignored and irrelevant and had appeared especially depressed and grumpy, now seemed his old self.

With the reopening of the Bureau for a few hours each week that summer, came more reports of supernatural favors. Father Bergeron, who was living at the rectory during the summer of 1936, recalled more than a half century later how, on numerous occasions, he was disturbed, while trying to study, by cries of "Miracle! Miracle!" which wafted through the open windows from lips of exulting throngs outside.

In August Brother André was again in the States. In Boston he told a reporter for the *Evening American:* "Always be prepared to die. We think least of the most important thing that is to happen to us. Death is all around us. It may happen at any moment. We should be ready for it." Asked about his opinion of America, he replied; "The United States — it is ever in my prayers. Always I pray for all in America. She must have even more faith. Throughout the world there is unrest today. There is unhappiness. The blame, it is the people's. They have little faith. Faith does not cure, but with the help of God and St. Joseph, faith helps to cure what is wrong with the world. When chaos prevails in the world, as it does today, we, each one of us, are to blame. We are lacking in faith."[30]

Father Cousineau began his tenure as superior by authorizing the construction of a Way of the Cross on the mountainside next to the basilica. This was a project long desired by Brother André, but one of which in later years the old man had almost come to despair. On November 2 Cousineau called a meeting of the Council of the Oratory. Architect Viau was present and warned that the frosts of another winter were likely to damage the structure irreparably. The members of the Council were at a loss as to how to solve the financial crisis. It was then that Brother André spoke. He suggested that the community make a procession, carrying a statue of St. Joseph to the open walls of the unfinished basilica. "Once he is placed there in the snow and cold, if St. Joseph wants to be covered, he will see to it."[31]

And so, on November 4, just two days after the meeting of the Council, the religious connected with the Oratory set out to climb the steep, winding, rubble-strewn mountain path that led to the unfinished basilica. Father Cousineau prayed the Rosary, with the others responding. Father Charron, who as Provincial still lived at the rectory, carried a large plaster statue of St. Joseph (obtained from the gift shop) that was to be placed within the walls. Leaning on the arm of Brother Placide, Brother André began the ascent, but could walk only part of the way to the top. The procession halted at the walls of the church, and, on the spot where plans called for the installation of a pipe organ, the statue was placed "as a permanent symbol of supplication to God." That night, one of Brother André's confreres heard him groaning and rushed into his room to find him speechless, clutching his throat. When he recovered his voice, the old man said, "Perhaps I dreamed it, but my throat hurts terribly. I think the devil was choking me. I guess he doesn't want a roof on the basilica. But I said to him, 'Don't you think one might desire death so that one might go to see the Good God?' That ended it. He fled."[32]

On November 6 Father Cousineau began negotiations with several financial institutions in hopes of obtaining a loan. In the meantime Brother André decided that it was time for another trip to the States. He wanted to go to New York City to drop in on John D. Rockefeller, Sr., the billionaire oilman, several years his senior, who was noted (at least in recent years) for his generous gifts to charitable causes. And so in mid-November he set out by car for New York with one of his faithful companions. He seemed strong and cheerful during the three days he spent with his friends, the pious spinster Ryan sisters of West 60th Street in Manhattan and their aged father. Stopped in a traffic gridlock on Fifth Avenue, Brother André responded to Miss Mary who asked him how he liked the city, "It's much too slow for me!"[33] One night he partook, uncharacteristically, of a large piece of steak and a dessert. Although he was unable to arrange a meeting with John D., the Rockefeller Foundation gave him a "generous" check for the basilica.

From New York, Brother André headed north to visit his relatives. In West Warwick, Rhode Island, he stayed at the home of Aurore Lawrence. "He just visited with me a short time," she recalled many years later. "He was old, but not feeble. He was very alert."[34] Jules Cayer, with whom he stayed in New Bedford, recalled, "He was very, *very* feeble. He was so feeble he hesitated to come up the stairs. I offered to carry him up. He was insulted! 'I can get up myself,' he said, and he did, but with very, very great difficulty."[35] Brother André's last stop was at Woonsocket, Rhode Island, where he stayed several days with the Guerin family, receiving three to four hundred visitors a day! At night, however, Mrs. Guerin heard him groaning in pain. After several days, when he awoke, he declared, "I'm sick. We've got to get back to Montreal." Handing out medals and telling well-wishers, "These are the last medals I'm ever going to give,"[36] he left the States for the last time.

By December, Father Cousineau had met with success and obtained loans from several financial institutions, loans which amounted to the $1.2 million that was necessary to save the Oratory. The loans had to be approved by the General Council of the Order, and they were, on December 16. The next day Cousineau set out to obtain the approval of acting Archbishop

Gauthier, and asked Brother André to pray for his success. "Do you have a St. Joseph medal?" he was asked. "No, Brother," he replied. Handing him a medal, André told him: "Well, here is one to keep in your hand all through your interview with Monsignor Gauthier. And if you can, slip it in his desk."[37]

Gauthier approved the loans, and Cousineau moved quickly to get the construction started again. He obtained the services of the celebrated church architect, Dom Paul Bellot, a French Benedictine, who decided, instead of the original plans for an ornate, baroque interior, to opt for a clean, stark, modernistic style. Bellot came to the Oratory and conferred with Brother André on the change of plans. The old man said that he was pleased with them.[38]

Just before Christmas, Brother André was talking to Father Clément. Only in his late fifties, the former superior had been forced to relinquish his remaining responsibilities at the Oratory, worn out (in the words of those who would write his obituary a few years later) by the "misery and excruciating pain" of "an insidious inward disease" which he bore "in silence with a beautiful smile." On this occasion, Father Clément was jubilant. "Brother André," he told his friend, "you were right in saying you would live to see your basilica."

"I never said I would live to see it *finished*," André corrected him. When Clément asked if he would like to see the structure complete in his lifetime, the Brother replied, "I put myself completely in God's hands."[39]

As days went by Brother was even more negative about the possibility of living to see the church complete. "It's certain that the basilica will be continued," he remarked. "I am useless now. It's time for me to go. I've done all I had to do. The work has no need of me now."[40]

Chapter Twelve

My Work is Done

The end was near at hand. Brother André managed to see pilgrims for a few hours on Wednesdays and Sundays, but each session, he confided, proved to be "another day in purgatory." Constantly dizzy and nauseated, he vomited blood and suffered excruciating pains in the chest. His abdomen was swollen, his bowels locked, his living failing. Yet he never complained, nor even showed the slightest interest in his condition.

Christmas Eve he was well enough to visit some patients in a Montreal hospital and attend most of three services at the Oratory that night. Midway through the third he became so dizzy that he had to be helped to his room. Later that night Father Clément came in to see him and found him lying fully clad upon his bed, with an expression of joy so sublime that the former superior was amazed. Brother André declared that he was happy because, within a year or two, Masses would be celebrated in the new basilica.

"And you will be there!" insisted Clément.

Brother André shook his head and said calmly that this would be his last Christmas "here below." He then expressed his concern for Pope Pius XI, who was then reported gravely ill. "The Pope will not die," he said. "It is I who will die in his place."

"We need your help," said Clément, almost pleading.

"My work is done. And besides, if you can do things here, just think of how much you can do in heaven."[1]

The next day Brother André went to dinner with the Claudes and told them that this would "probably" be his last Christmas on earth. When Claude said that the Oratory needed him, André responded as he had to the similar remark by Father Clément: "If you can do good on earth, you can accomplish far more in heaven." As on the night before, Brother André spoke of the Pope's illness. "The life of the Pope is precious and important for the good of the Church. The life of Brother André has no importance. I am already very old and I would be ready to disappear very soon to prolong the life of the Pope."[2]

December 26, at the home of Joseph and Albertine Pichette, Brother André, rising from the table, commented, "That's strange. I feel a pain in my legs that I've never had." Nevertheless he went on a hospital call, to see the stepfather of Father Cousineau. As Pichette drove him back to the Oratory, they passed the little old-fashioned St.-Laurent Hospital in the suburb of that name. Brother André commented on how lovely the nursing sisters there were to the patients, adding, "What a beautiful place to go to die."[3]

He returned to his room in the rectory that evening, never again to arise on his own power from his bed. Brother Placide was assigned to care for him. The sick man asked to be rubbed with the St. Joseph medal, but the ministrations had no effect on the pains in his chest and abdomen.

On the last day of 1936 Father Cousineau conferred with Dr. Lamy. The physician thought that Brother André had suffered a mild heart attack, but did not believe that death was necessarily imminent, although he acknowledged the possibility that his ninety-one-year-old patient could go at any time. Believing, however, that hospitalization was now appropriate, Lamy went to Brother André and suggested admission to the large modern Montreal Hotel-Dieu. Making no objection to the idea of going to a hospital, Brother André asked if, instead of the Montreal Hotel-Dieu, he might go to the Hospital of St.-Laurent. Lamy agreed, and at 8:30 that night, wrapped in blankets and only his weathered face visible, Brother André was placed in an ambulance. "I look like someone going to the North Pole," he remarked to Brother Placide, who accompanied him. During the course of the ride, complaining of suffocation, André asked in vain to be released from the straps by which he was bound to his stretcher.

The Hospital of St.-Laurent, run by the Sisters of Hope, was an ancient facility that looked like a big frame house. Sister Marie-Camille Fortin, one of the nurses assigned to Brother André, was ordered to admit "no visitors, with rare exeptions."[4] She was told that Brother André was being admitted because his stomach could no longer retain food and because he was run down.

Although Sister Marie-Camille later said that she and the other nurses hoped that Brother André would recover, they found him almost totally helpless. Nauseated to the point that he required a basin because of continual vomiting, André could tolerate nothing in the way of nourishment except a teaspoon of water mixed with cognac every five or six hours. The hospital staff tried in vain to prepare food that the old man's stomach would hold. Aware of their consternation, Brother André suggested to the nurses (who prepared the meals), "Boil some water, mix a little flour and salt, then pour it in the boiling water and stir to form a little gruel." The first time Sister Marie-Camille fixed this, she used cornstarch instead of flour, thinking to make it more palatable. When André threw it up, he chided, "Sister, you didn't put flour in it." So the Sister made a gruel using flour instead of cornstarch, and this time Brother André was able to retain the nourishment.[5]

When it came time to bathe the patient, Sister Marie-Camille was uneasy, aware of Brother André's reputation for modesty. Nervously she told him, "Brother, I must give you your bath." André made no objection, and she and another nurse proceeded to sponge bathe his entire body. The patient said nothing about his own embarrassment, but, expressing concern for the sensibilities of the nurses, commented, "This is very humiliating for you."[6]

New Year's Day Father Cousineau found him in great pain. "Yes, I'm suffering," André admitted, "but I thank God for according me the grace of suffering, since I have so great a need for it. One doesn't think about death enough." He continued in this vein, saying, "Sickness is a good thing, because it helps us reflect on our past life and make reparations through penitence and through suffering." Finally he bade the superior, "I have something to ask you. Pray for my conversion."[7]

On the morning of January 2 there was a turn for the worse as Brother André experienced increasing pain and numbness on his left side. It was determined that he was suffering from hemorrhaging in his brain — a stroke. Throughout the day the paralysis slowly spread over the affected side, although his reason and his ability to speak remained intact. The doctors also noted signs of failing kidney function. The pain was so intense that morphine was administered, and the injection brought relief for about an hour. But when he realized that he had been given a pain-killer, Brother André was deeply distressed and insisted, "Do not give me drugs."[8] He told Sister Marie-Camille, "I have more faith in prayers than in pills,"[9] and bade her rub him with the St. Joseph medal. There was no relief. "Why don't you ask St. Joseph to heal you?" she asked. "I can do nothing," he replied.[10] Still refusing pain medication, he moaned, from time to time, "My God, how I suffer!" After one "violent attack of pain," he declared, "The Great Almighty is coming!"[11] He also remarked, "Heaven is so beautiful that it is worth all the trouble with which one prepares for it."[12]

Brother André continued to be concerned about the health of the Pope (who would survive another two years). He insisted that the death of Pius XI would prove "a disaster" for the Church. "Does our Holy Father suffer much? . . . My hand is swollen . . . I am paralyzed . . . just like the Pope." Still troubled about the Spanish Civil War, he offered his life "for bloodstained Spain."[13]

Even so, Brother André retained his sense of humor. When he rang the buzzer to summon a nurse, he would frequently apologize, "It's your old nuisance calling you again." He joked about his paralyzed arm, in which he suffered terrible pains, saying, "My arm is a communist. It doesn't like me and makes me suffer, cruel thing!"[14] Sister Marie-Camille was struck by the fact that her patient never complained and never seemed to worry. Once, when she was feeding him, André spoke to Marie-Camille at some length. "You have a vocation of patience," he remarked. "Not like yours. I couldn't force myself to answer so many people," she replied.

To this André responded, "If people would tell us right away what they want, it would be less tiring, but, anyway, there is so much misery!"[15] Continuing, he went on to recall incidents from the past, such as the healing of Pichette's thumb, which he remembered thus: "One of my good friends had a pain in his thumb. At first he saw a charlatan, then a doctor, and finally he went to pray at the Oratory and to see Brother André, who told him, 'The charlatan took your dollars, the doctor your pains, and now St. Joseph is going to heal you.' "[16] Speaking of the Oratory, he declared: "It will go forward. The temple of St. Joseph will be completed." Reliving his ministry once more, he told the sister; "What misery there is in the world! I was in a position to know! I had to be lawyer, doctor, priest. But the Good God helped. How powerful He is!"[17]

On the fourth of January, André remarked to his nurse, "How good God is! How beautiful! How powerful! He must indeed be beautiful, since the soul, which is but a ray of His beauty, is so lovely."[18]

Towards midnight on the fourth, the pain grew yet more atrocious and Brother André murmured, "Mary, sweet mother, mother of my sweet Saviour, be merciful to me and help me!"[19] Early on the morning of the fifth, he tried to say something, but all that could be made out was, "St. Joseph." Towards dawn he was heard to moan, "Oh, my God, how it hurts! Oh, I suffer!"[20]

By now it was apparent that the end of Brother André's earthly pilgrimage was close at hand. At eight on the morning of the fifth, Father Charron, in the presence of other members of the community, administered the Last Rites to the invalid, who was now comatose. That day newspapers throughout the world proclaimed the imminent demise of Montreal's "Miracle Man." The *Washington Post,* for example, ran headlines: "Canadian Miracle Shrine Guardian is Believed Dying," and reported: "Brother André, Miracle Man of Montreal and Guardian of the New World's most revered shrine, where thousands believe that they have received divine cures, lay near death today."

Hospital authorities, now that the "Miracle Man" was unconscious, allowed the public into the white-washed little room where the old man lay in his death agony. Hundreds of people

— according to Sister Marie-Camille, as many as a thousand — filed through the room, staring at the wasted form and touching the hands and feet with medals, crucifixes, and other religious articles. Some people begged the comatose man, "Good Brother André, when you are in heaven, remember me!"[20]

By 11:30 that evening, there was no one in the room but members of his community, who were reciting the Litany for the Dying. As they did so, the moaning ceased and the rattling breath grew more regular. At ten minutes before one on the morning of the sixth of January, 1937 — the Feast of the Epiphany — Brother André, with an expression of peace and calm on his face, drew up his feet, yawned, and sagged. The two doctors in attendance listened for a heartbeat and declared him dead of a cerebral hemorrhage brought on by arteriosclerosis.

Once more the hospital was opened to passersby as thousands of the faithful were allowed to file past the corpse as it lay on its deathbed. Again rosaries and crosses were brought in contact with the now lifeless form. At 7:30 the funeral directors arrived to take measurements for a wooden coffin. "Out of respect" the body was not embalmed, but Doctors Lamy and Riopelle decided to remove the heart so that it could be venerated as a relic. So they opened the chest, removed the organ, washed it, placed it in a bottle of alcohol, and placed the bottle in the office of the hospital superintendent. While the body was still open, Lamy took pieces of cloth and drenched them in Brother André's blood to give to the nurses who had cared for him. After a death mask was made, the body was returned to St. Joseph's Oratory, while bells all over Montreal tolled the passing of the beloved Miracle Man.

Accompanied by scores of clergy and laypersons, the coffin was moved back to the Oratory, where it was placed in the Votive Chapel of the Oratory, behind the Crypt Church. There the assemblage chanted the "Magnificat": "My soul doth magnify the Lord, and my spirit hath rejoiced in God my Saviour . . ."

Brother André had died on a Wednesday. All day and all night Thursday and Friday, despite snow and ice, a continuous procession of the faithful streamed by the open wood coffin. From all corners of the North American continent people were

195

arriving by car, train and plane, to wait in the biting cold for hours for the opportunity to gaze at the face of the beloved wonder-worker, now slumbering in death, and to touch his form with medals and beads.

Saturday, January 9, a crowd of thousands followed the coffin in a freezing rain to the Montreal Cathedral, many slipping and sliding during the three-mile trek. After the celebration of a Requiem Mass, multitudes followed the coffin as it was borne back to Mount Royal. The weather was now so brutal that people stumbled in the slashing icy downpour and by the score went crashing to the glazed pavement. The throng, which had numbered in the thousands when the coffin left the Cathedral, had been reduced to little more than a hundred by the time the earthly remains of Brother André were placed in the vestibule of the College of Notre-Dame, on the spot where his doorkeeper's lodge had stood.

A few hours later, the body was conveyed across the street and again laid out in state at the Oratory. The procession of faithful grew and grew until on Sunday it looked to Father Bergeron as if "the mountain were being assaulted. All cars in Montreal seemed to have but one destination, the Oratory. Railway trains from all parts of Canada and the United States were bringing thousands who came to see for the last time the Apostle of St. Joseph. In no time, there were nearly a hundred thousand on the church grounds. The large esplanade was transformed into a field of closely-packed human beings resembling a field of thickly-sown wheat; the mountainside had become a forest of sheaves, thick-set and upright, bound together in one sheaf."[21]

For twenty-four hours a day, until Tuesday, people waited up to six hours for the privilege of viewing the remains of Brother André. One hundred and twenty people a minute filed by the coffin, two by two. Between Monday noon and Tuesday morning more than 300,000 persons passed by the bier. Brother Placide wrote, "At the foot of the hill the automobiles rumbled all night like the thunder of a steel mill. The trolley cars kept running as close together as they could, bringing thousands and thousands of people to the gates, and . . . the grounds of the Oratory were filled to overflowing. The regular trolleys were insufficient and the tramway company recalled ancient wrecks from years of retirement and pressed them into service."[22]

Despite the fact that Brother André's body had not been embalmed and it was now nearly a week since his death, there was neither odor nor sign of decomposition. Cousineau noted that the face looked "calm and serene, its ascetic features seemingly accentuated."[23] A physician who examined the body at this time was amazed that the hands and feet were still supple.

Cardinal Villeneuve, Archbishop of Quebec, arrived Monday night and tried to make his way through the crowds to view the body, but the crush of the throng made it impossible. He commented to Father Cousineau, "I have often read in the lives of the saints that so great a concourse of people came to view their remains that the high prelates could not get near them. I always thought it was a pious exaggeration, but yesterday evening it was proved to me to be authentic."[24]

Cures were reported. One of them concerned a little boy named Arthur Ducherme, whose arm was paralyzed as the result of an accident. When the boy's mother touched Brother André's body with the child's useless arm, the boy immediately regained sensation and mobility. Because the hand remained stiff, it was questioned whether the grace constituted a real miracle. To the child and his mother, the improvement in his condition constituted a divine favor wrought through Brother André.

Just before the funeral on Tuesday, the coffin was carried outdoors into the midst of the sea of humanity thronging the hillside. Then it was returned to the Oratory and placed before the altar in the church. The Requiem Mass — attended by the Mayor of Montreal, the Canadian Secretary of State and the Prime Minister of the Province of Quebec, Maurice Duplessis (a former pupil at Notre-Dame) — was sung by Bishop Eugene Limoges. The sermon was preached by Cardinal Villeneuve, who said:

> Whatever be the reputation of her children for virtue, the Church requires that, at their funeral services, prayers be said and supplications be made for the human frailties in their lives. She forbids us to anticipate the judgment which she reserves to herself, upon the heroicity of their

virtues and the certainty of their entrance into heaven. With all respect to Holy Church, however, we may sa̱ that today we celebrate the feast of humility.

On the tomb which guards the mortal remains of this virtuous Apostle of Saint Joseph, Brother André, we may read these three words, *'Pauper, Servus, Humilis.'* *Pauper,* that is to say, 'poor,' the religious that we so often came to see at the Oratory; *Servus,* 'servant,' the co-adjutor brother, the last in rank in his community; *Humilis,* so little in his own eyes, without any suspicion of the throngs his death would bring together.

The Cardinal continued, comparing Brother André to St. Joseph and holding up the little doorkeeper as an embodiment of the doctrine of humility. He closed, bidding worshippers to:

look to the life beyond and think of the seal that the Lord puts on the life of the humble. No prince of the Church or of the State could have a funeral such as this, which affects the inmost sentiments of the heart, as we can testify today. Remember then Brother André's words and hear him repeating them to us still: *Ite ad Joseph* [Go to Joseph].[25]

Chapter Thirteen

Blessed Brother André

T here are three steps on the road to sainthood. There is first a study of the life, which, if favorably concluded, leads to the conferral of the title "Venerable." The second involves a study of the reputation for miracles and may result in "beatification," or the bestowal of the title "Blessed." The third step further examines the reputation for miracles, and, if this phase is brought to a favorable conclusion, the subject is canonized, or proclaimed a saint. Beatification authorizes public veneration on a local level, with a Mass and an Office of Prayer in the name of the person so honored. Canonization permits such observances on a world-wide level.

Brother André was not long in his tomb when the "process" was begun which would result in his beatification within less than a half-century. Despite the occasional criticisms to which Brother André had been subjected over the years by certain members of the community, not a single objection was voiced to Father Cousineau concerning the introduction of "The Cause of Brother André." The very year of André's death, Father Bergeron was called upon to document the Brother's life and work in a biography. That same year Monsignor Gauthier ordered a "preliminary inquiry" into the possibilities of beatification. Three years later, Monsignor Joseph Charbonneau, who had succeeded Gauthier as Archbishop of Montreal, set up a board known as a "Tribunal" to interrogate witnesses. Over the next decade, in accordance with canonical procedure, the Archdiocese of Montreal held three "trials" in which the Tribunal sought to determine whether André had practiced "to a heroic degree" the virtues considered essential for beatification.

The first trial was the Trial of Writings, which was extremely brief, since the literary remains of Brother André consisted of three brief and practically inconsequential letters dictated to family in the 1870s. During the "Informative Trial" dozens of witnesses were questioned about André's virtues, and the purpose of the "Non-Cult Trial" was to ascertain that people were not anticipating the judgment of the Church by offering public devotions to Brother André.

Perhaps the most crucial of the trials was the Informative Trial, in which André's friends and associates were questioned closely about their knowledge of his life. It was the duty of the Tribunal not only to glean all the positive information on his life and character, but to make careful inquiry concerning any activities or characteristics that might disqualify him for further consideration for the highest honors of the Church. The "Devil's Advocate," the official whose duty it was to raise objections, was most concerned with the complaints, sometimes voiced against Brother André in his day, that through his frequent and lengthy trips, the founder of the Oratory had not been as faithful to the life of his community as he might have been. In connection with this endeavor, the testimony of Brother André's confreres was unanimous that the frequent trips, all authorized by his superiors, were not taken for pleasure, but as the result of the unusual ministry to which God had called him. There were the inevitable questions about possible breaches of the vows of poverty, chastity, and obedience, and concern raised about the Brother's celebrated temper. But after several years of study, the Archdiocese concluded that the "Cause for Brother André" was ready to be submitted to the Vatican.

In 1955 the printed record of the archdiocesan investigations was submitted to the Sacred Congregation of Rites. This committee in the Vatican examines its cases in the order in which it receives them, and since there were twenty-one cases ahead of that of Brother André, it was three years before any further action was taken. Then, in April, 1958 the Congregation took up the case, to decide whether the Cause for Brother André was to be dropped or recommended for further study. After three years, in November, 1960, the cardinals of the Congregation of Rites recommended to the Pope that the Cause be approved for further consideration. So, with the "placet" seal of John XXIII, the Cause was officially introduced to "Court." Whereas trials had been held by the Archdiocese of Montreal in the 1940s, a new series of Apostolic Trials began in Vatican City, in which the members of the Congregation of Rites combed through the same material that had been studied in Canada. They even arranged for interviews with the survivors of the group of witnesses who had testified two decades earlier.

As part of the Apostolic Trials, the tomb of Brother André was opened. The Code of Canon Law specifies that as a part of the process of beatification, the purported grave of any "Servant of God" be opened and the remains identified. The reason for this is probably the prevention of the traffic in false relics which made the Church appear ridiculous in the Middle Ages. And so, in December, 1963, in the presence of fifty witnesses, the bones of Brother André were retrieved and examined. As the blackened, mummified body was removed from the rotted coffin, the top part of the skull fell off onto the floor, leaving only the lower jaw attached to the rest of the mummy. Dr. Jean-Marie Rossel, who, along with the aging Dr. Lamy conducted the examination, expressed his amazement at the excellent state of preservation of an unembalmed corpse that had lain entombed for more than a quarter century:

> Normally I would have expected to find only a few scattered bones on the bottom of the casket, but the fact is that we actually found ourselves in the presence of a corpse literally mummified, which is to say that the skin, having dried up and hardened, completely covered the skeleton; and though the corpse had lost most of its internal organs through dehydration and hardly weighed a dozen pounds, the form of the body was perfectly recognizable. The head alone, the soft parts of which had been destroyed, was reduced to the skeleton state.

The excellent state of preservation in which the bones of

Brother André were found was attributed by Dr. Roussel not so much to miracle as to the method of interment, which allowed only warm, dry air to reach the cadaver, causing it to shrivel rather than rot. The investigators also examined the heart of Brother André, which had been on display in a glass case in the Oratory Museum. This, like the corpse, was declared authentic. After the examinaion, the heart was returned to the display case and the bones to the sarcophagus.[2]

Over the next year a volume called the *Positio*, containing the records of all the proceedings, was prepared and submitted to the sacred congregation of Rites, which in turn, gave copies of it to nine judges, each of whom was to study the case independently, over a period of nine months and subsequently prepare a "brief" of about 100 pages.

In the meantime the bishops of Canada formally requested Pope Paul VI to grant the Cause of Brother André a dispensation from the ecclesiastical law that specifies a fifty-year interval between the death of a "Servant of God" and the commencement of the final study of virtues. Two months later, on June 11, 1977, the Pope granted the dispensation.

On December 20 of the same year, the briefs prepared by the nine judges were turned over by the Congregation of Rites to the Congregation for the Causes of Saints. The judges, independently, had all reached a positive decision. "Not a single reservation was expressed."[3]

On February 21, 1978 the cardinals of the congregation for the Causes of Saints voted to ratify the decision of the judges. On April 13, Pope Paul voted to ratify the decision of the Congregation and, two months later, he read a formal "decree on the heroicity of the virtues of Brother André" and declared him "Venerable," declaring that the "Servant of God" had "practiced all the virtues in heroic degree."[4]

Before a "Venerable" Servant of God can be beatified, the Church must certify at least one genuine miracle. *The New Catholic Encyclopedia* states that miracles "constitute an unequivocal proof of the approval given by God to the person and life of the future *beatus* or saint." Father Bernard Lafreniére, Vice-Postulator for the Cause of Brother André, stated in 1987: "A miracle is a sign of the presence of God. The Church never tries to prove the existence of a miracle as such.

She seeks only to prove a *reputation* of miracles. That is, the Church seeks to confirm that a particular community of the faithful believes that the miraculous has occurred in answer to prayer. In order to be declared miraculous by the Church, a healing (which is the easiest type of miracle to study and document) must be beyond the laws of nature and a sign from the Lord.[5]

In seeking a certifiable miracle, Church authorities consider instances of recovery from serious illness or injury which involve either the cure of a complaint judged incurable by medical science, or the disappearance — more rapid than scientifically explicable — of a potentially curable condition. Meticulously documented cases of this nature are given, individually, to two medical experts for consideration. Studying the case *independently,* both must concur that the cure was extraordinary and inexplicable scientifically, if the case is to receive further consideration. If only one of the doctors is convinced that the case cannot be scientifically explained, the matter is dropped. If both agree that the healing is medically inexplicable, the case is forwarded to a group of four doctors. All four must be strangers to the others and none may be familiar with the case they are about to consider. Again the four doctors study the case independently, without consulting their colleagues until they have drawn their own conclusions. If more than one adjudges the case to be capable of scientific explanation, the case is dropped. If only one expert dissents, the entire panel of four is assembled. If the other three doctors fail to convince the fourth, the case is dead. If all four experts now favorably concur, the case is forwarded to a group of seven other doctors, all unfamiliar with the case and with each other. They, too, study the documentation independently. If more than one member of the group writes an unfavorable review, the case goes no further. If all the members unanimously agree that the cure under consideration is beyond the explanation of "state-of-the-art" medical science, the case is referred back to the Congregation for Causes of Saints.

To prove the occasion for a beatification, a miracle must have taken place after the death of a "Servant of God." Therefore, none of the numerous healings attributed to Brother André in his lifetime could be considered in the beatification proceedings. Shortly after his death, a Medical Office was set up at the Oratory under Dr. Lamy, to study reported posthumous miracles, screening for those cases with the potential of meeting the criteria of the Church. Brother Robert Montcalm, assistant to the Vice-Postulator, estimated in 1986 that between 1937 and 1977 approximately 125,000 cures had been claimed. Of these, only about 200 were sufficiently documented or sufficiently dramatic to warrant further study. In these instances, the subjects were sent a questionnaire with such queries as, "When were you taken sick?"; "From what sickness were you suffering?"; "What is the name of the physician you consulted?"; "Did the doctor say that a cure was possible?"; "What treatment did you undergo?"; "Have you been to a hospital?"; "What was the exact date of your cure?"; "Is your cure complete?" Mlle. Lucienne Nault, who assisted Dr. Lamy in the Medical Office, recalled in 1986: "The cured person had to write a testimony and accompany that with a testimony from a doctor. That was sent to me at the Oratory. I would copy the testimony . . . I had to send for hospital records. Most doctors were cooperative. Occasionally a patient would refuse to get the records and occasionally a doctor would refuse."[6]

By the mid-1960s, from over two hundred dossiers, the files of three miracles were selected to be forwarded for consideration to the Sacred Congregation of Rites. One concerned a Sister Frodebert, a nun who invoked Brother André the day after his death and was instantly healed of a chronically inflexible knee. The second concerned a Miss Breton, who had suffered for ten years from an ear disease called otitis. After treatment by several specialists, she was declared "chronically ill." According to Miss Nault, "There was always pus draining from the ear, always great pain in the ear and head."[7] On the afternoon of April 28, 1940, Miss Breton went to pray at Brother André's tomb and was cured instantly. It was, however, the case of Joseph Audino that most impressed the Congregation and was sent to the Congregation for the Causes of Saints in 1979. It was the latest, it was the most dramatic, and it was backed by the most thorough documentation. The Congregation had in hand a 585-page medical report and more than 140 x-rays. Members of the Congregation flew twice to Rochester, New York to hear witnesses and held thirty sessions during which fourteen persons were called upon to testify.

Audino, a wealthy home-builder in a suburb of Rochester, New York, was in his late forties in 1955 when he was diagnosed as suffering from reticulum cell sarcoma. This illness is a type of cancer which originates not in one, but in many organs, and is therefore especially difficult to treat. After three years of treatment by the finest oncologists in America, his physicians, Philip Rubin and Seymour Levitt, who would describe his case in the *Journal of Nuclear Medicine,* entertained little hope. The cancer was affecting nearly every organ in the patient's body, the liver was "swollen to the size of a medicine ball" and "his bone marrow was so totally suppressed that it could no longer produce red and white blood platelets."[8] Dr. Rubin recounted, "We thought it was all over ... very, very few make it back once the disease has progressed as far as it did."[9]

According to Father Lafrenière, Audino was not a churchgoer. Yet, in 1951, when one of his children was seriously ill, having learned about the Oratory from a doorman at the old Laurentian Hotel while on a trip to Montreal, he went there with his wife to pray. "Something came over me I cannot describe or explain," he said a quarter-century later. "I didn't know too many prayers, but in my own words I asked Brother André to help our daughter and make her well. I left there feeling that I had talked to someone who heard me."[10] The daughter recovered.

When his cancer was first diagnosed, Audino began to pray to Brother André. When, on July 24, 1958, he was informed that his condition was "terminal" he asked Brother André "to tell my doctors what to do to save me."[11] Later that day Dr. Rubin asked him if he would try an experiment wherein a small amount of radioactive gold would be injected into his veins. "I wasn't out to cure him," insisted Rubin. "I was out to shrink his liver and make him as comfortable as possible."[12]

Three weeks after the injection of the gold there was no improvement. On the contrary, on August 14, Audino's doctors were convinced that the end was only hours away. That night, however, the patient, who had been running a fever of 105, suddenly fell into a deep sleep. The next morning he awoke convinced that he was entirely cured. Over the next few weeks doctors made an extensive series of tests — which failed to find any evidence of cancer, only days after similar tests had revealed a body riddled with metastases.[13]

Dr. Rubin, a Jew, admitted that Audino's cure was "by any medical measure, a kind of miracle." There were two possible medical explanations for the recovery. "Either Audino's cancer happened to distribute itself among his organs in precisely the same fashion as the radioactive gold that was injected into his system, or the cancer underwent a highly unlikely spontaneous remission."[14] Rubin insisted that the medical odds of a patient in Audino's condition being cured of reticulum cell sarcoma "at the advanced state of the disease were a million to one, even with the gold treatment." This experimental approach, incidentally, was tried on many other cancer sufferers and never worked, leaving Rubin, Leavitt, and other oncologists to conclude that radioactive gold therapy is "essentially useless in the treatment of cancer."[15]

Audino, who survived an operation for lung cancer in 1976, was still giving interviews as late as 1979. At that time the old man urged all sick persons to have faith and pray to something or someone. "Who's your god? Your god is a telephone pole? Okay, pray to a telephone pole, but, dammit, pray to something!"[16] The staff of the Oratory believe that Audino lived until 1982.

On June 19, 1980, the panel of medical specialists engaged by the Congregation for the Causes of Saints, citing sixteen new files of cures "to indicate the permanence of the reputation of miracles attributed to the intercession of Brother André,"[17] voted to beatify Brother André. Finally, on May 23, 1982, Pope John Paul II formally declared "The Miracle Man of Montreal" "Blessed" Brother André Bessette.

Brother André's friends and admirers hope that the day may not be distant when Blessed André is declared Saint André. For this to occur, another miracle — one occurring *after* beatification — must be certified. Father Lafrenière stated in 1987: "At the present time the Cause is not so spectacular as it was in the early 1980s, just before the beatification. Then we received many cases [of reported miracles] and I had the conviction that the Lord wanted this to happen then. The only thing I can say is whenever the Lord wants Brother André to be declared a saint, He will supply the miracles. I believe He can do it. Right now it is a matter of keeping the eyes and ears open. We listen to people. We see them and go to the doctors to establish a file as accurately as we can. We have several cases we are studying, but we are not ready to ask the bishop to conduct the formal study."[18]

The Basilica was finally completed in 1967 and continued to draw large congregations in the late 1980s, even as church attendance among Roman Catholics in Canada was declining precipitously. Even midweek Masses at the Crypt Church were still well-attended. A prominent French-Canadian religious scholar told a reporter in August, 1987; "I know a great many people who won't go to their own parish churches but go to the Oratory instead . . . I think it is in large part a nostalgia . . . In the Oratory, it's more like the old days: the church is full and everyone is singing and worshipping." Father Marcel Lalonde, Rector of the Oratory, in the same review, agreed that the Oratory's continuing appeal had much to do with its traditional liturgy and approach to spirituality. Attendance at Mass showed continued growth throughout the 1970s and 1980s. Father Lafrenière, who estimated the yearly volume of pilgrims at two million, said that in a fifteen-year period ending in 1985, the rate of visitors grew two to six percent each year.[19]

What is the relevance of Brother André to the modern world? Father Lalonde declared that André: "represents hope for the little man, the person without much money, the sick person. He himself was poor. He wasn't a priest. He had no power except for the power of the little people, those who suffer and who pray. He goes beyond all the usual categories. He shows that in life there is something you can have confidence in."[20]

Father Lafrenière insists that Brother André's message is: "God exists and not only does He exist, but He cares. He is interested in what happens in your life. Brother André used to say, 'The Lord has His ears close to your mouth when you pray.' He is right next to you when you pray. People knew that Brother André was close to the Lord. People wanted to be near a real believer, to experience a relationship with someone close to God. St. Joseph's Oratory began even thirty years before the first chapel existed. The Oratory existed in the doorkeeper's room in Notre-Dame College. St. Joseph's

Oratory is, above all, a movement of prayer. Brother André accepted to pray with the sick and then the signs would come and the people would experience the wonders of the Lord. It was a prayer movement that grew up around a man. It caused problems in the school and was moved to a trolley stop, then it provided itself with a wooden chapel, then a large chapel, then a church, and then a basilica. It has become a mission to reveal that God exists, He cares, He is near, He loves us, and can do something, giving signs of His presence, His love, and His care."[21]

Perhaps the aspect of Brother André's life and ministry that most commends itself to this or any other time is his theocentricity — his God centeredness. Brother's entire life revolved around his service to his God. There was no time in his life for himself — every day, every hour, every minute of his existence was lived for God and for his fellow men. Spectacular was his cheerful forgetfulness of his own desires. So dedicated was he to his Lord and to his fellow human beings that he took never a thought for his own comfort, his own pleasure, or, for that matter, for his doubt or fear. Early in life he seemed totally empty of self, or of anything that did not proclaim unwavering love and confidence in God. It was from this singleminded Godfullness and the radiant and powerful faith that proceeded from it, that the Oratory movement was born, a movement by which men and women, even a half century after its author was called to glory, perceive the presence and the peace of God, even amid grief and trouble, and through which the sanctity of Blessed Brother André shines forth most brilliantly even in the waning years of the twentieth century, as a beacon to a darkling world.

Chapter Notes

Chapter One

1. Etienne Catta, *Le frere Andre (1845-1937) et l'Oratoire Saint-Joseph du Mont-Royal.* (hereafter designated CATTA) (Montreal, 1965), p. 603
2. Sacra Congregatio pro Causis Sanctorum, *Marianapolitana Beatificationis et Canonizationis Servi Dei Fratris Andreae (in saec. Alaphridi Bessette) E Congregatione a S. Cruce. Summarium.* (hereafter designated SUMMARIUM). (Rome, 1976). pp. 847-848
3. CATTA, p. 584
4. Ibid., p. 599
5. Ibid., p. 600
6. SUMMARIUM, pp. 457-458
7. CATTA, p. 603
8. Ibid., pp. 615-616
9. Interview of Brother André by Frederick Griffin from *Toronto Star,* December 21, 1931. (hereafter designated GRIFFIN)
10. *The Oratory,* July-August, 1977, p. 6
11. Ibid., p. 9
12. Ibid.
13. Ibid., p. 7
14. Interview of Brother André by Leon Gray from Montreal *La Patrie,* July 5, 1936. (hereafter designated GRAY)

Chapter Two

1. *The Oratory,* July of 1983, p. 11
2. Alden Hatch, *The Story of Brother Andre and the Shrine on Mount Royal.* (hereafter designated HATCH) (New York, 1959). p. 32
3. GRAY
4. SUMMARIUM, p. 924
5. CATTA, p. 113
6. Ibid.,
7. Ibid., p. 120
8. HATCH, p. 34
9. SUMMARIUM, p. 925
10. Ibid., p. 941
11. CATTA, p. 143
12. Ibid.
13. SUMMARIUM, p. 319
14. Ibid., p. 120
15. Ibid.
16. Ibid.
17. Ibid.
18. SUMMARIUM, p. 925
19. Ibid., p. 600
20. CATTA, p. 120
21. Ibid.
22. SUMMARIUM, p. 146
23. Ibid.

Chapter Three

1. CATTA, p. 167
2. *The Oratory,* April, 1963, p. 6
3. CATTA, p. 178
4. Ibid., p. 179
5. *The Oratory,* April, 1963, p. 7
6. CATTA, p. 182
7. Ibid., p. 191
8. SUMMARIUM, p. 6
9. Ibid., p. 199
10. Ibid., p. 193
11. Henri-Paul Bergeron,

Brother Andre, C.S.C.,
The Wonder Man of
Mount Royal. (hereafter
designated BERGERON)
(Montreal, 1937) p. 30
12. *The Oratory,* March, 1963,
pp. 6-7
13. Ibid., p. 7, 31
14. CATTA, pp. 193-195
15. HATCH, p. 57
16. CATTA, p. 195
17. SUMMARIUM, p. 576
18. CATTA, p. 218
19. Ibid., p. 199
20. Ibid., p. 195
21. Ibid., p. 200
22. Ibid.
23. Ibid., p. 201
24. Ibid., p. 203
25. Ibid.
26. BERGERON, p. 125
27. Ibid.
28. Ibid., p. 136
29. Ibid., p. 122
30. Ibid., p. 137

Chapter Four

1. CATTA, pp. 208-209
2. Ibid., p. 209
3. Ibid.
4. Ibid.
5. Ibid.
6. Ibid.
7. GRAY
8. CATTA, p. 214
9. GRAY
10. CATTA, p. 215
11. BERGERON, p. 70
12. Ibid., p. 71
13. Ibid.
14. Ibid.
15. CATTA, p. 243
16. George Ham, *The Miracle*
Man of Montreal. (here-
after designated HAM) (Toronto, 1922) p. 2

Chapter Five

1. CATTA, p. 228
2. Ibid.
3. Ibid.
4. Arthur St.-Pierre, *St. Jo-*
seph's Oratory of Mount
Royal. (hereafter designated ST. PIERRE) (Mont-
real, 1927) pp. 97-98
5. CATTA, p. 250
6. ST. PIERRE, p. 34
7. Montreal *La Presse,* May
25, 1906
8. BERGERON, p. 65
9. HATCH, p. 81
10. SUMMARIUM, p. 16
11. CATTA, p. 357
12. Ibid.
13. Ibid.
14. ST. PIERRE, pp. 53-54
15. HATCH, p. 83
16. CATTA, p. 250
17. Montreal, *La Patrie,* January 10, 1910
18. Quebec City *Action So-*
ciale, May 28, 1910
19. Montreal *La Patrie,* May
25, 1910
20. Montreal *La Presse,* August 1, 1910
21. CATTA, p. 295
22. Ibid.
23. Ibid. p. 306
24. Ibid. p. 308
25. Ibid.
26. Ibid. p. 357
27. HATCH, p. 89
28. Ibid. p. 87
29. CATTA, p. 313
30. Ibid.
31. HATCH, p. 91
32. HAM, pp. 53-54
33. SUMMARIUM, p. 50
34. Albert Cousineau, C.S.C.,
Brother Andre as I Knew
Him. (Montreal, 1960) p. 15

Chapter Six

1. Telephone interview with Jules Cayer, East Freetown, Massachusetts, October 21, 1987. (hereafter designated CAYER)
2. CATTA, p. 200
3. Micheline Lachance, *Le frere Andre: l'historie de l'obscur portier qui allait accomplir des miracles.* (hereafter designated LACHANCE) (Montreal, 1979) p. 184
4. HATCH, p. 130
5. Ibid., p. 132
6. BERGERON, pp. 63-65
7. SUMMARIUM, p. 89
8. Ibid., p. 99
9. Ibid.
10. Ibid., pp. 20-25
11. CATTA, pp. 429-434
12. SUMMARIUM, p. 451

Chapter Seven

1. Interview with Father Henri-Paul Bergeron, Montreal, August 4, 1987
2. BERGERON, p. 100
3. Philip Schaff, ed., *A Select Library of the Nicene and Post-Nicene Fathers of the Christian Church, Vol. IV, St. Augustin: The Writings Against the Manichaeans and Against the Donatists* (New York, 1901) pp. 321-322
4. Saint Augustine, *The City of God* (trans. Gerald C. Walsh and Daniel J. Horan) (New York, 1954) p. 451
5. Saint Augustine, *The City of God* (trans. Marcus Dods) (New York, 1950) pp. 822-823
6. Ibid., p. 823
7. Ibid., p. 828
8. Benjamin Warfield, *Miracles: Yesterday and Today, True and False* (Grand Rapids, Michigan, 1965) pp. 53-54
9. Ewald Plass, ed., *What Luther Says: An Anthology* Vol. II (St. Louis, 1959) p. 957
10. Ibid., p. 954
11. Ibid.
12. John Wesley, *Works,* Vol. V (New York, 1856) p. 706
13. Warfield, op. cit. p. 6
14. American Classics, *The Diary of Cotton Mather,* Vol. II (1709-1724) (New York, 1911) pp. 16-17
15. SUMMARIUM, p. 489
16. Ibid., pp. 487-488
17. Ibid., p. 488
18. Ibid., p. 485
19. Ibid., p. 96
20. Ibid., p. 13
21. Ibid.
22. CATTA, p. 600
23. Ibid., p. 601
24. Ibid., p. 606
25. SUMMARIUM, p. 26
26. Ibid., p. 624
27. Ibid., p. 485
28. Interview, Father Bernard Lafreniére, August 5, 1987
29. CATTA, p. 651
30. SUMMARIUM, p. 486
31. BERGERON, p. 74
32. Ibid., pp. 75-76
33. Ibid., p. 80
34. SUMMARIUM, p. 328
35. Ibid., p. 462
36. Ibid.
37. CATTA, p. 343
38. Ibid., p. 344
39. Ibid., p. 345
40. Ibid.
41. Ibid., p. 348
42. Ibid., p. 349

43. Ibid., p. 350
44. SUMMARIUM, pp. 1005-1006
45. HAM, pp. 21-24
46. Ibid., pp. 34-36
47. "La Guerison de Martin Hannon," *Annales de Saint Joseph* Vol. 13, no. 3, March, 1924, pp. 105-119
48. ST.-PIERRE, pp. 65-66
49. Ibid., p. 67
50. Ibid., 68
51. ST.-PIERRE, pp. 69-70
52. Ibid., pp. 70-76
53. HAM, p. 33
54. ST.-PIERRE, pp. 81-88
55. Ibid., pp. 79-80
56. GRIFFIN
57. ST.-PIERRE, p. 77
58. GRIFFIN
59. Ibid.
60. ST.-PIERRE, pp. 89-93
61. SUMMARIUM, p. 660
62. Interview with Father Henri-Paul Bergeron, August 4, 1986 and August 4, 1987
63. CATTA, p. 575
64. SUMMARIUM, p. 692

Chapter Eight

1. Interview with Brother Robert Montcalm, C.S.C., Montreal, August 5, 1987
2. SUMMARIUM, p. 849
3. Ibid., pp. 658-659
4. Letter, Mrs. Aurore Snow Lawrence to Rev. C. Bernard Ruffin, October 14, 1987 (hereafter designated LAWRENCE)
5. SUMMARIUM, p. 823
6. Ibid., p. 61
7. Ibid., p. 92
8. Ibid., p. 584
9. Ibid., p. 65
10. Ibid., p. 691
11. BERGERON, p. 85
12. SUMMARIUM, p. 691
13. Ibid., p. 51
14. Ibid., p. 928
15. Ibid., p. 933
16. Ibid., p. 946
17. Ibid., pp. 112-113
18. Ibid., p. 928
19. Ibid., p. 468
20. Ibid., p. 93
21. CATTA, p. 588
22. SUMMARIUM, p. 37
23. Ibid., p. 696
24. Ibid., p. 338
25. Ibid., p. 101
26. Ibid., p. 580
27. BERGERON, p. 118
28. Ibid.
29. Scrapbook in Archives of Oratory of Saint Joseph
30. SUMMARIUM, p. 27
31. BERGERON, p. 114
32. LACHANCE, p. 240
33. CATTA, p. 580
34. Ibid.
35. BERGERON, p. 114
36. CATTA, p. 579
37. SUMMARIUM, p. 614
38. BERGERON, p. 106
39. SUMMARIUM, p. 600
40. Ibid. p. 594
41. Scrapbook in Archives of Oratory of Saint Joseph
42. SUMMARIUM, p. 618
43. Ibid., pp. 43-44
44. Ibid., p. 583
45. Ibid., pp. 43-44
46. LAWRENCE
47. CAYER
48. SUMMARIUM, p. 889
49. GRIFFIN
50. SUMMARIUM, p. 42
51. Ibid., p. 933
52. Ibid., p. 926
53. Ibid., p. 658
54. Ibid., p. 689
55. GRIFFIN
56. Ibid.
57. SUMMARIUM, p. 615

58. CAYER
59. SUMMARIUM, p. 42
60. Ibid., p. 613
61. Ibid., p. 113
62. Ibid., p. 664
63. Ibid., p. 594
64. Ibid., p. 114
65. Ibid., p. 47
66. Ibid., p. 489
67. Ibid., p. 698
68. Ibid., p. 506
69. Ibid., p. 101
70. Ibid., p. 11
71. LAWRENCE
72. SUMMARIUM, p. 114
73. Ibid., p. 115
74. Ibid., p. 619
75. Ibid., p. 494
76. Ibid.
77. Ibid., p. 576
78. Ibid., p. 937
79. Ibid., p. 437
80. Ibid.
81. Ibid., p. 591
82. Ibid., p. 458
83. Ibid., p. 97
84. Ibid., p. 324
85. BERGERON, p. 154
86. SUMMARIUM, p. 687
87. Ibid., p. 93
88. Ibid., p. 33
89. Ibid., p. 886
90. Ibid.
91. BERGERON, p. 137
92. SUMMARIUM, p. 467
93. Ibid., p. 33
94. Ibid., p. 35
95. HATCH, p. 161
96. CATTA, p. 647
97. Ibid., p. 653
98. SUMMARIUM, p. 601
99. Ibid., p. 118
100. Ibid.
101. Ibid., p. 691
102. Ibid., p. 584
103. Ibid.
104. Ibid., p. 332
105. Ibid., p. 57

106. Ibid., p. 694
107. Ibid., pp. 481-482
108. Ibid., p. 482
109. Ibid., pp. 601-602
110. Ibid., p. 53
111. Ibid., pp. 51-52
112. Ibid., p. 55
113. Ibid., p. 56
114. Ibid.
115. CATTA, pp. 844-845
116. Ibid., p. 848
117. LACHANCE, p. 268
118. GRIFFIN
119. BERGERON, pp. 104-105
120. SUMMARIUM, p. 107
121. Tom Sinclair-Faulkner, "Sacramental Suffering: Brother Andre's Spirituality," *La Societe Canadienne d'Histoire de l'Eglise Catholique,* 1987, p. 67
122. Ibid., p. 125
123. Ibid., p. 127
124. SUMMARIUM, p. 552
125. Ibid.
126. Ibid., p. 108
127. CATTA, p. 599

Chapter Nine

1. Burlington *Free Press and Times,* September 10, 1919
2. *Plattsburgh Press,* September 24, 1932
3. Burlington *Free Press and Times,* September 10, 1919
4. Ibid.
5. Ibid.
6. Telephone conversation with Mrs. Albert Sharron, Jr., February 14, 1988
7. Scrapbook in Archives of Oratory of Saint Joseph
8. Ibid.
9. SUMMARIUM, p. 587
10. LACHANCE, p. 201

11. Ibid., pp. 204-205
12. Ibid.
13. Ibid.
14. Scrapbook in Archives of Oratory of Saint Joseph
15. LACHANCE, pp. 204-205
16. Ibid.
17. Scrapbook in Archives of Oratory of Saint Joseph
18. Ibid.
19. HATCH, p. 132
20. Ibid., p. 140
21. Scrapbook in Archives of Oratory of Saint Joseph
22. HATCH, p. 141
23. CATTA p. 786

Chapter Ten

1. HATCH, pp. 122-123
2. SUMMARIUM, P. 467
3. CATTA, p. 764
4. LAWRENCE
5. CAYER
6. SUMMARIUM, p. 885
7. Ibid., pp. 931-933
8. Ibid.
9. CAYER
10. SUMMARIUM, p. 885
11. LAWRENCE
12. CAYER
13. LAWRENCE
14. CAYER
15. SUMMARIUM, p. 931
16. CAYER
17. Ibid.
18. SUMMARIUM, p. 928
19. Ibid., p. 947
20. CAYER
21. HATCH, p. 125
22. CAYER
23. SUMMARIUM, p. 955
24. HATCH, pp. 121-122
25. O. A. Boyer, *She Wears a Crown of Thorns: Marie Rose Ferron (1902-1936) Known as 'Little Rose'* *The Stigmatized Ecstatic of Woonsocket, R.I.* (Mendham, New Jersey, 1958) p. 136
26. Ibid., pp. 79ff
27. Ibid., p. 30
28. CATTA p. 775
29. CAYER
30. LAWRENCE
31. CATTA, p. 771 and LAWRENCE
32. SUMMARIUM, p. 1020
33. CATTA, p. 782
34. Ibid., p. 766
35. Scrapbook in Archives of Oratory of Saint Joseph
36. Ibid.
37. SUMMARIUM, P. 967
38. Scrapbook in Archives of Oratory of Saint Joseph
39. CATTA, p. 780
40. Scrapbook in Archives of Oratory of Saint Joseph
41. Ibid.
42. BERGERON, p. 117

Chapter Eleven

1. CATTA, p. 795
2. Ibid.
3. Ibid., p. 806
4. Ibid., p. 799
5. Ibid., p. 807
6. Ibid., pp. 807-808
7. LACHANCE, p. 299
8. Ibid., p. 303
9. Ibid., p. 304
10. SUMMARIUM, p. 595
11. HATCH, p. 117
12. CATTA, p. 733
13. SUMMARIUM, p. 454
14. CATTA, p. 819
15. LACHANCE, P. 325
16. Interview with Father Bernard Lafreniére
17. SUMMARIUM, p. 501
18. Ibid.

19. Ibid., p. 577
20. BERGERON, p. 139
21. Ibid., p. 106
22. LACHANCE, p. 290
23. BERGERON, p. 103
24. LACHANCE, p. 354
25. Scrapbook in Archives of Oratory of Saint Joseph
26. CATTA, p. 828
27. Ibid., p. 824
28. Ibid.
29. SUMMARIUM, p. 619
30. GRIFFIN
31. SUMMARIUM, p. 500
32. HATCH, p. 158
33. HATCH, p. 160
34. LAWRENCE
35. CAYER
36. CATTA, p. 863
37. Ibid., p. 830
38. HATCH, pp. 158-159
39. SUMMARIUM, p. 601
40. BERGERON, p. 163

Chapter Twelve

1. BERGERON, p. 164
2. SUMMARIUM, pp. 118-119
3. LACHANCE, p. 368
4. SUMMARIUM, p. 568
5. Ibid., p. 569
6. Ibid., p. 568
7. Ibid., p. 422
8. SUMMARIUM, p. 571
9. Ibid.
10. BERGERON, p. 164
11. SUMMARIUM, p. 429
12. Ibid., p. 571
13. BERGERON, p. 165
14. Ibid., p. 166
15. Ibid.
16. SUMMARIUM, p. 570
17. Ibid.
18. Ibid.
19. BERGERON, p. 166
20. SUMMARIUM, p. 570
21. Ibid.

22. BERGERON, p. 167
23. Ibid., p. 174
24. Scrapbook at Archives of Oratory of Saint Joseph
25. Ibid.

Chapter Thirteen

1. News Release, Oratory of Saint Joseph, 1982, pp. 1-2
2. *The Oratory.* February, 1964, pp. 24-26
3. News Release, p. 3
4. Ibid.
5. Interview with Father Bernard Lafrenière
6. Interview with Mlle. Lucienne Nault, Montreal, August 4, 1986
7. Ibid.
8. *Maclean's,* February 7, 1977
9. Ibid.
10. Rochester *Democrat and Chronicle,* July 25, 1976
11. *Maclean's,* February 7, 1977
12. Rochester *Times-Union,* August 11, 1978
13. *Maclean's,* February 7, 1977
14. Rochester *Times-Union,* August 11, 1978
15. *Maclean's,* February 7, 1977
16. Rochester *Times-Union,* August 11, 1978
17. News Release, p. 3
18. Interview with Father Bernard Lafrenière
19. Montreal *Gazette,* August 1, 1987
20. Ibid.
21. Interview with Father Bernard Lafrenière

Index

A

Abundius (Brother) — 53, 57, 122, 176, 182

Aldéric (Brother) — 41-42, 51

Alexander (Brother) — 42

Ambrose (Saint) — 82

André (Brother)

  and America — 19-20, 67, 158-159, 162-174, 184, 186-188

  ancestry — 13-14

  appearance — 3, 69, 127-128, 163

  birth — 12

  Cause for Beatification — 199-207

  childhood — 13, 15-17

  on Communism — 184, 193

  criticism of his ministry — 47, 49-51, 54-55, 60-62, 121, 124, 155-158, 182

  death — 195

  diet — 19, 37, 128-130, 166, 179

  as doorkeeper of College of Notre-Dame — 29-30, 34-39, 48-49, 57

  education, lack of — 15-17, 19, 136

  exhumation of remains — 201-202

  funeral ceremonies — 197-198

  healings — 4-9, 41-46, 55-62, 72-79, 92-120, 138-139, 153-156, 170-173, 176-178, 181, 184-185, 197, 204-206

  health — 8, 17, 20-21, 28-29, 33, 36-38, 129-130, 173-174, 178-179, 183

  humor, sense of — 30, 78, 134, 159, 161, 165, 193

  irritability — 9, 124-126, 168-169

  last illness — 189-194

  ministry to penitent — 179-150

  ministry to sick — 2-5, 7-10, 61-62, 65, 77-80, 86-91, 120, 142-143, 164-165, 167-168, 178-179, 186-187, 194

  money, attitude towards — 10, 52-53, 56, 133-135, 158, 187-188

  mystical phenomena, reputed — 79, 140-148, 180-188

  and Oratory of Saint Joseph — 51-58, 62-63, 67-68, 159-160, 175-176, 183-189, 194

  personality — 10, 17-19, 21-22, 36-37, 122-124, 131-133, 136, 166, 168, 180

  Protestants, attitude towards — 138-139

  relatives, relations with — 31-33, 66-67, 162-163, 165-167, 181, 188

  religious devotions — 17-19, 22, 37-38, 130, 135-138, 165-167

  Saint Joseph, devotion to — 4, 10-11, 47, 63, 88-89, 96, 122, 136, 169

  suffering, attitude towards — 89, 91, 130, 143, 150-151, 181-182, 192-193

  travels — 19-20, 158-159, 162-174, 183-184

  vocation — 18-19, 23-25, 27-29, 32-33

  women, attitude towards — 21, 125-126, 132-133, 169

  work history (in youth) — 15, 17, 19-21

  youth — 17-23

Anne-de-Beaupré (Saint), church of — 1, 102-105, 116-117, 152
Anthony, A.H. (Mrs.) — 139
Archambault (Dr.) — 98-99
Aubry, George (Dr.) — 73-76
Audel, Rosaire (Father) — 78
Audino, Joseph C. — 204-205
Augustine of Hippo (Saint) — 82-83

B

Baker, Seth — 155
Belanger, Ernest — 95
Bellot, Paul (Dom) — 189
Benedict XIV (Pope) — 84
Bennett, Richard (Prime Minister) — 183
Bergeron, Henri-Paul (Father) — 31, 80, 92, 118-119, 125-127, 136, 186, 196, 199
Bertrand, Louis — 73-74, 107-108, 120
Bessette (Mlle.) — 173
Bessette, Alfred — see André (Brother)
Bessette, Alphonsine (Mrs. Boulet) (1847-1934) (sister of Brother André) — 14, 17, 66-67, 166, 181-182
Bessette, André — see André (Brother)
Bessette, Angelique (nee Georges) (grandmother of Brother André) — 13
Bessette, Anne (nee Seigneur) (ancestress of Brother André) — 13
Bessette, Basile (uncle of Brother André) — 15
Bessette, Benoni (uncle of Brother André) — 15
Bessette, Claude (1841-1929) (brother of Brother André) — 14, 16, 19-20, 66, 162-163, 165-166, 181
Bessette, Clothilde (nee Foisy) (1814-1857) (mother of Brother André) — 14-16, 18, 147
Bessette, Clothilde (1833-1836) (sister of Brother André) — 14
Bessette, Elisa (1854-1858) (sister of Brother André) — 14
Bessette, Eusèbe (uncle of Brother André) — 13
Bessette, Henry (nephew of Brother André) — 166-167, 169, 181
Bessette, Homer (Dr.) (cousin of Brother André) — 173
Bessette, Isaac (1807-1855) (father of Brother André) — 13-16
Bessette, Isaïe (1837-1920) (brother of Brother André) — 14-16, 20, 66, 181
Bessette, Jean (ancestor of Brother André) — 13
Bessette, Joseph (1778-1851) (grandfather of Brother André) — 13
Bessette, Joseph (1840-1905) (brother of Brother André) — 14, 16, 19-21, 66
Bessette, Joséphine (1849-?) (sister of Brother André) — 14, 19-21, 66
Bessette, Léocadie (Mrs. Lefebvre) (1835-1916) (sister of Brother André) — 14-17, 20, 66-67, 129, 165-167, 181
Bessette, Marie (Mrs. Cayer) (1843-1874) (sister of Brother André) — 14-16, 19, 66

217

Bessette, Napoleon (1838-1928) (brother of Brother André) — 14, 16, 19, 66, 162-163, 181
Bessette, Ubald (Dr.) (cousin of Brother André) — 183
Bessette, Virginie (1852-1852) (sister of Brother André) — 14
Bessette, Xavier (uncle of Brother André) — 15
Boisvert, Ludger — 6-7
Boulet, John — 97-98
Boulet, Néré — 66
Bourget, Ignace (Archbishop) — 25, 29, 53
Boyer, Onesimus (the Rev.) — 169
Bréton (Mlle.) — 204
Brousseau (M. and Mme.) — 144
Brownrigg (Mrs.) — 58-59
Bruchési, Paul (Archbishop) — 50, 54, 56-57, 60-64, 68-69, 79, 89, 143, 152, 160
Bruhlmann, (M. and Mme.) — 93, 120
Buchand, Joseph — 26

C
Cardinal, Albert (Mme) — 97
Catta, Etiénne (Canon) — 146-147
Cayer, Jules — 66, 129, 131, 164-168, 170, 188
Chagnon, Sam — 114-115, 120
Chambon, Marie-Marthé (Sister) — 10, 136, 146
Charboneau, Joseph (Archbishop) — 199-200
Charrette, Joseph (Dr.) — 49, 54-56, 73
Charron, Albert (Father) — 182, 185-187, 194
Chrysostom, John (Saint) — 82
Civil War (American) — 19-20
Civil War (Spanish) — 184, 193
Claude, Azarias — 3, 43-44, 71-73, 77, 88-89, 119, 123-126, 131-134, 140, 144, 158, 191
Claude, Marguerite — 72
Clément, Adolphe (Father) — 59-60, 80, 102-103, 114, 116, 134, 145, 159, 168, 174-175, 179, 182, 189-190
Comeau, Frank (Mrs.) — 129, 137-138, 166-167
Cormier, Dominique — 164
Cornish, Frank (the Rev.) — 169
Cousineau, Albert (Father) — 88, 122, 125, 132, 182, 186-189, 191-192, 197, 199
Crypt Church — 68-69, 119, 152, 159-160, 175-176, 195, 207
Cyr, Roland — 177-178

D
Dagneau, P.C. (Dr.) — 104-106
Deguire, Emile (Father) — 89-90, 122-123, 126-129, 131, 140-141, 178-180
Delara, J.J. — 128
Demers, Pierre — 17-18

Depression (1930s) — 19, 183-185
Desgrosseilliers family — 93
Desjardins (M.) — 4-5
Desjardins (M.) — 7
di Maria, Pietro (the Rev.) — 160
Dion, Georges (Father) — 54-56, 59, 61, 65, 70-71, 74, 132, 153
Donohue, James W. (Father) — 185
Doran, John — 158
Doyon, Germaine — 115-119
Drolet, Luci — 94-95
Ducharme, Arthur — 197
Dufresne, Henri (Dr.) — 106-107
Defresne, J.O. — 106
Duplessis, Maurice — 37-38, 197
Duquette, Joseph (Abbe) — 180

E
Elisha — 40, 87
Elsburg (Dr.) — 172
Erard, Philip — 173

F
Fabre, Adélard — 92-93, 135-136, 141, 161
Falardeau, M.A. (Dr.) — 109
Fallon, Michael (Bishop) — 160
Fatima, Our Lady of — 86
Ferron, Marie Rose — 169-170
Foisy, Claude — 14
Foisy, Martin — 14
Foisy, Ursule (nee Barsalou) — 14
Forbes, Joseph (Archbishop) — 175
Fortin, Marie-Camille (Sister) — 192-195
Frances of Rome (Saint) — 147-148
Frodebert (Sister) — 204

G
Gagnon, (Mlle.) — 58
Ganz, Arthur — 78, 93, 134, 137, 142-144, 164
Gastineau, Jules (Father) — 26, 29
Gauthier, Georges (Archbishop) — 143-144, 160, 189, 199
Gauthier, L.O. (Dr.) — 111
Gauthier, Raoul (Chief) — 77-78, 180
Gelineau, Francis Xavier — 172-173
Geoffrion, Louis (Father) — 48-49, 51, 175, 181-182
George V (King of Great Britain) — 11
Gertrude of Helfta (Saint) — 10, 136
Giacomini (sculptor) — 69
Gilbert, Arthur — 109

Gilbert, F.G. (Dr.) — 107
Gingras, Adolphe J. (Dr.) — 117
Goodwin (Dr.) — 172
Gorcha (Dr.) — 181
Gravette, Camile — 171
Griffin, Frederick — 114, 130, 149
Grothé, Armand (Mme.) — 95
Guerin, Michael — 50-51
Guerin (Mrs.) — 188
Guertin, Yvonne — 58
Gunn, Alexander — 50
Guy, Pierre (Father) — 29

H
Ham, George (Colonel) — 46, 99-101, 108
Hannon, Kathleen — 105
Hannon, Martin — 58, 102-106
Harbour (Canon) — 175
Henri (Brother) — 48, 54
Hitler, Adolf — 11, 184
Hogan, Fred — 97
Holy Cross, Congregation of — 22-27, 31, 34-35, 40, 51-52, 67-68, 131, 158
Hughes, Albert (the Rev.) — 46, 86

I
International Eucharistic Congress (1910) — 59
Irenaeus (Saint) — 82

J
Jansoone, Frédèric (Father) — 46
Jenner, Edward — 28
John XXIII (Pope) — 201
John Paul II (Pope) — 206
Johnson, Stephen — 181
Joncas, Onézime — 155
Joseph (Saint) — 4-10, 14, 18, 22, 27-28, 34, 38, 41-48, 51-55, 58, 61-63, 69,
    72, 76-77, 87-89, 94, 109-110, 114-116, 120, 122-123, 130, 136, 139, 141,
    150-151, 156, 160, 166-167, 169, 174-178, 181, 193, 196-198

K
Kelly, Edward J. (Sergeant) — 184-185

L
Labonté, Elphège (Father) — 89-90, 130, 140, 142
Lacroix, Joseph — 105
Lafleur, Attaria (nee Lefebvre) — 123, 129, 165-167
Lafrenière, Bernard (Father) — 202, 205-207
Lalonde, Joseph (Father) — 60

Lalonde, Marcel (Father) — 207

Lamy, J. Lioney (Dr.) — 88, 117-120, 122, 128-129, 131, 133, 156-157, 178-179, 191, 195, 201, 204

Lawrence, Aurore (nee Snow) (Mrs.) — 122, 129, 133, 165-167, 170-171, 188

Leblanc (Sister) — 126

Lebou (Mr.) — 67

Lecavalier, Benjamin (Father) — 52, 54, 175

Lefebvre, Camille (Father) — 29

Lefebvre, Joseph — 20, 66-67

Lefebvre, Joseph, Jr. — 167

Léon (Brother) 121

LeRoux, Antonio — 96

LeRoux, Gabrielle — 96

LeRoux, Marguerite — 96

Letendre (Dr.) — 143

Levesque, Mathilde — 94

Leroyer (Sister) — 179

Levitt, Seymour (Dr.) — 205

L'Heureux, Ephrem — 101

L'Heureux, Joseph — 101

Limoges, Eugene (Bishop) — 197

Little Sisters of the Holy Family — 161

Lord, William — 176

Louage, Augustin (Father) — 35-37, 48

Lucas (Mrs.) — 73

Ludger (Brother) — 141

Lussier, Leopold — 180

Luther, Martin — 84-85

M

Malenfant, Joseph — 69-71

Marcoux, Joseph (M. and Mme.) — 119

Marguerite d'Youville (Blessed) — 14

Marie-Rose Durocher (Blessed) — 14

Mather, Cotton (the Rev.) — 85-86

Mather, Samuel (the Rev.) — 85-86

Maynard, Lionel — 97-99, 107, 120

McGinley, Roger (the Rev.) — 168

McPherson, Aimee Semple — 86

Mercier, Antoinette — 58, 111, 113, 119

Mercier, Jeanne — 113

Miville, Eugénié — 66-67

Montcalm, Robert (Brother) — 204

Moreau, Basile (Father) — 24-25

Morin, Felix I. — 172-173

Moses — 81

Mullen, James E. — 172-173

Mundelein, George Cardinal — 160
Mussolini, Benito — 11, 184

N
Naaman — 40, 87
Nadeau (M.) — 78
Nadeau, Rosalie (nee Foisy) — 16-18, 31-33
Nadeau, Timothée — 16-17, 31-33
Neumann, Therese — 170
Newman, John Henry Cardinal — 84

O
Oratory of Saint Joseph — 1-2, 7-8, 53-60, 62-65, 67-75, 77-79, 90-97,
    101-107, 110-111, 113, 115-122, 133-136, 138, 140-141, 147-148, 152-153,
    155-160, 164, 174-180, 182-183, 185-191, 194-198, 200, 204-205, 207
Origen — 82
Osée (Brother) — 36
Ouimet, Louis — 17, 20, 22
Ovide (Brother) — 45

P
Paine, Henry E. — 171
Paine, Suzanne (nee Boulet) — 66, 97, 123, 166-168, 171
Panneton (Dr.) — 76-77
Paradis (Miss) — 67
Parizeau, Leo (Dr.) — 155-158
Paul (Saint) — 150
Paul VI (Pope) — 202
Perrier, Philippe (Abbe) — 60
Pichette, Albertine (Mme.) — 179, 183, 186, 191
Pichette, Joseph — 4, 6-7, 73-77, 89, 91, 107, 123, 125, 128-129, 131,
    133-135, 142, 144-148, 164, 179, 183, 186, 191, 194
Pio (Padre) — 133, 140, 145, 170
Pius X (Pope) — 58
Pius XI (Pope) — 190, 193
Piuze, L.J. (Dr.) — 107
Placide (Brother) — 159, 191, 196
Provençal, André (the Rev.) — 22-23, 27
Provost (Mrs.) — 170-171

R
Raymond, Philippe — 176-177
Revolution (American) — 15
Rézé, Joseph (Father) — 28
Richard, Calixte — 57
Riopelle (Dr.) — 195
Rochette, Arthur — 109-111
Rockefeller, John D., Sr. — 188

Rouleau (Dr.) — 76-77
Rouleau, Felix Cardinal — 175-176
Roosevelt, Franklin Delano — 11, 184
Roussel, Jean-Marie (Dr.) — 201-202
Roy, Alfred (Father) — 153, 158-161, 174
Rubin, Philip (Dr.) — 205-206
Ryan Sisters — 188

S

Saint Joseph Medal — 4, 9, 40-41, 45, 48-52, 55-56, 64, 73-74, 78, 87-89,
        93-95, 99, 101, 109, 111, 116, 139, 171, 176, 179-182, 188-189, 191, 193
Saint Joseph Oil — 4, 9, 40-43, 45-46, 48-50, 55, 73, 80, 88-89, 93, 96, 101,
        109, 139, 156, 171, 176-177, 179
St.-Laurent (M.) — 43
St.-Martin, Alphonsine — 106
St.-Pierre, Arthur — 102, 104-111, 113-115
Saint Stephen Oil - 83
Savaria, J.T. (Canon) — 60
Sharron, Marie (nee Valle) 153-155, 166
Sharron, Roswell — 154
Smallpox epidemic 28, 42
Snow, Clothilde (nee Lefebvre) (Mrs.) — 181
Spanish influenza — 79
Springer, Edward (the Rev.) — 20
Stanhope, Alfred — 113-114, 119
Sylvestre (Father) — 18-19

V

Valois (Father) — 155
Veilleux, Charles Eugene — 107
Vianney, Jean-Marie-Baptiste (Saint) — 86
Viau family — 171
Victoria, Queen of Great Britain — 13
Villeneuve, Jean Cardinal — 197-198
Villeneuve, Marie (nee Lefebvre) — 174

W

Walsh (Mr.) — 164
Wesley, John — 85
Williams, Howard S. (Dr.) — 117
World War I — 65, 68-69, 78-79, 125, 152